OPPORTUNITIES AND DANGERS OF SOVIET-CUBAN EXPANSION

OPPORTUNITIES AND DANGERS OF SOVIET-CUBAN EXPANSION

Toward a Pragmatic U.S. Policy

RICHARD J. PAYNE

with a foreword by Roger Fisher

STATE UNIVERSITY OF NEW YORK PRESS

Published by
State University of New York Press, Albany

© 1988 State University of New York

For information, address State University of New York
Press, State University Plaza, Albany, N.Y., 12246

Library of Congress Cataloging in Publication Data

Payne, Richard J., 1949–
    Opportunities and dangers of Soviet-Cuban expansion : toward a
pragmatic U.S. policy / Richard J. Payne.
       p. cm.
    Bibiolgraphy: p.
    Includes index.
    ISBN 0-88706-796-4.   ISBN 0-88706-797-2 (pbk.)
    1. United States--Foreign relations-- Soviet Union.   2. Soviet
Union--Foreign relations--United States.   3. United States--Foreign
relations--Cuba.   4. Cuba--Foreign relations--United States.
5. United States--Foreign relations--1981–   I. Title.
E183.8.S65P4 1988   87-26778
327.73047--dc 19

10 9 8 7 6 5 4 3 2 1

For my parents and my son, Jason

Contents

Foreword

In this thoughtful and provocative book, Richard Payne adopts a rare stance for an academic analyst: the stance of the responsible critic. He examines the past conduct of U.S. foreign policy not just to describe and criticize, but also to prescribe workable alternatives that will enhance the effectiveness of U.S. foreign policy. This book is a model for how scholars can make their work relevant to the urgent problems of the world. It will help the next generation of U.S. policy-makers cope with the new pragmatism of Soviet foreign policy, the breakdown of the bipolar world, and the continuing risk of nuclear holocaust.

In Professor Payne's view, the conduct of U.S. foreign policy has foundered on its preoccupations with the ideological contest with communism and with military force as both the measure of American "power" and the principal instrument of foreign policy. The preoccupation with ideology has led policymakers to focus on differences in the positions of the United States and the Soviet Union at the cost of not seeing where the two countries underlying interests are shared or at least parallel. The preoccupation with mililtary force has led to too hasty and too frequent resort to militaristic options for dealing with international conflicts at the cost of finding more effective and less dangerous solutions. These approaches constitute a formula for repeated failure, as the case studies of Soviet and Cuban involvement in Afghanistan, Nicaragua, Southern Africa, and the Commonwealth Caribbean demonstrate.

Professor Payne's formula for a systematically more successful handling of foreign policy begins with a clear-headed — not emotional — assessment of the different kinds of U.S. *and Soviet* interests at stake in any given conflict. Such an assessment by our officials would enable them to see not only where U.S. and Soviet interests differ but also where they create opportunities for joint gains. Another key element of the suggested strategy is a concerted effort to understand Soviet perceptions of reality, of the nature of the Soviet/Cuban relationship, of their objectives in the Third World, and of their political, economic, and social ties with the countries they seek to influence. While many scholars today focus on the technical and strategic capabilities of the superpowers' arsenals, Professor Payne understands that security and survival in the nuclear age depend on the *thinking* of those responsible for weapons use. And so the most pragmatic foreign policy is one directed towards understanding and influencing the way the Soviets think.

A third element of the approach is to rely on negotiation. Professor Payne wisely assumes that negotiations that take a joint problem-solving approach to our shared and conflicting interests are a sign of strength and confidence.

In his introduction, Professor Payne observes that in the nuclear age, a "policy of confrontation which tends to make the world riskier for the Soviet Union also increases our own risk." This observation poses a severe test for those who would advise U.S. policy-makers: their prescriptions should be good not only for the U.S., but should at the same time make the Soviet Union no less secure. Happily, the prescriptions in this book meet that test and, indeed, go beyond that: If both the United States *and* the Soviet Union follow his advice to negotiate rather than confront, to focus on underlying interests rather than conflicting positions, to understand each other's perception of reality rather than assume that their own view is the only correct one, and to focus on the kind of future we want rather than assess blame for the past, then both countries — and the rest of the world — will be safer and more secure.

Roger Fisher
Williston Professor of Law
Harvard Law School

Acknowledgments

I am indebted to many students, colleagues, and friends who have made significant contributions to this book. I would like to thank my students who helped me refine my ideas by raising questions and offering suggestions on resolving conflicts between the Soviet Union and the United States. Special thanks is due to Sam McLean, Elizabeth Wilp, Karen Talkington, Sandy Parker and Kurt Cruppenink for their insights and interest in my work. I am extremely grateful to Garold Cole for providing invaluable assistance in locating materials at Milner Library, and to Helga Whitcomb for her unsurpassed enthusiasm, dedication, and skill in obtaining materials through the Inter-Library Loan system. I am deeply indebted to Sharon O'Connor, Doris Poiriez, and Iris Baird for typing the manuscript, and Kenton Machina for his computer expertise. I would also like to thank Joanne Long and Kay Gibbons of the Graphics Department for preparing the maps, and Virginia Owen, Dean of the College of Arts and Sciences at Illinois State University, for assisting my research efforts. I owe a special debt of gratitude to my editors Peggy Gifford and Elizabeth Moore for their confidence in my work and careful editing of the manuscript, and to the anonymous reviewers for their helpful comments.

Hibbert Roberts, Chairman of the Political Science Department at Illinois State University, read the entire manuscript and offered many specific suggestions for improving it. His support and encouragement over the years is greatly appreciated. Many colleagues read parts of the manuscript and made insightful comments. Richard Jacobs read the chapter on Nicaragua, Ronald Pope and Pat Risso read the chapter on Afghanistan, and Denis Thornton and Richard Hartwig reviewed the Commonwealth Caribbean chapter. I would like to thank Professor Roger Fisher of Harvard Law School and the Harvard Negotiation Project for encouraging me to focus on negotiations as an instrument of conflict resolution and for his suggestions for improving the first chapter.

I wish to express special thanks to Barbara Heyl, Ana Maria Downs, and Patricia Colter for editing several chapters, and to Susie Pope for her careful proofreading of the entire manuscript. Ana Maria Downs, Charlotte Thomas, Linda Levinson, Kathy Bowen, Sandra Hall and

Melissa McKinney provided valuable research assistance, and Mark Feaster was extremely helpful with the index.

I am grateful for the support of many friends, especially William and Maria Brisk, Donald and Arlene Winslow, Linaya Leaf, and Ellie Duax. Above all, I would like to thank my parents for teaching me to question, and my son Jason for his questions, insights, and his focus on the future.

Introduction

Technological revolutions profoundly affect international relations and many aspects of life within nations. Nuclear technology, with its accompanying threat of a global thermonuclear war, forces us to question the conventional opinion that strategic advantage is derived solely from military might and the prevalent attitude that Soviet interests around the world, especially in Third World countries, always oppose U.S. interests. The argument that a confrontive stance toward Moscow is required to prove our military supremacy (to ourselves as well as to the world community) is not only shallow and dangerously shortsighted, but demonstrates a lack of imagination and creativity essential for survival in a nuclear age. It ignores the fact that nuclear weapons have created unprecedented interdependence among nations by inextricably linking the fate of all humanity. A policy of confrontation which tends to make the world riskier for the Soviet Union also increases our own risk. Our survival (as well as theirs) depends on how they perceive us, how we perceive them, and each country's self-perception.

The paradox of the nuclear age is that nuclear weapons provide peace because they assure mutual destruction; but any miscalculation by the superpowers contains the risk of pushing the world from peace to a thermonuclear holocaust. Military technology, which is supposed to provide greater security, provides some security at the same time that it makes us ultimately more vulnerable. Under these circumstances, military solutions to crisis situations become less desirable. Nevertheless, we find that violence and counterviolence continue to underlie contemporary approaches to political crisis management in general, and U.S. policy toward Soviet-Cuban activities in particular. Although each conflict presents dangers as well as opportunities, preoccupation with military solutions prevents American foreign policymakers from taking advantage of such opportunities.

Strongly influenced by proponents of so-called "power politics" and "political realism," the architects of U.S. foreign policy continue to emphasize military force as the principal instrument of foreign policy. This approach inevitably generates militaristic options to international conflicts and diminishes our prospects for less dangerous solutions. Combined with hateful rhetoric and ideological hostility, the conventional approach to crisis resolution makes war a self-fulfilling prophecy. Numerous historical examples suggest how we define a situation profoundly affects our actions. Governments have embarked on suicidal missions because they perceived war as the only alternative to a decline in their power. Afraid of appearing weak, they marched confidently into wars that resulted in incalculable costs for all involved, costs that were seriously underestimated by those initiating the conflicts.

Previously, each major advance in military technology was seen as a permanent deterrent to war, but each was eventually used to inflict the unimaginable destruction it was intended to prevent. Instead of emphasizing the power of ideas, persuasion, and negotiation, and taking greater responsibility for their actions, many world leaders allowed technology to control their actions. Unfortunately, an understanding of the painful consequences of such decisions seems to elude contemporary world leaders who believe that nuclear technology will save us.

While few scholars underestimate the potential for thermonuclear war between the United States and the Soviet Union, a large majority continue to focus on the technical and strategic capabilities of the weapons rather than on the thinking of those responsible for their use. So deeply ingrained is the belligerent approach to problem-solving that negotiation as an important aspect of national power is generally dismissed if it is not accompanied by the threat of force.

This book rejects the fatalism characteristic of contemporary American relations with the Soviet Union and Cuba, and suggests that through negotiating, deemphasizing ideology, and focusing on problems that provide opportunities for Soviet-Cuban involvement, the United States can have a pragmatic, workable, and efficient foreign policy in relation to Soviet-Cuban activities in the Third World. An underlying assumption is that negotiation is not only a sign of strength but also a necessity in the nuclear age. Our choice is increasingly narrowed to one between peaceful resolution of superpower conflicts or general global catastrophe. How we think will determine our future. Each conflict presents dangers as well as opportunities for superpower cooperation.

Moscow's ability to achieve its objectives in the Third World depends on Soviet power, local conditions, and how the U.S. responds to perceived threats. The success of U.S. foreign policy depends on a realistic assessment of the limits of military power, sensitivity to Third World problems beyond the context of communism and anticommunism, acceptance of change, our willingness to allow others to play the leading role when appropriate, and our ability to use Soviet-Cuban activities to our advantage.

Suggesting less traditional ways of addressing Soviet-Cuban involvement in Third World conflicts is inherently risky because it challenges how we habitually think about and react to communism and change in Third World countries. Any departure from accepted, even anachronistic, views of conflict resolution is vulnerable to criticism. Furthermore, because it is generally much easier to make recommendations than to implement them, it is risky to attempt less traditional solutions to conflicts involving the Soviet Union and Cuba. Nevertheless, in light of recent U.S. foreign policy failures in the Third World, more realistic approaches to Soviet-Cuban activities are obviously needed.

Soviet-Cuban Activities: Toward a Pragmatic U.S. Policy

A primary objective of U.S. foreign policy is the prevention of Soviet-Cuban involvement in Third World conflicts. This concern affects East-West relations in areas such as trade, arms control, and cultural exchanges; influences various guerrilla movements to vie for U.S. support in essentially internal political struggles; and sharpens the debate within the United States and among our allies about the wisdom of making foreign policy based primarily on anticommunism. A pragmatic foreign policy is guided less by ideological considerations and more by a careful assessment of each conflict in order to formulate an effective and efficient response that will achieve desired objectives. This book examines several Third World conflicts the Soviet Union and Cuba are involved in and suggests a more pragmatic U.S. policy for each particular regional problem.

The first step toward an effective U.S. policy in relation to Soviet-Cuban military involvement in foreign countries is to clearly define U.S. interests and objectives in those areas, particularly where there is a high probability of social and political conflict. This requires prioritizing those interests to determine what kind of Soviet behavior we would find unacceptable and the nature of our response, if any. It also means that the United States must in effect decide the price it is willing or able to pay to protect those interests when challenged by the Soviet Union and Cuba. A related impediment to a successful U.S. foreign policy is the erroneous belief that U.S. resources and power are virtually unlimited. This prevents us from being more careful about defining and prioritizing our interests. Unless the limits to U.S. power are taken into account in strategic planning, foreign policy will continue to flounder. If our interests and aspirations are out of balance with our capabilities, our credibility will be proportionately diminished because of the inherent failures in such an approach. To reduce the temptation for Soviet-Cuban involvement in Third World conflicts, the United States must send Moscow and Havana credible diplomatic and military signals that will influence their perceptions of American resolve. This would also discourage the Soviet Union and Cuba from committing their resources in high-risk areas. One advantage of clearly defining our interests and demonstrating our commitment and resolve is that it would send the Soviets and Cubans a credible threat before they make substantial military and ideological commitments that are difficult to reverse.[1] For example, failure to clearly define our interests in Afghanistan before the 1979 Soviet invasion made it extremely difficult for us to convince Moscow and others that Afghanistan was important to the United States. On the other hand, we have carefully articulated our security concerns in the Caribbean and Central America and, as Grenada demonstrated, neither Moscow nor Havana doubted America's resolve to protect its interests.

Implicit in the above discussion is the need for anchoring foreign policy to a concrete idea of national interest and distinguishing different kinds of interests in order to avoid a universalistic approach that makes it virtually impossible to set priorities. National interests may be defined as a finite set of intrinsically important goals either essential or beneficial to the country's survival, its prosperity, the psychological well-being of its population, or any combination of these.[2]

Donald Nuechterlein has developed a four-tiered scale of priorities as the basis for defining more precisely the value a nation attaches to specific foreign policy issues.[3] In order of importance, this scale includes: 1) Survival interests, where a country's existence is at stake; 2) Vital interests, where serious damage to the nation could result if strong measures are not taken within a relatively short period of time; 3) Major interests, where the country could be seriously harmed if it fails to counteract an unfavorable development abroad; 4) Peripheral or minor interests, where little harm will result if a "wait and see" policy is adopted.[4]

U.S. reaction to Soviet-Cuban activities in the Third World indicates a lack of clearly defined interests as well as failure to make a distinction between primary and secondary concerns. There is a general tendency at the national level to regard all crisis areas as vital to U.S. security interests, especially when the crisis is perceived in an East-West context. One can seriously question whether Afghanistan and Ethiopia are as important as Nicaragua and the Commonwealth Caribbean.

Policymakers use the term "vital interests" so loosely as to render it meaningless, confusing, and therefore dangerous. The following table might be helpful in deciding if a Third World conflict in which there is Soviet-Cuban involvement can affect the United States' vital interests.

Table I Criteria for Determining Vital Interests

Value Factors	Cost/Risk Factors
Proximity of the Danger	Economic Costs of Hostilities
Nature of the Threat	Military Costs of Hostilities
Economic Stake	Estimated Casualties
Sentimental Attachment	Risk of Protracted Conflict
Effect on the Balance of Power	Risk of Enlarged Conflict
	Risk of Public Opposition
Support of Allies	Risk of Congressional Opposition
National Prestige at Stake	Risk of World Opposition

Source: Donald Nuechterlein, *America Overcommitted: U.S. National Interests in the 1980s* (Lexington, Kentucky: University of Kentucky Press, 1985), p. 19.

Based on these criteria, a policymaker should be able not only to determine vital interests, but also the choice of instruments for dealing with Soviet-Cuban activities in the Third World.

While most American presidents have shared the view that the United States cannot abandon competition with the Soviet Union (and Cuba) in any part of the world, they have differed in terms of the instruments they select. President Reagan for example, decided to emphasize both military and economic measures to implement foreign policy objectives. By 1985 the Reagan doctrine, involving support to insurgent groups fighting against Soviet-Cuban supported regimes as well as improved trading opportunities for Third World exporters, was clearly articulated in relation to Angola, Afghanistan, the Commonwealth Caribbean, Nicaragua, and, to a lesser extent, Ethiopia.[5] Reagan's attempts at diplomacy as an instrument of foreign policy have been less obvious. His approach to the Soviet Union has been characterized by sharp oscillations between conciliation and acrimony. The most obvious and dramatic example of this is the 1986 Iceland Summit with Gorbachev, viewed by Michael Mandelbaum and Strobe Talbott as breaking with virtually all precedents of U.S.-Soviet relations and as one of the most extraordinary encounters in the annals of high-level diplomacy[6] Reagan's lack of preparation and the confusion about what was discussed during the Summit underscored his difficulty in using diplomacy to protect U.S. interests. Presidents Nixon and Carter, on the other hand, emphasized preventive diplomacy and economic aid as the most appropriate instruments for competing with Moscow in the Third World in the post-Vietnam era.

Before we can pursue preventive diplomacy we must take inventory of our resources. What factors favor Soviet-Cuban involvement? What do they have working against them? What do we have that will enable us to frustrate Soviet objectives? It is generally agreed that violence in Third World societies is beneficial to Soviet objectives whereas peaceful change is favorable to the United States. There is also general agreement that the Soviets are not highly regarded or liked in Third World countries, especially in Africa. Their isolation places them at a definite disadvantage when dealing with racial and cultural differences. Furthermore, their ideology has grown tired and outdated for the more sophisticated leaders of developing countries. Moscow cannot afford significant economic assistance to Third World countries; Cuba is a very expensive exception. But the Soviet Union has problems closer to its own frontiers. There is increasing evidence that the Kremlin's grip on Eastern European societies is weakening. The elites of these countries are increasingly outspoken in their yearning for autonomy at a time when Soviet citizens as well as many leaders, including Gorbachev, are communicating their dissatisfaction with attempted economic reforms, continued shortages, and the bureaucratic stranglehold on the economy.[7]

The United States is limited by its anticommunist ideology and reluctance to support the changing of the status quo in societies where there are pressures for change. Institutional arrangements and the system of checks and balances, deliberately designed to protect freedom domestically, sometimes work to the detriment of an effective foreign policy. However, the successful working of these institutions domestically is a factor that can also be made to work for us externally. U.S. power abroad is most clearly identified not so much with military might as with its ideals and political values, which provide hope around the world. In addition to the power of principle, U.S. human and material resources are of great consequence. Despite overt hostility to U.S. policies in many parts of the Third World, a distinction is generally made between the government and the people. Compared to Soviet citizens, Americans integrate easily in most societies and are viewed positively. There is also strong convergence between Third World interests in economic development and the United States' ability to provide technology, capital, managerial expertise and access to markets. After taking inventory, we must consider how we can use what we have to accomplish our objectives. The approach that is most consistent with American ideals and political realities is preventive diplomacy.

In order to have a more pragmatic policy toward Soviet-Cuban activities in the Third World, it is imperative that we develop a better understanding of the Soviet society, foreign policy objectives of the USSR in the Third World, and the nature of the Soviet-Cuban link. Greater knowledge of and communication with the Soviets could convert actions that are conventionally viewed as liabilities into assets, reduce unnecessary bloodshed and destruction of material resources, enable policymakers to work with the Soviets in areas of mutual interest, and achieve a stable world order consistent with the United States' role as a global power.

UNDERSTANDING THE SOVIETS' REALITY

So concerned are American policymakers with not being too soft on communism and not allowing the Soviets to threaten U.S. security in remote and previously neglected areas of the world that little time is spent trying to see the world from the Soviet perspective. It is even regarded as somewhat heretical to attempt to see their reality. However, this is exactly what must be done if we realistically expect to influence their behavior, take advantage of their activities, and communicate U.S. objectives to the Soviet leadership. America's historical experience, vastness, isolation, abundance of natural resources, and commitment to freedom and entrepreneurship, among other qualities, have combined to shape the American character. The American view of reality is strongly influenced by the nation's past. The Soviets have also constructed a reality based on their history. Both realities are equally valid; both lead to a feeling of self-righteousness. A state's reality, like that of the individual, is constructed from the sum total of its remembered experiences.

A key factor influencing the Soviet construction of reality is their weakness. Although militarily strong, the Soviet Union remains an essentially weak society. Indeed, it is this sense of vulnerability that forces them to allocate much of their resources to being militarily strong. Their history, unlike U.S. history, is replete with invasions and devastation. They have never been secure and therefore elevate security above all else. As Joyce notes, Americans should always remember that Russia's exaggerated need for security can make them dangerous and that threatening the Soviets is often counterproductive.[8] Because they are weak, they cannot appear to be weak. A corollary of insecurity is the tendency to be suspicious, and extremely cautious. Consequently, the Soviets demand such a high degree of security from their neighbors that they eventually dominate those countries militarily or at least make sure that they are militarily superior. Understanding this Soviet reality could have influenced Carter to take a different approach to Afghanistan. While this means that the U.S. must maintain an adequate defense, definition of adequacy must take several factors into consideration. The USSR's economic weaknesses, social and technological problems and the decline of its appeal to Third World leaders, and the obvious costs of maintaining an empire prevent it from becoming a world-devouring monster[9]. Moscow's preoccupation with economic and job security allows workers to feel so secure that productivity is extremely low due to absenteeism, poor job performance, alcoholism, and a lack of motivation. This ultimately restrains Moscow's global ambitions, especially in nonmilitary areas.

Putting ourselves in the Soviets' shoes, as it were, would also help us to understand that competing with them militarily gives them the advantage. That is their strength. Their experiences with wars, particularly World War II in which they lost approximately 20 million lives — forty times the number of Americans killed in that conflict — influence their perceptions of the world today. World War II became the Great Patriotic War because it touched practically every family and united them against Germany. Visitors to Moscow, Leningrad, Kiev, and elsewhere are constantly reminded of the war's pervasive and devastating impact. Most cities have war memorials and elaborate rituals to constantly remind people that they must be vigilant to prevent such a recurrence.[10] Under these circumstances the government can get the support of all Soviet citizens, including the dissidents, when threatened by the United States that is perceived by the Soviet Union as a determined effort to disregard their legitimate interest in safeguarding national security or keeping their role in world affairs consistent with their status as a superpower and near-equal of the United States.

SOVIET EXPANSION

Excessive concern with security is a significant factor influencing Moscow's relationship with neighboring states as well as Third World countries. And since World War II, U.S. foreign policy has focused on effective ways of restraining the Soviets. Several reasons have been advanced to explain Soviet global activities in general. A major argument is that contemporary Russia is essentially a continuation of prerevolutionary Russia and that current leaders are the inheritors of the expansionist, imperialist czars. The Soviet empire today, just as in the czarist period, provides not only prestige but also security. This view holds that in order to maintain control over what it has, the internal dynamics of imperialism compel the Soviets to control more. In Afghanistan, for example, one argument is that the Soviets want not so much unlimited power as unlimited security.[11] A second and widely-held explanation for Soviet expansion is that it is the essentially defensive reaction of an insecure state to perceived external threats. Soviet leadership, it is argued, lacks internal legitimacy and must justify itself by creating and then reacting to external threats. Third, Soviet expansion is an expression of Marxist-Leninist ideology, which gives the Soviet Union a special mission to make the world communist. The corollary of this view is that the Soviets are guided by a systematic grand strategy[12] and will utilize proxies such as Cuba to assist in the achievement of global domination in direct competition with the West, particularly the United States.

Given the complexities of any nation's foreign policies, it is likely that Soviet leaders are motivated by a combination of all the above reasons. Since the Kremlin operates under circumstances in the internal environment similar to those which influence a nation's behavior externally, it is also likely that rather than a long-term systematic grand strategy, Soviet policy is more accurately characterized by short-term decision making, contradictions, and inconsistencies.[13] In light of the nature of its domestic political system the Soviet Union is probably better able to manage these contradictions than the United States. On the other hand, the external environment is less hospitable to Soviet foreign policy ambitions and more conducive to a U.S. foreign policy, which is consistent with fundamental American values and political ideals.

This is especially applicable to the Third World, an area where Soviet-Cuban involvement clearly escalated, beginning with Soviet-Cuban military support for the Popular Movement for the Liberation of Angola (MPLA) in 1975.

The United States' sharp reaction to this new stage of Soviet-Cuban military involvement is due in part to the American perception of Soviet interests as being determined primarily by East-West relations. Brezhnev and other Kremlin leaders indicated to Washington that detente would not preclude Soviet support for liberation movements in the Third World. Nonetheless, when the Soviets backed the Cuban initiative and decided to fully support the MPLA, they were seen by Washington as violating the spirit and meaning of detente. The Soviets were, in fact, reluctantly honoring a commitment made openly to liberation movements.[14] This action was also consistent with their objective of trying to get Western, primarily U.S., recognition of their status as a global power, which entitled the USSR to spread its influence by diplomatic, military, economic, and political means like any other major power, such as Britain, France, Germany, and the United States. The Soviet leadership, as well as informed Soviet citizens, given their feelings of inferiority and insecurity, take special pride in their country's status as a super-power. Having achieved strategic parity with the United States and the ability to project their power globally, the Soviets are claiming the right to participate in the regulation and resolution of important international issues and conflicts.[15]

Soviet foreign policy toward the Third World has become complex and marks a departure from the Brezhnev era during which Moscow was willing to pay a fairly high price for its empire. Gorbachev's drive to ac-celerate development of the Soviet economy, combined with a wide-ranging reassessment in elite Soviet policy circles of Moscow's relations with the Third World, influenced him to adopt a low-cost foreign policy that included substantial reductions in arms to various Third World clients.[16] Regimes such as Nicaragua, Angola, Ethiopia, and even Afghanistan were expected by the Kremlin to develop their economies primarily through their own effort, as Moscow focused attention on its own domestic problems and became increasingly aware of the complex-ities of the Third World. Furthermore, unlike previous Soviet leaders, Gorbachev requires concrete foreign policy successes, the most impor-tant being improved relations with the United States and Western Europe, especially in the area of arms control.[17] This does not mean that efforts to undermine U.S. interests in developing countries were aban-doned. On the contrary, the Soviet Union under Gorbachev is pursuing a more pragmatic policy at a time when the U.S. approach to the Third World is more influenced by ideology.

The basic objectives of the new Soviet policy are to improve the country's image worldwide, to integrate the Soviet Union more into the world economy, and to exert influence in regional conflicts by develop-ing stronger ties with non-Marxist countries while maintaining those with traditional allies.[18] Strengthening ties with nonaligned non-Marxist states is a low-cost policy designed to create both economic and political oppor-tunities for Moscow. Gorbachev's visit to Latin America in 1987, Moscow's relatively moderate approach to the Middle East crisis, and its decision to allow Soviet tankers to transport Kuwaiti oil through the Per-sian Gulf are examples of this new diplomacy.[19]

Washington's failure to develop a pragmatic policy to deal with the contemporary Soviet approach to the Third World could be extremely costly. U.S. policy of containing communism that polarizes Third World countries into mutually exclusive camps, pro-Soviet, or pro-West, and stresses military confrontation over diplomacy is likely to be counter-productive. As Buchanan observes, confrontation deepens Third World military dependence on and ideological identification with the Soviet Union.[20] In order to develop a more effective policy toward Soviet-Cuban activities, it is important to analyze the nature of the Soviet-

Cuban link. Understanding it might provide insight into how Washington can decrease Moscow's influence in the Third World.

THE SOVIET-CUBAN LINK: COOPERATION AND CONFLICT

Despite the continuing debate among scholars regarding the relative amount of independence exercised by Cuba in the conduct of its foreign policy toward radical Third World regimes, the general assumption in Washington is that Cuba is a Soviet proxy and that its policy objectives and activities are an extension of Moscow's.

That the Soviet-Cuban link is strong cannot be disputed. It is estimated that a Soviet Brigade of 2,600–3,000 men is located near Havana. Carter's demand that they be withdrawn focused attention on this aspect of the Soviet-Cuban relationship. There are also between 6,000–8,000 so-called civilian advisors in Cuba. The Soviets give Cuba $4–5 billion annually, which is approximately one-fourth of that country's GNP, and pay up to four or five times the world price for Cuban sugar. In April 1986 Moscow signed economic and trade agreements with Cuba providing for $3 billion in new credits, a figure which represents a 50 percent increase in Soviet assistance to that country for the 1986–1990 period. Overall, Cuba receives approximately 51 percent of all Soviet foreign aid.[21] Soviet arms deliveries to Cuba since 1960 have been about $2.5 billion; and a joint scientific and economic commission has brought direct Soviet participation in planning and other aspects of the economy. Cuba's debt to the Soviet Union exceeds $25 billion,[22] and there is little possibility of repayment. Although this alliance is very expensive for Moscow, Gorbachev has underlined the Soviet Union's commitment at a time when it is focusing on its own economic problems. But what are the foreign policy implications? Is Cuba repaying Moscow by being an instrument of its policy designs?

It is generally agreed that the Soviet-Cuban alliance which grew gradually was, to a large extent, a consequence of U.S. determination to punish Castro by isolating him in Latin America and the Caribbean and detroying Cuba's economy through embargoes. Initially, Moscow demonstrated little interest in the Cuban revolution. The first Cuban-Soviet economic transaction occurred in April of 1959, when the Soviets decided to purchase 170,000 tons of sugar, 30,000 tons less than they had bought from the previous government of Batista in 1958. In February 1960, Moscow offered Castro a $100 million credit to buy equipment. However, not until May of 1960 did Cuba and the Soviet Union actually establish diplomatic relations.[23] Growing U.S. hostility and belligerent rhetoric on both sides pushed Cuba closer to the Soviet camp. In other words, it can be argued that there is a direct relationship between U.S. unremitting hostility toward Cuba, the consequent deterioration in U.S.-Cuban ties, and the development of Soviet-Cuban links. For example, in the first week of July, 1960, when the United States significantly reduced Cuba's sugar import quota, the Soviet Union stepped in to take up the slack, saving Cuba from economic ruin. Despite the Soviet subsidy, between 1963 and 1965 only an unsteady, uneasy relationship existed between Cuba and the Soviet Union.[24] That Castro was unwilling to substitute dependence on the United States with dependence on the Soviet Union is demonstrated by a deliberate attempt by Castro to have an independent foreign policy. In fact, Castro's international ambitions and practices were in direct conflict with Soviet policy objectives. This is particularly true in Latin America and Southern Africa, where Cuba supported revolutionary groups.

In Latin America, the Soviets disliked the Castroites' refusal to allow "objective conditions" to ripen. Castro, who was essentially independent during this early period, saw U.S. imperialism as the principal enemy, but he bitterly resented socialist governments that gave aid to Latin American oligarchs and hampered the work of the guerrillas who were the genuine revolutionaries.[25] Specifically, Castro was actually sponsoring guerrilla warfare in countries such as Venezuela, Colombia, Brazil, Argentina, and Peru while the Soviet Union was endeavoring to establish and maintain normal economic and diplomatic relations with them. Castro's decision to downgrade support for these groups in particular and for armed struggle in general was influenced by direct Soviet economic pressure on Cuba in 1967–1968 and the failure of Cuban-sponsored insurgencies on the ground.[26] Nevertheless, Cuba's preoccupation with armed struggle and commitment to becoming the Third World's revolutionary leader had a negative impact on the Soviet Union's efforts in Latin America.

The differences between Cuban and Soviet foreign policies were even more distinct in Africa. Evidence indicates that Castro's African policies in the late 1960s and early 1970s were developed and implemented quite independent of the Kremlin. Long before joint Soviet-Cuban operations in Angola and Ethiopia, Castro had been actively supporting various groups. Castro sent advisors to the Congo in 1961; Cuban troops assisted the Ben Bella regime in Algeria in a border conflict with Morocco in 1963; Cubans trained guerrillas in Guinea; and in the mid-1960s Havana established close military and political ties with the Popular Movement for the Liberation of Angola. These activities were not affected by relations between Moscow and Havana.[27] As Duncan contends, the Soviet Union was reformulating its African policies at a time when Cuba's ideological adherence to internationalist solidarity in support of African liberation movements was on the ascendancy.[28] However, later operations in Angola and on the Horn of Africa showed a more complex relationship between Havana and Moscow.

Castro's mismanagement of his economic and political resources, combined with the effectiveness of the U.S. policy of hostility, forced Cuba to abandon some of its relatively independent internal economic policies and foreign relations by 1968, and Cuban opposition to the conduct of Soviet policy decreased. The most discernible shift came with the Soviet invasion of Czechoslovakia in 1968 to terminate the liberalization attempts by the Communist Party there. Unlike the 1968 "Prague Spring," when the Cuban government was essentially neutral and the Cuban people demonstrated their support for the Prague government, subsequent Soviet suppression of Czechoslovakian attempts to pursue policies of which Moscow disapproved were regarded by Castro as politically correct and therefore necessary and justifiable.[29] Cuba, it is argued, gradually yielded one sphere after another of its domestic and foreign policy to Soviet tutelage, relinquishing the revolution's original goal of political and economic autonomy.[30] The loss of independence is seen as corresponding with Cuba's growing dependence on Moscow for its economic and political survival. This view is misleading.

Soviet-Cuban activities in Angola, the Commonwealth Caribbean, and Nicaragua were initiated by Havana. In these areas Cuba strongly influenced the Soviet decision to become involved. Obviously the Soviets perceived various benefits that would be derived from joint interventions, and Castro could not have been as effective without Soviet logistical support, sealift capabilities, and weapons and supplies. But because of the Soviet Union's dependence on Cuban ground forces in both Angola and Ethiopia for advancing Moscow's objectives, Cuba emerged with increased influence in its relationship with the USSR.[31] Therefore, although Cuba is a strong supporter of some Soviet foreign policies, because of Havana's dependence on Moscow, it can also be argued that the relationship between the two countries is best thought of as a tight alliance. It is not a simple case of a puppet responding to its master's will.[32] Cuba needs Moscow's backing in order to continue playing such an important role in world affairs, a role clearly inconsistent with Cuba's size and resources. Moscow, on the other hand, benefits from Cuba's activities. It would seem that there is essentially a convergence of interests. What is often overlooked is that the massive Soviet investment in such a strategic ally as Cuba, provides the latter with influence over the former.

One must be careful to distinguish among Soviet-Cuban partnerships in different parts of the world. Whereas the Soviets were obviously interested in enlisting the Cubans as surrogates on the Horn of Africa, they appeared less enthusiastic about what the Cubans were doing in

Latin America and the Caribbean in the 1960s. Perspectives on Soviet interests and Cuba's role as a Soviet surrogate in Latin America and the Caribbean are more complex and contradictory than those in Africa. By challenging the United States in its own backyard, the Soviets expect to gain significant political advantages and to have greater freedom to act in areas of more immediate strategic interests, above all the Persian Gulf and Indian Ocean. They regard the Caribbean as a hinterland on whose stability freedom of U.S. action in other parts of the globe depends. The Soviets, according to this view, profit from the troubles of others and continue directly, or through surrogates, their clandestine material support for revolutionary or anti-status quo forces everywhere.[33] This perspective is consistent with the view that the Caribbean is part of Soviet global strategy and that Cuban gains are tantamount to Soviet gains.

Another view, similar to the first, is that the Soviets see developments in the Caribbean as favorable to the advancement of their interests. Their establishment of a political-military base in Cuba and leftism in the Caribbean provide additional opportunities for the USSR to augment and establish commercial and political relations with the region as a counterweight to U.S. influence. They hope to capitalize on local nationalists' frustrations with the strong impact of the United States on the region.[32]

Contradicting the first two viewpoints is the perspective which holds that even though there are close similarities between Cuban and Soviet foreign policies, the total overlapping of Soviet and Cuban interests in the Caribbean may be exaggerated. This controversial opinion of the Soviet-Cuban alliance is best articulated by LeoGrande, who contends that some Cuban foreign policy initiatives, among them Cuban activities in the Caribbean region, seem to be of little concern to the Soviet Union. LeoGrande argues that:

> Although the Soviets have not, as far as is known, tried to restrain Cuban behavior, they have shown remarkably little enthusiasm for creating other Cubas in the region. The Soviet Union has refused to underwrite the expenses of socialist construction in such countries as Jamaica, or Nicaragua. The Soviet economy can ill afford to finance any more Cubas in the Caribbean, especially because they would provide only a marginal strategic gain over the existing partnershp with Cuba itself.[35]

Indeed, Cuban, not Soviet, objectives are paramount in the Caribbean and Latin America. It is in this region that Cuba's independent foreign policy and its influence on its relationship with Moscow are clearly manifested.

Departing from the position it adopted in the 1960s, the Soviet Union shifted in the mid-1970s toward the Cuban view of conflicts in the U.S. sphere of influence. In addition to Cuba's success in Angola, Castro also had successes in Nicaragua, Grenada, and El Salvador to convince Moscow that Cuba's perspective on revolutionary opportunities in the region was far more accurate than the Soviets had been inclined to think.[36] Castro's understanding of Caribbean politics and close friendship with leaders such as Michael Manley of Jamaica and Maurice Bishop of Grenada provided him with leverage in his relationship with Moscow. In addition, Cuba's geographic proximity to areas of conflict facilitated the application of its military capabilities, allowing it to project its own brand of power and to increase its prestige in the region and the Third World while depending on Soviet economic and military support.[37]

The Soviet Union, on the other hand, regards the Caribbean as being of less strategic value and does not want a direct confrontation with the United States. Nevertheless, given the ideological and strategic rewards Moscow derives from creating problems for its rival in its own backyard, the Soviets demonstrate a willingness to back Cuba in its support for armed struggle,[38] a fact underlined by Gorbachev's decision to increase economic and military assistance to Castro. The idea that Cuba is simply carrying out Soviet policy objectives is incorrect. There is an obvious convergence of interests as well as a relationship characterized by mutual dependence. It is more accurate to see the Soviet-Cuban alliance as one in which influence flows in both directions at various times over different issues and in different Third World conflicts.[39] Just as the Soviets took the initiative to invade Afghanistan without Cuban support, Castro was not reluctant to assist the Sandinistas prior to 1979. Under Gorbachev, the Soviet strategy in the Third World and its ties with Cuba are likely to be based more on pragmatic considerations than ideology.

The Soviet Union is turning its attention inward and focusing on domestic problems that are demanding attention. During what could be regarded as a transitional stage, it is anticipated that although the Soviets will continue to take advantage of crises in Third World countries and elsewhere, this will be a period in which domestic economic issues will be of paramount importance and foreign policy a secondary concern.[40] Furthermore, there are other restraints on Soviet expansion in the Third World. These include the vulnerability of Third World governments to being overthrown, the divergence of Soviet and Third World interests, nationalism, and the fact that regional and local Third World conflicts could easily put Moscow in the crossfire of ethnic, religious, and nationalist clashes.[41] Many developing countries are likely to attempt to pursue independent foreign policies instead of falling victim to a new form of colonialism.

TOWARD A PRAGMATIC U.S. POLICY

Despite significant changes in the post-World War II international environment, American foreign policymakers continue to operate within a framework that is no longer suitable for an effective, long-range, pragmatic foreign policy, especially in relation to Soviet Union-Cuban activities in Third World countries. Indeed, the traditional approach to foreign policy making is counterproductive; very costly in terms of prestige, money, and power; extremely dangerous in the nuclear age; and, inadvertently, assists the Soviets and Cubans in achieving their objectives.

In the process of resolving conflicts, the general tendency on the part of individuals and governments alike is to focus on what we should do rather than what we want done, who is best suited for doing it, and what price we can afford. Specifying the objective must be the beginning of analysis.[42] The starting point should be the other government's problem. The key question to answer is what decision we wish them to make or refrain from making. Once we have identified this, the immediate step is to develop various strategies for influencing events in the direction favorable to us. We would also take into account what restraints on Soviet behavior, for example, might realistically be expected. Obviously, this can be extremely difficult under the most propitious circumstances. However, it is a crucial challenge that policymakers must confront for U.S. foreign policy to be successful.

A major objective of American foreign policy is to prevent Soviet-Cuban involvement in Third World conflicts. How can we get them to do this? How can we take advantage of their activities to accomplish it? Contrary to the conventional approach, the Soviets and Cubans can be instrumental in their own removal from areas of U.S. interest if we can use their activities to change the conditions which are conducive to their involvement. This requires an accurate assessment of the problem. In South Africa, for example, the problem is not communism but rather the denial of basic human rights to the vast majority of the population by the white minority government that, in turn, creates a climate that facilitates and encourages Soviet-Cuban involvement. In this case, the U.S. might find it advantageous not to oppose the Soviets but to explore ways in which the Soviets can assist in making the South African government implement fundamental changes that would safeguard basic human rights and consequently remove opportunities for future Soviet-Cuban influence. There are obvious dangers to this approach. The Soviets could benefit from their role in resolving conflicts. However, Third World nationalism and desire for economic growth are likely to reduce Soviet-Cuban influence. Despite significant differences between the two superpowers, competition in the Third World is not always a zero-sum game. When interests coincide, the United States should not hesitate to cooperate with the Soviet Union, overtly or covertly. This is especially appropriate in situations where there is a high probability that the side supported by the Soviets will eventually assume power. It is generally more costly to attempt to resist major developments than to accommodate to them. Compared with the Soviet Union, the United States is better suited to capitalize on contemporary changes because such changes are essential and consistent with American political ideals. It is the Soviets who face an uphill battle in a world dominated by nationalism.[43] Although not risk-free, this might be an extremely effective, low-cost policy.

What is suggested is that foreign policy objectives must be rational, clearly defined, and part of a long-range policy framework. Such an approach could help to preserve U.S. prestige and power by enabling the U.S. to resist impulsive decision making and avoid those situations which diminish its credibility and, consequently, its power. It might also influence policymakers to consider more options rather than simply reacting instinctively to Soviet-Cuban activity. For example, the Soviet invasion of Afghanistan could have been used: 1. to advance U.S. foreign policy objectives in Asia in particular and the Third World in general; 2. to provide leverage against Iran, the Arab oil producing countries, and Pakistan; and 3. to drive a wedge between Havana and Moscow. By emphasizing that the Soviet invasion was a direct and immediate threat to Pakistan rather than to the U.S., certain concessions that could not be hoped for under ordinary circumstances might have been obtained without putting U.S. reputation in jeopardy by making threats against the Soviets that Washington was unable or unwilling to enforce. As Fisher contends, the "location of the critical ingredients of power is in the minds of those who pay attention to what those with power say or do."[44]

By promptly reacting to the Soviet invasion as a major threat to U.S. security interest, the U.S. government failed to utilize Moscow's actions to put pressure on Pakistan to respect basic human rights, and thereby eliminate a potential threat to Pakistan's security. Pakistan was inadvertently given leverage over U.S. policymakers. Pakistan almost gained concessions from the Carter administration but refused Carter's offer of military aid, referring to it as "peanuts." Reagan's decision to give Pakistan $3.2 billion in military assistance in an effort to counter the Soviet occupation of Afghanistan did not persuade the Soviets to leave. Reagan's action could eventually be a self-defeating blunder that will stir up anti-Americanism in both Pakistan and India and enable the Soviet Union to make significant diplomatic and political advances in southwest Asia through its relationship with India without direct military involvement.[45] The complexity of political interests and alliances in the region defy simple East-West assumptions which underlie U.S. policy.

In our haste to do something, anything, about Soviet-Cuban "expansionism" we often overlook the fact that Cubans and Soviets do not have perfect foresight and that they occasionally make serious mistakes for which they pay an extremely high price. Their foreign policies, like those of any nation, are not cost-free. Reminding ourselves of this in a conflict situation would reduce our tendency to react frantically. By being more patient and taking into consideration the complexities of international relations, the United States could capitalize on Soviet-Cuban mistakes and explore ways in which to profit from them. In other words, their policies, whether successful or not, could provide a wide range of foreign policy opportunities for a United States with an inventive rather than a reactionary approach to foreign policy. Taking advantage of Soviet-Cuban miscalculations could eventually prove discouraging for Moscow and could influence the Soviets and Cubans to more carefully evaluate possible negative political and military consequences of their activities in foreign countries. Such an approach might ultimately diminish international conflict and simultaneously reduce the tremendous costs to the United States which are almost inevitable when conflicts are indistinguishably viewed as East-West (USSR-U.S.) confrontations. Soviet difficulties in Afghanistan, a conflict which has already lasted longer than World War II, with which older Russians are so preoccupied, has significant implications for Soviet society and the Third World. It provides an excellent example of how Soviet miscalculation can hurt them without affecting the U.S. adversely. Promptly instituting a grain embargo, only to have it lifted shortly thereafter by Reagan, eroded U.S. credibility and aborted possible opportunities for improving U.S. policy in that area. It further diminished U.S. power due to the perception that the policy was ineffective because the Soviets successfully stood up to the power play in an area where it was unrealistic to expect the Soviets to jeopardize, from their perspective, vital security interests. By failing to put themselves in the Soviets' shoes, both Carter and Reagan squandered U.S. credibility in reacting to the invasion of Afghanistan.

DEVELOPING A LONG-RANGE FOREIGN POLICY

There is general consensus on the need for a long-term comprehensive foreign policy in relation to the Soviet Union. Such a policy would include: identifying appropriate strategies while assessing the means and resources available for implementing them; evaluating the risks and costs of attempting to achieve our objectives; finding and promoting interests we have in common with other nations, including the Soviet Union; determining the kind of world order which is feasible, given the realities of the current international system; and exercising patience and flexibility. Unlike domestic policy, in which either Congress or the president may assume leadership responsibilities, foreign policy planning requires presidential initiative and direction. The fundamental requirement is the establishment of a national consensus, one that would encompass not only members of the administration but key members of both parties in Congress, the press, and powerful interest groups. These groups must believe in the legitimacy of the policies. Policy legitimacy requires the president to convince those mentioned above of two things: 1) that the policy is consistent with deeply-held national values and will actually contribute to their enhancement; and 2) that the long-term objectives can be achieved.[46] One advantage of having a well-thought out, legitimate foreign policy is that it provides the president with sufficient flexibility to formulate and implement policy without being so vulnerable to pressures inherent in the open, democratic society that Tocqueville and others have discussed.[47]

A long-range foreign policy would also demand changes in the bureaucracy, which are likely to be resisted. Bureaucratic political struggles, delays, fear of rocking the boat, the tendency to reward conformity rather than encourage critical thinking and imagination all combine to frustrate attempts to devise an effective policy. Former Secretary of State Kissinger articulated the relationship between bureaucratic behavior and foreign policy, noting that the large number of lawyers in government is partly responsible for the *ad hoc* nature of foreign policy because they are trained to deal with actual rather than hypothetical cases.[48]

But this problem is deeply rooted in American culture and contemporary society. As George Ball observed, the way we live, including our dependency on television and visual impressions, reinforces the short attention span of most Americans.[49] We react impulsively to first impressions on policy questions. This impulsiveness, by encouraging a "now" focus, limits our ability to utilize past experiences constructively or to have a realistic assessment of the future. There are two main causes of this behavior: inattention on the part of most citizens; and the need to appeal to an inattentive audience.[50] Given the impact of public opinion on decision making and competition between news organizations, the impulsive view developed by the general public influences those whose survival depends on their popularity to also adopt an impulsive view. By working with the "relevant" public, the press, and Congress, the president can mitigate the negative effects of impulsiveness and ultimately reduce its occurrence. However, preoccupation with the containment of communism often exacerbates the problems and inadvertently assists the Soviets and Cubans to achieve their objectives.

ANTICOMMUNISM IS NOT A POLICY

Anticommunism has emerged as the dominant ideology in a country whose founding principle was the establishment of a righteous community in an evil world. Failure to understand the persistence of this cultural trait in foreign policy diminishes the prospects of fashioning a policy that can be reasonably efficient and successful. Although Nye correctly points out that inconsistency and incoherence generally characterize American foreign affairs and are deeply rooted in our political culture and institutions,[51] there is another side to this. The foundation of American assumptions which influence policy has remained solid. It can be summarized in terms of good versus evil. Since World War II America has been consistently anticommunist. Anticommunism as an ideology carries all the dangers inherent in an ideology.

Ideology undermines reality by isolating problems from the turbulent stream of change and treating them in splendid "abstraction from the whirl and contingency of life."[52] Thus, despite the status of the Soviet Union as a superpower with an awesome nuclear arsenal that can destroy the world, it is regarded by the U.S. as not having legitimate interests outside its borders which all great powers, including the United States, have traditionally pursued. Indeed, the legitimacy of the Soviet Union itself is challenged. The pervasive fear of communism precludes an objective view of reality. This anticommunist mentality creates its own set of perceptions which become a self-confirming, self-perpetuating force, to be treated as creators and actual components of political reality.[53]

Perceptions in the U.S.-Soviet rivalry are extremely important, especially when analyzed in the context of strong anticommunist sentiments. The perception of a crisis or event that actually occurs is the one which requires the least reorganization of a person's other ideas.[54] Not surprisingly, both superpowers generally assume the worst about the other's intentions and regard adopting a "worst case" approach as only prudent.[55] Their perceptions and assumptions about each other are usually unreflective, visceral, and deterministic.[56] A very good example of this is the Angolan crisis. Both superpowers intervened on the basis of miscalculations, misperceptions, poor intelligence and faulty judgement.[57] The United States was so convinced that The National Front for the Liberation of Angola (FNLA) and Union for the Total Independence of Angola (UNITA), with South African support, could defeat the Cuban-backed MPLA that it essentially derailed the possibility of a negotiated settlement. The Soviet Union followed Cuba's lead and committed significant military resources to a client state that has yielded few tangible benefits. Another example of misperception relates to Nicaragua. American policymakers generally assume that the Sandinistas are inexorably on the path to establishing a Soviet outpost and ignore Nicaragua's internal dynamics. Unfortunately, as chapter four discusses, U.S. policy toward Nicaragua has been essentially counterproductive, and has contributed to Soviet-Cuban influence in that country.

Despite the obvious complexity of world politics and the dynamism which characterizes Third World politics and society, the United States continues to view the Soviets and Cubans as being responsible for developments which are perceived as inimical to U.S. security interests. Conflicts and conquests, friends and enemies, issues and interests are judged within the very narrow framework of Soviet-U.S. rivalry. The world, from America's view, is divided into two mutually exclusive groups, the evil communists and the righteous anticommunists. To form alliances simply on the basis of anticommunism, or anti-Soviet Union in the case of U.S. ties with China, ignores the logic of international relations and has serious consequences for U.S. foreign policy. As Harrison comments:

> No foreign policy of global leadership based on the resumption of a pervasive Soviet-U.S. rivalry can restructure world politics into the simple, sometimes appealing, but anachronistic hierarchy of the Cold War. Such a misreading of international trends threatens the Soviet Union and offers the unsettling prospect of damaging U.S. economic and security interests in key regions of the Third World. Moreover, it may inflict further damage on the U.S.-West European alliance. . . .[58]

Setbacks for the United States would be regarded by Moscow as a positive development.

Assuming that all countries will follow either the United States or Soviet Union ignores the cardinal principle of international politics — national interests. Given the balance of terror, it is imperative that policymakers take into consideration the aspirations and interests of other states. This translates into a shift away from attempting to impose unilateral decisions on our Western European allies and the Third World to a policy of accommodating their interests and consulting them prior to making decisions which affect them or require their participation.

The problem created by anticommunism is that it overlooks the multiplicity of interests and diversity of existing political regimes. For example, while Europeans, Africans, Asians, and Latin Americans may be concerned about Soviet-Cuban expansionism, their interests and perceptions of the impact of Soviet-Cuban activities will not necessarily coincide with Washington's. Although West Germany opposed the invasion of Afghanistan, it had to take into consideration its ties to East Germany and trade relations with the Soviet Union. For Third World countries, especially those in southern Africa, racial inequality is a more immediate concern than communism. Therefore, it is unlikely that they will passively follow the United States' policy of supporting Savimbi, who is trying to overthrow the Soviet-Cuban backed MPLA government with South African assistance.

The intractability of U.S. anticommunist ideology was demonstrated by President Carter, who began his term in office with an admonition regarding the danger of inordinate fear of communism and a strong appeal for human rights in South Africa, only to end it with increased emphasis on the dangers of communism in southern Africa and the threat of the Soviet brigade in Cuba which had in fact been there for several years. The obvious consequence was further erosion of U.S. credibility. The Russians refused to leave, and Carter later found their presence acceptable. Reagan's anticommunist approach escalated nuclear demonstrations throughout Europe, perhaps to the advantage of the Soviet Union, and divided Western Europeans over the building of the Soviet pipeline. Both examples indicate that to focus solely on a confrontationist policy vis-à-vis Moscow is actually self-defeating. Given the military might of the Soviet Union, the instability inherent in the process of political development, Americans' indifference to Third World problems, their preoccupation with domestic economic conditions, and their fear of nuclear war, it is unrealistic to expect a confrontationist policy to be successful. On the contrary, it prevents us from taking advantage of Soviet-Cuban activities by foreclosing options other than confrontation.

THINKING ABOUT THEIR CHOICES

A pragmatic foreign policy takes into consideration the choices available to the other side or, more precisely, their perception of choices. In Grenada, for example, their Bishop regime viewed Cuban assistance as essential to alleviating that small island's poverty. Sending the Cubans home would have been self-defeating, especially in light of Washington's refusal to make any conciliatory gestures toward Bishop when he visited the United States shortly before his assassination and the subsequent

U.S. invasion. Perhaps the most obvious case of where the other side cannot accept U.S. proposals for conflict resolution is Nicaragua. Reagan is essentially asking the Sandinistas to abdicate their control. By funding the Contras, providing massive amounts of military aid to El Salvador, Honduras, and Guatemala, and by conducting large-scale military exercises in neighboring Honduras, the United States inadvertently influenced the Sandinistas to move even closer to Cuba and the Soviet Union in order to obtain weapons to defend itself.[59] From the Nicaraguan perspective, their choice was between giving in to Washington's demands and survival.

Another problem discussed in the book, Soviet-Cuban activities in Angola, might be resolved if we focused more precisely on the Angolan perception of their choice. As Table II indicates, it is difficult for the MPLA to say yes to Washington's demands that the Angolan government negotiate with Savimbi after sending the Cuban troops back to Havana, especially in light of South Africa's military raids on Angola and its continued cooperation with Savimbi's forces.

Similarly, U.S. policy toward Afghanistan could be more effective if policymakers focused not only on the limits of U.S. power in the region, our national interests at stake, the political and military complexities of the entire region, and the composition of the Afghan resistance movement, but also on the Soviets' perception of their choices. This does not suggest that we stop military assistance to the resistance movements or agree with Moscow's reasons for invading; it simply asks that we try to understand the Soviets' reality in order to deal more pragmatically with the problem.

How the United States responds to Soviet-Cuban activities in the Third World should depend on our national interests there and our ability to project our military and economic power to influence the outcome. None of the countries examined can be regarded as places where vital U.S. interests are at stake, and only the Caribbean and Nicaragua may be classified as areas where the United States has major interests. The tendency to regard all countries in which Moscow and Havana are involved as vital undermines our ability to deal more effectively with resolving the conflicts. Furthermore, Washington's emphasis on communism obscures the role of indigenous forces in the process of change in Third World countries, and failure to separate internal factors from the East-West context reduces the probability of conflict resolution or of diminishing Soviet-Cuban influence. This is particularly true of South Africa and Nicaragua. On the other hand, American policymakers avoided the trap of universalism on the Horn of Africa and adopted a very pragmatic policy in relation to Soviet-Cuban activities.

When formulating and implementing a pragmatic U.S. foreign policy *vis-à-vis* Soviet-Cuban activities, several questions must be raised.

Table II Perception of Choice: The MPLA in Angola

QUESTION: *Shall we send the Cubans home?*

If we say yes	*If we say no*
South Africa continues to dominate Namibia	Defend ourselves against UNITA
No protection against an invasion by South Africa	Protect the revolution
Support violence by UNITA	Protect the oil companies
Divide the ruling group	
More economic turmoil	Stand firm
No protection for oil, the main source of income	Safeguard political power
Risk the revolution	Will not become vulnerable to South African military raids
Risk civil war	
Lose Soviet-Cuban assistance	Will not alienate Soviet-Cubans
Risk losing political power	
But:	*But:*
Perhaps Washington will stop assisting UNITA and pressure South Africa to withdraw from Namibia	The civil war will continue
Angola will have more resources for economic development	Economic decline will accelerate
The MPLA will appear reasonable	Washington will focus on Cuba instead of the real problems
	Expense for keeping Cubans continues
	Appear unreasonable

Source: The author is indebted to Roger Fisher, Professor of Law at Harvard Law School and Director of the Harvard Negotiation Project, for this idea.

In each case, policymakers should ask how deeply involved are U.S. interests? How can our allies assist us in achieving our objectives? Are our interests compatible with theirs? To what extent can the U.S. influence the outcome and at what cost? What is the nature of the regime in internal debates and governmental decisions? If our policy is unsuccessful, can we leave the situation without jeopardizing broader U.S. interests? As these questions suggest, patience and flexibility rather than

Table III   Perception of Choice: The Soviets in Afghanistan

QUESTION: *Should we leave Afghanistan?*

If we say yes	*If we say no*
We undermine Soviet credibility	We strengthen our credibility
We allow the U.S. to influence the new regime	
We risk losing other countries (the domino theory)	We prevent Western influence in a border state
We acknowledge defeat on our own border	
We fail to project our power in the Gulf	We expand by adding another country
We appear weak	
Wisdom of leadership's decision to invade would be questioned	We can project our power in the Gulf
We lose Afghanistan as a base	Leadership appears strong

But:	
We save lives	We appear strong
We reduce negative world opinion	
We improve ties with India	
We improve ties with Moslem countries	
We have more money for the domestic economy	*But:*
	We lose more lives
	We spend more money on the war
	We appear unreasonable
	We continue to suffer from negative international opinion

ideological purity are essential components of a pragmatic U.S. foreign policy.[60]

Furthermore, closer analysis of the groups we assist, an objective assessment of Soviet-Cuban interests, and an examination of the perceptions of those we are trying to influence might improve U.S. policies. Perhaps the most obvious example of the dangers of not carefully scrutinizing the groups we assist relates to the Contras in Nicaragua. Another is UNITA in Angola. Instead of supporting a group primarily on the basis of anticommunism, the United States might ask two questions before it embraces their cause: 1. Is the resistance group self-generated and inherently strong? 2. Is it supported by regional consensus, so that we can count on moral and political support for our policies as well as for our client?[61] In both Nicaragua and Angola the answer to these questions is negative. Secondly, an objective assessment of Soviet-Cuban involvement might show that opportunities exist for cooperation and mutual restraint. As long as Third World conflicts are perceived as a zero-sum game, broader interests of the superpowers such as arms control, trade, and global order are likely to suffer.[62]

Although the Soviet Union and Cuba might want to reduce their commitment to Third World regimes such as Angola and Nicaragua, Washington seems oblivious to exploring ways to help make their decision easier. It seems reasonable to conclude that Washington generally ignores the major lesson of the Cuban missile crisis; namely, that if an adversary wants to retreat, a face-saving avenue should be provided.[63] Finally, the realities of the countries we are trying to influence are important factors influencing Soviet-Cuban success or failure. Most Third World states are reluctant to allow an increase of Soviet-Cuban influence in their affairs, and political volatility and highly personalized domestic politics may actually reduce Soviet-Cuban influence overnight as governments and personalities change.[64] A pragmatic U.S. policy toward Soviet-Cuban activities must take all of these factors into consideration. When this is done, as the Horn of Africa demonstrates, U.S. policy in the Third World might be more successful.

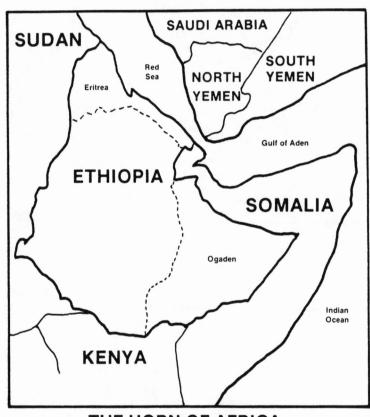

THE HORN OF AFRICA

2

The Horn of Africa: U.S. Pragmatism, Not Paralysis

The pragmatism of United States' policy on the Horn of Africa was demonstrated by American restraint in the face of unprecedented Soviet-Cuban military intervention in the region on behalf of Ethiopia. The United States, despite pressure for a belligerent reaction, carefully assessed its interests on the Horn; its ability to influence local events; the cost of direct military confrontation with the Soviet Union and Cuba; indigenous factors and their impact on Soviet-Cuban influence; the broader implications for its interests in Africa; and its role as global power. This approach represents a significant departure from previous policy in relation to Soviet-Cuban activities in Angola. By focusing on national interests rather than being preoccupied with anticommunism, American policymakers skillfully avoided Somalia's attempt to involve the U.S. in what was essentially a regional quagmire, in the name of frustrating the ambitions of the Soviet Union, a country with which Somalia was so recently closely allied.

Somalia's own actions, invading the Ogaden and terminating the Treaty of Friendship and Cooperation with Moscow, showed that its interests, not the Soviet Union's, predominated. The same is true of the relationship between Ethiopia's new leaders and the United States. Indeed, as Ottaway observed, the degree of success or failure of the great powers in the Horn was based not so much on how skilled their policies were as on the compatibility that existed at different times between their goals and those of Ethiopia and Somalia.[1] Because both external actors put their interests ahead of ideology, conflict between local actors

27

deescalated. What this suggests is that, given the relatively low level of interest of both superpowers in the region and the fragility or tenuousness of their influence because of the area's volatility, Washington and Moscow might be able to cooperate for mutual benefit and work toward a negotiated settlement of various disputes. Economic problems on the Horn should facilitate diplomatic efforts to resolve some of the major conflicts.

Ethiopia and Somalia, two of the poorest countries in the world, remain extremely dependent on foreign aid. Their emphasis on military solutions to their problems drains resources which could be allocated to much-needed economic development, especially in agriculture. As is generally the case in Africa, rapid population growth, government mismanagement, and dependence on foreign food aid combine to exacerbate political problems and challenge governments' stability.

Despite Ethiopia's revolution and Somalia's repudiation of its treaty with Moscow, war continues in the Ogaden, Eritrea, Tigre, and elsewhere; approximately 8 million Ethiopians are at risk due to drought and famine; Somalia is confronted with over 1 million refugees; and the per capita income for Ethiopians is less than $140 a year. More than ten years after the revolution, the current situation in Ethiopia is hauntingly reminiscent of conditions which contributed to the fall of Haile Selassie and the emergence of the Dergue in 1974. Soviet-Cuban activities have not altered these realities, and the root causes of the problems that have plagued the Horn for over two decades persist.

Boundary problems, common to most African countries created by colonial rulers, are at the heart of Ethiopia's continuing conflict with Eritrea and Somalia. Failing to conquer Ethiopia, the Italians carved out a colony along the Red Sea, called it Eritrea, and governed it as a separate political entity from 1890 until World War II. Even before the Italians gained control over Eritrea it was set apart politically and culturally from Ethiopia. Unlike Ethiopia, which remained primarily a Christian country surrounded by Islamic states, Eritrea retained strong ties with the Arab world, was part of the Ottoman Empire from the sixteenth to the nineteenth century, and was occupied by the Egyptians in the 1860s, shortly before Italy arrived. Again, unlike Ethiopia, which continued to be essentially a feudal society, Eritrea experienced agricultural, educational, industrial, and administrative development under colonialism. Only after Italy was defeated in World War II did Haile Selassie seriously attempt to annex Eritrea in order to have outlets to the Red Sea, thereby altering Ethiopia's landlocked status.

The United States, France, Britain, and the Soviet Union favored an autonomous Eritrea, federated with Ethiopia, a position strongly endorsed by the UN General Assembly. This did not deter Selassie from endeavoring to annex Eritrea. Through a combination of bribery, intimidation, and force Selassie succeeded in gaining sufficient votes in parliament to make Eritrea another province of Ethiopia in November 1962. This marked the beginning of the Ethiopian-Eritrean conflict.

Ethiopia's conflict with Somalia over the Ogaden region, where many Somalis live, is also relatively recent, dating back to 1935. During World War II the Italians governed the Ogaden but were soon replaced by Britain. In 1946 Britain proposed the Bevin Plan, which called for a Somalia containing the majority of ethnic Somalis within its boundaries.[2] This meant that the Ogaden and the Northern Frontier District of Kenya, where Somalis make up the majority of the population, would be considered part of Somalia. Opposed by both the United States and the Soviet Union, Britain decided to abandon the Bevin Plan and withdraw from the Ogaden. Ethiopia's interest in the Ogaden coincided with Britain's departure. Nevertheless, the boundary dispute remained dormant until Somalia became independent in 1960. Despite widespread acceptance of the sanctity of colonial boundaries by the vast majority of African states and the Organization of African Unity, Somalia persisted in claiming territories clearly within the boundaries of Ethiopia and Kenya. American interests in Kenya and Ethiopia prior to the 1974 coup as well as its wider African interests militated against support for Somalia's irredentism.

U.S. RELATIONS WITH ETHIOPIA PRIOR TO 1974

Unlike the Commonwealth Caribbean, Central America or even southern Africa, Ethiopia did not evoke any strong emotional feelings on the part of American foreign policymakers. U.S. interests in Ethiopia were clearly defined and limited. The extent of U.S. involvement in Ethiopia was determined primarily by strategic considerations and, to some extent, on a degree of admiration for Emperor Haile Salassie. When Britain withdrew from Ethiopia in 1953, the United States signed a defense-cooperation treaty with Ethiopia to replace Britain. It was the strategic importance of the Horn, its location at vital transportation routes that attracted American defense planners to Ethiopia. The Horn is situated directly along the straits of Bab el Mandeb that control one entrance to the Red Sea, and looks across the Red Sea and the Gulf of Aden to the Arabian Peninsula. It lies at one end of the transit route between the Mediterranean Sea and the Indian Ocean via the Suez Canal and the Red Sea. When much of the ocean-going traffic went through the Suez Canal, the Horn enjoyed considerable strategic value. Nowadays, many ships are too large to utilize the Suez Canal, and the geographic location of the Horn has been diminished by modern technology and modern military realities. However, it is argued that the growing dependence of industrial countries on Persian Gulf oil renders the Horn strategically important because it could serve as a base to interrupt the flow of oil.[3] While it is unlikely that the Soviet Union would risk attacking U.S. ships, small groups of terrorists could effectively harass shipping. Thus, the threat to U.S. oil supplies comes primarily from instability on the Horn rather than from Soviet port facilities in the region.

American ties with Ethiopia under Selassie stemmed mostly from U.S. interest in using the Kagnew military base at Asmara in Eritrea as a major communications facility. Kagnew, an integral part of the U.S. global intelligence network, was used to monitor Soviet activities. In return, Ethiopia received significant amounts of economic and military assistance. Between 1953 and 1978 the United States provided approximately $350 million in economic assistance and $300 million in military aid to Ethiopia. Agriculture, education, and health were the major areas in which U.S. financial assistance was concentrated. Despite the attempted coup in 1960, Ethiopia remained relatively calm and there was no serious military conflicts in the region. The number of American personnel stationed in Ethiopia grew to about 3,000 by 1971. However, increased guerrilla activity in Eritrea, Ethiopia's inability to defeat the insurgents, and modern technology radically altered the United States' perception of its interests in Ethiopia. President Nixon, realizing that Kagnew would be an easy target of the Eritrean liberation movements, decided to end U.S. use of the facilities.[4]

This decision was facilitated by satellite communications with submarines and U.S. access to former British military bases on Diego Garcia in the Indian Ocean. By 1976 only 35 Americans were stationed at Kagnew.

Developments in Ethiopia and Haile Selassie's response to them contributed to a change in U.S. policy toward Ethiopia and the emergence of the Dergue. Apart from the fact that revolutions in technology and communications made Ethiopia less significant strategically, Haile Selassie's decision to terminate relations with Israel following the Arab-Israeli conflict in 1973 reduced Ethiopia's usefulness as an ally in the Middle East. Furthermore, evidence of change in Ethiopian society was all too obvious to be ignored by Washington.

The feudal nature of Selassie's control of Ethiopia was challenged by many educated Ethiopians and members of the armed forces, several of whom were trained in America. As the largest recipient of U.S. Peace Corps volunteers, Ethiopia found it virtually impossible to exclude ideas that challenged the status quo. Although the United States was concerned about communist expansionism in Africa, it was not persuaded that military aid could solve Ethiopia's problems, which were rooted in poverty and imperial rule. When Emperor Haile Selassie visited Washington in 1973, shortly before his downfall, to obtain $500 million in military assistance including jets and tanks, Washington demonstrated its displeasure with Selassie by refusing to grant his request. The United States continued to suggest land reform, greater civil and political freedoms, more autonomy for Eritrea, and a stronger role for the Ethiopian parliament. Selassie, however, was more concerned about sustaining imperial rule than with significantly reforming the society.[5]

STARVATION AND THE RISE OF THE DERGUE

Mass starvation and the Emperor's insensitivity to the plight of his people paved the way for his demise and provided opportunities for Soviet-Cuban involvement on the Horn of Africa. From 1970 through 1972, drought plagued Ethiopia's northern highlands. Approximately five hundred people were dying each day, despite the availability in Addis Ababa of food donated by the United States and other Western countries. Rather than aggressively confronting the problem, the government decided to suppress information from the Ministry of Agriculture about crop failures and projections of widespread food shortages[6]. Having lost many of their plow oxen, and being severely malnourished, Ethiopian farmers could not exploit the long rains which finally came in 1973. Consequently, they migrated to the cities to avoid death. Selassie's indifference and inability to admit the seriousness of the crisis met with severe criticism from a broad cross-section of the Ethiopian population, Western governments, and private groups. More than 100,000 people perished from starvation between 1970 and 1974.

Mismanagement of the famine combined with continued fighting in Eritrea and escalating oil prices in 1973 to cripple the government in Addis Ababa and fuel widespread dissatisfaction. The ailing Emperor's son and successor, Crown Prince Asfa Wossen, being paralyzed, could not provide continuity in the imperial rule enjoyed by his father.This only served to exacerbate an already hopeless situation. Taxi drivers protesting higher fuel prices, school teachers and civil servants demanding improved salaries, decided to go on strike. They were joined by the Labor Federation and others. The net result was economic paralysis and escalating demands on the government. Nor was the civilian population alone in its dissatisfaction with conditions in Ethiopia. Troops of the second division who were protesting low pay, poor living conditions, and the military stalemate in Eritrea, decided to arrest their commanding officers. Mounting public pressure forced Selassie's cabinet to resign, but its replacement was not spared demands from teachers, enlisted men, students, municipal workers, and a plethora of other groups for higher pay, a new constitution, and land reform.[7] Revolutionary sentiment was by now contagious. All sectors and classes of society were affected. The Ethiopian Parliament, composed mainly of conservative landowners, introduced a bill to establish privately owned newspapers and radio stations and to abolish governmental control of the media. The usually quiet Moslems shattered the myth that Ethiopia was predominantly Christian by staging the largest demonstration ever held in Addis Ababa (approximately 100,000 marchers) to demand religious equality and the separation of church and state.[8] Lacking flexibility characteristic of developed societies, Ethiopia moved rapidly toward chaos. Under these circumstances, military force generally prevails, and the armed forces moved in to fill the vacuum.

In April 1974 representatives of the military formed the Armed Forces Coordinating Committee, or Dergue, to restore order and govern the country. The Dergue moved quickly to consolidate its control by arresting prominent political and administrative personnel on charges of "betraying" the Emperor and allowing the famine to reach disastrous proportions, and replacing members of the Emperor's close advisers with Dergue supporters. Clearly, Haile Selassie was powerless to prevent the revolution or to protect himself from the revolutionaries. On September 12, 1974, New Year's Day in Ethiopia, Dergue representatives removed the Emperor from his National Palace, transported him to army headquarters in a Volkswagen, and issued a proclamation deposing him. Strikes, demonstrations, and protests of any kind were outlawed. Although promising "change without bloodshed" the Dergue engaged in one of the bloodiest reigns of terror in recent history. Internal rivalries led to the arrest and immediate execution of 59 Dergue members suspected of plotting "a counter-revolutionary" coup, on Bloody Saturday November 23, 1974. Violence against ordinary Ethiopians, especially students, escalated and spread to the inner circles of the Dergue. Power struggles within the Dergue were resolved through extermination. February 3, 1977, a Dergue meeting ended in a shootout between the relatively moderate Terefe Bante faction and the more radical faction led by Mengistu Haile Mariam in which Terefe was killed. After executing his opposition, Mengistu emerged as the unchallenged leader of Ethiopia. Approximately 100,000 Ethiopians were killed in revolutionary violence.

Preoccupation with consolidating power left the Dergue little time to implement many of the promised changes. Land reform, introduced immediately, was by far the Dergue's most important action. Private ownership of land and the system of tenancy were abolished. Peasant associations, formed to replace previous landlords, carried out mandated reforms. Most businesses were nationalized or brought under state control, and second homes and rental property were seized by the government[9]. New schools were constructed and health care improved for rural communities. However, promises of political freedom, freedom of the press, and rapid economic development remained elusive. Eritrea continued to drain the nation's few resources, and civil strife increased.

Despite serious reservations about the radical course of the revolution, the United States continued to supply Ethiopia with economic and military assistance. But Washington could not ignore gross violations of human rights. In April 1977, the American Military Advisory and Assistance Group in Ethiopia was virtually dismantled and Washington communicated its decision to terminate the Kagnew base agreement early. Mengistu, after considering this development for twenty-four hours, ordered the U.S. out of Kagnew within four days. Although the State Department expressed formal regrets over the deterioration of relations with Ethiopia, the United States was actually relieved to end what had become an embarrassment to the Carter administration and many Americans. Reports of possible Cuban ties with Ethiopia influenced Congress to cut off all funds for Ethiopia.[10] Somalia's decision to invade the Ogaden while Ethiopia was internally divided and at odds with the United States gave Moscow and Havana an opportunity to escalate their activities in Ethiopia.

SOVIET-CUBAN ACTIVITIES IN THE HORN OF AFRICA

Cuba's involvement on the Horn of Africa is much more recent than the Soviet Union's, and its interests less clearly defined. Unlike Angola, where Castro had close personal ties with Agostino Neto and could claim a certain cultural affinity with the region, Ethiopia was never really part of Castro's foreign policy agenda. Indeed, Cuba's limited engagement on the Horn was in support of the Eritrean liberation groups at war with Ethiopia. Castro's decision to commit about 13,000 troops to assist Ethiopia against former allies demonstrated that, unlike Angola, he was acting primarily to protect Soviet interests under Moscow's direction.

Believing in the "correlation of forces," Moscow seeks recognition commensurate with its great power status outside Eastern Europe. Direct competition with the United States for influence in Africa and elsewhere appears to be an important aspect of Soviet strategy. Naval forces off the east coast of Africa and elsewhere in the Indian Ocean are a valuable foreign policy instrument. They serve to improve Soviet capability to respond to regional crises, underscore their commitment to specific policies or local regimes, and support their efforts to either strengthen ties or destabilize individual governments.[11] As a global power with interests in the Indian Ocean area, the Soviets' use of port facilities on the Horn of Africa contributes to their ability to sustain worldwide deployments. For example, prior to obtaining access to Berbera in Somalia, the length of Soviet combatant deployments in the Indian Ocean was significantly reduced because of the long distance from the Soviet Union.[12] Access to port facilities in Somalia facilitated ship repair and maintenance. In addition to military considerations, Soviet dependence on the Indian Ocean as a source of protein should not be overlooked. Given the coastal states' control over their two hundred mile economic zones, a country with major interests in fishing would not be disadvantaged by maintaining a naval presence near areas where its fleets operate.

Soviet interest in the Horn of Africa in general and Ethiopia in particular predates the 1971 revolution. Instead of engaging in an ideological crusade, the Soviets were concerned about the area's strategic value and its domination by European colonial powers, especially Britain. Before the Italians settled in Eritrea Moscow had made several attempts to establish a Russian presence there. Ethiopia, however, was the African country in which Russia first played a significant role. As early as 1890 Russian delegations visited Ethiopia, and in 1895 an Ethiopian mission, largely military in composition, visited Moscow and returned with arms and promises of military and diplomatic cooperation.[13] During Ethiopia's war with Italy in 1896 a Russian officer advised the Ethiopian Emperor on military strategy. After Italy's defeat, the first for a European power in Africa, a Russian Red Cross mission visited Addis Ababa and set up a hospital. Diplomatic ties between the two countries were strong, and Russian officers not only served in the Ethopian army but also assisted in establishing the country's boundaries.[14] However, following Russia's defeat by Japan in 1905, contacts between Ethiopia and Russia declined dramatically.

It was not until after World War II that Moscow began to reestablish ties with Ethiopia, a country which was firmly allied with the United States. During UN debates on the future of Eritrea, the Soviet Union actually opposed Ethiopian attempts to annex that territory and clearly indicated its interest in playing a role in governing the former Italian possessions until they obtained their independence. Failing to persuade the UN to establish a trusteeship council for Eritrea and Somaliland, Moscow advocated immediate independence for Eritrea and voted against the General Assembly resolution approving Eritrean incorporation in Ethiopia as an autonomous unit.[15] Inadvertently, Soviet support of Eritrean guerrillas and its military assistance to Somalia eventually weakened Ethiopia and, ironically, provided Moscow an opportunity to establish close military ties with the beleaguered regime in Ethiopia, and achieve its original objective on the Horn of Africa.

Soviet involvement in Somalia was due in part to the lack of U.S. or Western European interest in that country, one of the poorest and most desolate in the world, and Soviet desire to have a base on the straits of Bab el Mandeb. Ethiopian-U.S. relations were strong and U.S. interests could be safeguarded without extensive activity on the Horn of Africa. Shortly after Somalia became independent, the United States, Italy, and West Germany offered it $10 million to strengthen internal security on the condition that it refrain from seeking military assistance from other sources, particularly the Soviet Union. Rejecting these limitations, Somalia accepted $55 million from the Soviet Union to equip an army that grew from 5,000 in 1962 to 20,000 by 1975. Moscow supplied tanks, MiG fighters, transport planes, and helicopters. Approximately 3,000 Soviet military advisers worked with Somalia's armed forces and be-tween 1,000 and 2,400 Somali military personnel were sent to the USSR for military training.[16] Nonmilitary aid included meat packing and fish-canning plants, an irrigation project, resettlement of nomads following Somalia's severe droughts, and a deep-sea fishing project. Despite Western reluctance to arm Somalia, economic assistance was provided. China, the UN, and many Arab countries also played a role in famine relief, health service, and economic development. In exchange for the aid, Somalia granted the Soviet Union access to various facilities around Berbera, including: 1. a deep-water port; 2. fuel storage facilities; 3. a 13,000 foot runway; 4. a tactical-missile and storage-handling capacity; and 5. a communications facility.[17] In 1974 the Treaty of Friendship and Cooperation was concluded between the two countries, setting a prece-dent in Africa.

Although the Soviets were not primarily interested in transforming Somalia into a communist state, they nevertheless strongly supported the creation of the Somali Socialists Revolutionary Party to replace the Supreme Revolutionary Council (SRC) formed in 1969 when Siad Barre seized power in a military coup. The SRC, due to its narrow power base, was relatively isolated from irrendentist pressures. The creation of the party provided a broader base of support for Somalia's leader, Siad Barre, but also rendered him more vulnerable to ethnic demands for regaining parts of Kenya and the Ogaden. Strong party organization and substantial military expenditures combined to undermine Moscow's posi-tion in Somalia and, ultimately, to act as a catalyst in altering alliances on the Horn of Africa.[18]

Other developments must be taken into consideration in order to understand the Soviet shift from Somalia to Ethiopia. Following the 1974 coup in which the Dergue seized power, Soviet leaders began to reassess their options in the Horn. The Dergue, far more revolutionary than Siad Barre, was regarded as a more compliant partner and more reliable than Barre whose links with conservative Arab countries were well-known. It has been suggested that historical ties between Russia and Ethiopia, and a certain similarity in their histories and background — Czar and Emperor, Orthodox and Coptic Christianity, neo-feudalism — may also have influenced Soviet thinking.[19] But there were abrupt changes. Somalia, Ethiopia, and the Soviet Union all seemed very cautious and more flexible ideologically. The Dergue experimented with establishing ties with China. Somalia courted the Arab states that had long attempted to woo it away from Moscow's influence; and the Soviet Union assumed the role of peacemaker on the Horn in order to maintain ties with Somalia while developing closer links with Ethiopia. Increasingly supportive of Mengistu, the Soviets endorsed Ethiopia's offer to negotiate a peaceful settlement of the Eritrean problem. Efforts to reduce tensions between Somalia and Ethiopia over the Ogaden were rejected by both countries. Socialist solidarity could no longer mask real differences between Somalia and Ethiopia, and conflicting interests of the former and the Soviet Union. Whereas the Soviet's unrealistically expected Somali restraint as a measure of gratitude for Soviet aid, Somalia anticipated Soviet backing in the name of anticolonialism, self-determination, and antiimperialism.[20] Moscow's desire to retain its position in Somalia and gain a foothold in Ethiopia simultaneously was now clearly impossible.

In May 1977, Mengistu returned from the USSR with a promise of $500 million worth of arms and assurances that Somalia would be restrained from invading the Ogaden. But arming Ethiopia was perceived as a direct threat by Somalia. Agreements between Moscow and Addis Ababa on economic-technical and cultural-scientific cooperation and on a consular convention were regarded as a violation of the Treaty of Friendship and Cooperation with Somalia.

Barre's perception that he had a military advantage over Ethiopia while it was fighting Eritrean guerrillas and fear of Mengistu's increasing military capabilities influenced him to invade the Ogaden in July 1977. But quick victory proved elusive because the Soviets began supplying arms to Ethiopia while restricting supplies to Somalia. Barre's visit to Moscow in August 1977 did not modify Soviet policy toward the conflict. Realizing that the Treaty of Friendship under the circumstances was a liability, Barre abrogated it in November 1977, partly to enlist Western support for his Ogaden operation. His assumption that his newly discovered anticommunism would attract significant military assistance from Washington was painfully inaccurate. Barre's action cleared the way for a massive air and sealift of Soviet arms to Ethiopia, the intervention of 1,000 Soviet military advisors and 14,000 Cuban troops. It is estimated that the Soviet Union gave Ethiopia $1 billion worth of aircraft, tanks, rocket launchers, helicopters, ammunition, vehicles, and other material. Western observers were now forced to reevaluate assumptions about Soviet airlift capabilities after seeing the efficiency with which it conducted its large overseas airlift, and its disregard for other countries' airspace; Cuba's participation also shattered the view that Castro acted independently of the USSR in pursuit of Cuba's goals.

Cuban interest and participation in the Horn of Africa dispute was virtually nonexistent before 1974. During the Angolan war, in which Cuba radically departed from previous policy by committing more than 25,000 troops to fight on foreign soil, Castro's attention shifted gradually to Somalia and several dozen Cuban military technicians were sent there. By 1976 this contingent was reinforced by approximately 500 soldiers. When the radical faction of the Dergue gained more control by eliminating opposition within the group, Castro's interest in Ethiopia increased. According to LeoGrande, Castro viewed the Ethiopian revolution as genuine, largely because a number of the Dergue's policies were similar to his own during the early years of the Cuban revolution.[21] Cuba's new relationship with Ethiopia was in direct conflict with its policy of supporting the Eritrean liberation movements fighting for an autonomous Eritrea; it was also contrary to Cuba's involvement in Somalia. Like the Soviet Union, Cuba attempted to negotiate a settlement of disputes between the contending factions but failed to persuade them to elevate antiimperialism above provincial interests. After Barre invaded the Ogaden, Raul Castro went to Ethiopia and later to Moscow to coordinate military strategy. Cuban troops, arriving in Soviet troop transports, and more than 1,000 Soviet military advisors prepared for a counteroffensive in the Ogaden. When Ethiopia launched its drive to recapture the Ogaden, the operation was planned by General Vasilli Ivanovich Petrov, deputy commander of all Soviet ground forces, and led by General Arnaldo Ochoa, Cuba's deputy minister of defence. Thirty Soviet pilots were sent to Cuba to replace Cubans flying combat missions. Having inside knowledge of Somali fighting tactics and military strengths and weaknesses, Soviet advisors and Cuban troops contributed greatly to Somalia's disastrous defeat, forcing Barre to withdraw from the Ogaden.[22]

Eritrea was more of an embarrassment for Cuba because it clearly demonstrated a reversal of Cuban policy. Agreeing with Moscow that a negotiated settlement giving Eritrea regional autonomy while being federated with Ethiopia is a reasonable solution, Cuba is painfully aware of the contradictions in its position. Having supported the Eritreans against Selassie's Ethiopia and recognizing Eritrean liberation movements as progressive, Castro attempted to minimize his embarrassment by resisting Ethiopian pressure for Cuban troops to become more directly involved in Eritrea with Ethiopian soldiers, on the grounds that the conflict is an internal matter and outside the current ground rules relating to Cuban troops in Ethiopia. The Soviets obviously found it difficult to reconcile their new policy of giving Ethiopia military assistance to counterbalance the large amounts they gave to Somalia before changing partners.[23]

Cuba's gains from its involvement on the Horn are as unclear as its interests. Moscow, on the other hand, has received tangible benefits. The USSR gained permission to anchor an 8,500 ton floating drydock, which was at Berbera in Somalia, at Dahlak Island, on the Eritrean coast. Dahlak also serves as a maintenance facility and supply depot for Soviet naval ships operating in the Indian Ocean and the Red Sea. According to the U.S. Defense Department, guided-missile cruisers and nuclear-powered submarines regularly call at Dahlak for repair and supplies.[24] Despite Moscow's huge investment of over $3 billion since 1975, Ethiopia has been reluctant to become a Soviet base. Many ordinary Ethiopians openly express their displeasure with the presence of over 1,500 Soviets in the country, and Mengistu waited until 1984 to establish a Communist Party, which had been demanded by Moscow in 1978. Addis Ababa generally supported the Soviet Union on international issues, refusing to condemn its invasion of Afghanistan. However, the view that Ethiopia remains a thoroughly communist state and that it is well on the road to becoming an African-style Cuba and a full fledged satellite of Moscow is not strongly supported by available evidence. The adoption of a constitution in 1987 which enshrines the Marxist ideals of Ethiopia's leaders and puts the country in ideological conformity with Moscow and its allies does not necessarily mean that Ethiopia will be another Cuba.[25] As Somalia vividly demonstrated, Soviet influence on the Horn is more apparent than real and, given the plethora of economic, political, and military problems plaguing Ethiopia, it is unlikely that the USSR will significantly improve its position there.

U.S. RESPONSE TO SOVIET-CUBAN INTERVENTION

The United States' response to the unprecedented Soviet-Cuban military involvement on the Horn of Africa represents a rare case of pragmatism in the face of communist expansion. Rather than focusing on communism as the major or sole factor in the crisis on the Horn, American policymakers took into consideration the fact that Somalia and Ethiopia were relatively insignificant in the overall scheme of national security interests. Even before Mengistu ordered U.S. personnel to leave Kagnew, the U.S. had virtually dismantled operations there because of technical advances and continued threats from Eritrean guerrillas. Thus Soviet gains in the Horn, if any, were not necessarily at the expense of the United States or its Western allies. Furthermore, U.S. options were severely limited by the chaos in Ethiopia and the nature of the conflict itself.

The Dergue, clearly anti-American, was disunited, with various factions violently contending for control. Under such circumstances it was extremely difficult for Washington to exert any meaningful influence on the Dergue, especially after more moderate leaders were killed. Somalia was not an attractive alternative, and could not be supported simply because it was opposed to Ethiopia which was now backed by Moscow and Havana. By rushing to Somalia's aid, the United States would have placed itself in the quagmire that Moscow helped to create by heavily arming Somalia. The disadvantages of escalating the crisis outweighed any possible advantages. Doing nothing was actually the appropriate policy, especially when considered within the African context. Somalia's invasion of the Ogaden ran counter to the Organization of African Unity's principle on the sanctity of colonial boundaries and threatened Kenya, America's most important East African ally. Focusing primarily on the Soviet-Cuban threat in this situation would have jeopardized much wider U.S.-African interests to the possible benefit of the Soviet Union. However, U.S. support of Ethiopia and opposition to Somalia would have strained relations with the conservative Arab states during the height of the oil crisis. Saudi Arabia and Iran, before the 1979 revolution, shared a common interest with the United States in moving Somalia into the "Islamic fold." Having succeeded in weaning the Sudan from the Soviet Union by offering it economic aid and $220 million to buy arms from the West to replace outdated Soviet weapons, Saudi Arabia decided to pursue the same policy in Somalia.[26]

Similarly, the Saudis regarded Eritrea's liberation movements' struggle against Ethiopia as part of the broader objective of reducing Soviet influence not only on the Horn but throughout the Middle East. American policymakers were therefore constrained by complex indigenous interests, many of which were contrary to the superpowers' goals in the region. The U.S. policy of noninvolvement removed it from entanglements in essentially local conflicts. The Carter administration refused to give Somalis any military aid and denied Saudi Arabia and Iran permission to transfer U.S. arms to Somalia as long as Somali troops were fighting in the Ogaden. Perhaps the most concrete action against Soviet-Cuban intervention was directed against Cuba. Carter, who had indicated rapprochement with Cuba by lifting the ban on U.S. tourism in Cuba and agreeing to an exchange of diplomatic Interest Sections, among other things, responded to Cuba's military involvement by terminating the process of normalizing U.S.-Cuban relations.[27]

The Iranian hostage crisis and the Soviet invasion of Afghanistan influenced the Carter administration to alter its policy toward Somalia as part of its overall Persian Gulf security strategy. Developments in both Iran and Afghanistan strengthened the position of National Security Advisor Zbigniew Brzezinski and others who had earlier advocated a policy of military confrontation with the Soviet Union and Cuba to check communist expansion. Furthermore, public opinion by early 1980 clearly favored a tougher approach to communism, and the emergence of Ronald Reagan as the Republican party's nominee pushed Carter to take more aggresive action against Moscow. Consequently, Carter negotiated with Somalia conditions of U.S. access to naval facilities abandoned by the Soviets at Berbera. The resulting agreement provided Somalia with $40 million worth of defensive weapons, including radar and anti-aircraft guns, in return for U.S. utilization of the naval base over a two-year period. Nevertheless, Washington remained doubtful of Berbera's strategic importance in the larger Middle East conflict, and increased aid to Somalia by only $4 million in 1982 to repair old storage and other facilities at Berbera for the benefit of the newly-developed Rapid Deployment Force. Somalia received additional military assistance in July 1982 to counter what was regarded as an Ethiopian military incursion in the Mudugh region on behalf of Somali dissidents trying to discredit the Barre government.[28]

In 1983 the Reagan administration placed greater emphasis on the military security components of its foreign aid programs to Somalia, partly to demonstrate resolve and ability to confront both Ethiopia and Libya, if necessary. In addition to granting Somalia $115 million for military purposes, Reagan committed $35 million to expanding the Berbera military base used by the Rapid Deployment Force. Furthermore, Reagan's interest in the region was underscored by Bright Star III, a military exercise involving approximately 8,000 troops of the Rapid Deployment Force in Egypt and Somalia between August 10 and September 10, 1983.[29] Nonmilitary assistance was primarily in the form of food and reforestation programs. Despite close military ties with Somalia, questions remained about the value and reliability of Somalia as an ally in the Horn.

U.S. policy toward Ethiopia continued to be ambiguous, partly because of Ethiopia's continuing crises and its relative unimportance to overall U.S. strategic interests. Following Ethiopia's nationalization of U.S. business, U.S. development aid was terminated in 1979 because of disagreements concerning compensation. Nevertheless, food aid continued to flow into Ethiopia, despite efforts by the Reagan administration to abolish the program on the grounds that food aid was diverted by Ethiopian officials to purchase Soviet weapons and pay the armed forces. The United States bought about a third of Ethiopia's coffee crop, making it one of Ethiopia's three main trading partners, along with the Soviet Union and Italy. Widespread American concern about starvation in Ethiopia, among other factors, moderated Reagan's anticommunist approach to the country.

ETHIOPIA IN CONTINUING CRISIS

Revolutionary ideology has not altered the major realities that confronted Ethiopia prior to the emergence of the Dergue. Fighting in Eritrea and Tigre continue unabated, without either side being able to achieve a decisive victory. Nor is this likely to change in the forseeable future. After more than twenty years of fighting—the longest and most costly liberation war in Africa—Eritrean guerillas are now better trained and more determined to achieve autonomy for the region. The Ethiopian government is forced to allocate much-needed scarce resources to fight Eritrean liberation and Tigray movements as well as other insurgency groups in the Woolo and Gondar regions of the north, the Oromo movements Bale and Sidamo, and Somali-supported guerrillas in the Ogaden. This high level of counterrevolutionary violence has helped to prevent the Ethiopian revolutionary government from consolidating its power and transforming the country into a communist state. Increasingly indebted to the Soviet Union for arms puchases, Mengistu's regime has failed to deliver on its promises to develop Ethiopia's economy and grant its people political freedom. With a per capita income of $140 a year, Ethiopia remains one of the world's most impoverished countries, and starvation is much worse now than in 1974 when Haile Selassie was overthrown.

Agriculture, the centerpiece of reforms by the Dergue and Ethiopia's principal source of export earnings, suffered tremendously under collectivization schemes implemented by Mengistu. These inefficient state farms took up 3 percent of Ethiopia's arable land, received 90 percent of all agricultural investment, but produced only 6 percent of the country's grain.[30] Despite the Dergue's initial emphasis on agricultural production, only 16 percent of Ethiopia's agricultural land is cultivated, and almost three-fifths of the total land area is under permanent pasture. Coffee still accounts for two-thirds of Ethiopia's foreign exchange.[31]

Widespread famine, chronic warfare with various secessionist movements, and military expenditures have alienated many middle class

Ethiopians whose salaries remained frozen while the cost of living increased approximately 200 percent. Although comprising a relatively small minority of Ethiopia's population, the middle class is extremely important because its administrative skills and technical knowledge are essential to the country's economic growth and political stability. Reminiscent of the situation prior to the 1974 coup, fuel prices are playing a key role in Ethiopia's current problems. About 8 percent of the country's petroleum comes from the Soviet Union and, despite relatively favorable pricing arrangements, about half of Ethiopia's export earnings are allocated for petroleum. In 1985 the government limited gasoline consumption to four gallons a week for private cars and imposed restrictions on the importation of new cars. These austerity measures affect all sectors of society, including the business community. Housing space is regulated by the government and construction of new homes was banned in mid-1985. In light of persistent economic problems Mengistu moderated his socialist rhetoric to attract Western finance, technology, and tourists.[32] Nevertheless, Mengistu established the Communist party of Ethiopia on September 12, 1984 to institutionalize and expand communism in the country, five years after the formation of a committee to organize a Communist party.[33]

Despite Mengistu's decision to make Ethiopia Africa's first communist state, several problems exist between Ethiopia and the Soviet Union. Improvement of economic ties with the West and growing dependence on Western food aid highlighted Ethiopia's disillusionment with Moscow's apparent inability to provide the necessary economic assistance to arrest the deteriorating situation in the country. Furthermore, Moscow's success in persuading Barre to accept a new Soviet ambassador to Somalia helped to increase Ethiopia's distrust of the Soviet Union. Primarily due to worsening economic problems, Ethiopia decided to reduce the estimated costs of $6 million a year for Cuban troops stationed there by sending most of them home in 1984. In light of Castro's prior commitment of Eritrean liberation groups and his refusal to allow Cuban troops to be directly involved in military operations in Eritrea, Ethiopia's decision actually removed one of Castro's greatest foreign policy embarrassments. Soviet-Cuban involvement produced no significant gains for Ethiopia. It is now all too obvious that Marxism-Leninism and Soviet and Cuban economic models are no panacea for Ethiopia's intractable political and economic problems.

MAINTAINING A PRAGMATIC POLICY

Careful analysis of American interests on the Horn of Africa, indigenous forces at work, the economic and political realities of the region, and broader U.S. interests in Africa suggest that avoiding direct military confrontation with the Soviet Union and Cuba demonstrated pragmatism, not paralysis, in U.S. foreign policy. Having determined that continuing conflicts on the Horn diminished its strategic value, even before Moscow changed partners, American policymakers skillfully avoided marching into the quagmire. U.S. security interests, not the fear of communism, influenced its response to Soviet-Cuban activities. Indeed, the Horn represents a case where ideological commitments played a secondary role to each actor's perceived interests. It is also a case where losses for all involved appear to be greater than their gains. Contrary to the general view, by investing the minimum amount of resources in the conflict the United States may actually be the greatest beneficiary in the long run, if it continues to avoid the zero-sum game mentality *vis-à-vis* the Soviet Union and Cuba. Given the fact that Mengistu eliminated members of the Dergue, and other Ethiopians who may have been supportive of Washington, U.S. contacts within the government or with specific groups in Ethiopia are limited and, consequently, its ability to directly influence the Dergue is diminished. However, there are several options available to the United States.

Work with the Soviets. Neither Moscow nor Washington stands to benefit significantly from the conflict on the Horn of Africa. The economic costs of supplying Ethiopia with weapons seem to outweigh any possible military and political benefits for Moscow. Compared to southern Africa or Nicaragua, Ethiopia does not elicit strong emotional responses or widespread political appeal. Both superpowers can cooperate to solve the Eritrean, Somali, and Ethiopian problems, thereby reducing their liabilities in the region and setting a precedent for superpower collaboration in the interest of regional stability. Despite the existence of a Communist party in Ethiopia, Ethiopian nationalism, the strength of religion in the country, overwhelming economic problems, widescale domestic conflicts, and Moscow's former ties with Somalia and Eritrean liberation movements may be ultimately detrimental to Soviet interests in Ethiopia. Moscow's inability to prevent Somalia from invading the Ogaden, setbacks in the Sudan, Egypt, Ghana, Zimbabwe and Mozambique, growing domestic demands from Soviet citizens for an improved standard of living, and more pragmatic leaders in the Kremlin combine to make the Soviet Union more cautious in the Horn.

Avoid Excessive Entanglements with Somalia. By maintaining a relatively neutral position on the Horn and not strongly supporting Somalia militarily, the United States will avoid antagonizing Ethiopia as well as the OAU, and be in a position to capitalize on future developments within Ethiopia. Large numbers of Somalis work in the Gulf States and the

Middle East, and Italy maintains strong economic ties with Somalia. Perhaps allowing Italy and the Arab states to play the leading role in Somalia would be more beneficial to overall U.S. interests. By not dominating Somalia, the U.S. is in a position to emphasize its commitment to nonalignment, independence for African states and support for the OAU's position of African boundaries.

Work with Allies in Ethiopia. Mengistu's disillusionment with the Soviets because of their inability to provide substantial economic assistance has increased economic opportunities for Western European countries in Ethiopia. The European Economic Community (EEC) is by far a more significant trading partner than the Council for Mutal Economic Assistance, (Comecon), and Ethiopia is growing more dependent on Western technology, capital, and tourists. In light of Ethiopia's continuing economic crisis, the United States should encourage its allies to maintain their foothold in Ethiopia to moderate the regime's socialist ideology and build closer ties with Ethiopians at all levels of society, especially middle class technicians and bureaucrats.

Cultivate Good Relations with Ethiopians in America. Many of Ethiopia's brightest citizens who are now exiled in the United States can provide a bridge between Washington and a future Ethiopian government. Focusing on their interests in a stable, pluralistic Ethiopia may eventually frustrate Soviet objectives that are inimical to ours on the Horn. Supporting Ethiopian civic organizations, providing financial assistance to Ethiopian students studying in the United States, and encouraging the exiles to participate in nongovernmental organizations involved in famine relief activities are steps which are mutually beneficial to the United States and Ethiopians.

Encourage Negotiations between Somalia and Ethiopia. Somalia's decision to invade the Ogaden reduced its ability to achieve a military victory over Ethiopia in the Ogaden. Working with the Soviet Union, the United States should try to persuade Somalia to abandon its claim over the region and agree to local self-government for Somalis living there. Furthermore, the United States should make every effort to support the dialogue initiated between the two countries at the East African Conference on Drought and Development in Djibouti on January 17, 1986.[34] The OAU should also be encouraged to be actively involved in mediation efforts.

Support Closer Ties between Somalia and Kenya. Relations between Kenya and Somalia have improved due to American pressure on Somalia to relinquish its claims to Kenyan territory populated by Somalis. Somalian-Kenyan friendship strengthens Kenya, a country in which the United States has important interests. Somalia's official pronouncement that it is content that the people of Kenya's North Eastern Frontier province have gained their independence as part of Kenya should be included as part of a formal agreement between the two countries.

Have Patience. Vital U.S. interests are not at stake in the Horn and neither Somalia nor Ethiopia evokes strong emotional reactions from Americans. Therefore, there is no need for precipitate action or alarm over Ethiopia's relationship with Moscow. The Soviets' own economic problems serve as a check on their ability to provide economic assistance, which is essential for the perpetuation of a strong communist regime in Ethiopia.[35]

U.S. pragmatism on the Horn of Africa is due to several factors. Unlike Nicaragua, the Commonwealth Caribbean or southern Africa, Ethiopia and Somalia did not evoke the strong American emotions which usually encourage an ideological approach to foreign policy. Because of the traditionally low priority accorded to much of Africa by American foreign policymakers, Africanists in the State Department were relatively unopposed in their view that the U.S. should examine Soviet-Cuban activities on the Horn within the African context. Equally important were Carter's genuine efforts, prior to the 1980 re-election campaign, to rid Washington of its inordinate fear of communism, and to focus on human rights.

Furthermore, U.S. interests on the Horn were easily identified. When Kagnew lost its military significance there was no reason for the United States to continue its involvement in Ethiopia. Supporting Somalia would have jeopardized U.S. ties with Kenya and other African countries because of their widespread acceptance of colonial boundaries. Finally, Reagan made Central America his primary foreign policy concern, and showed greater interest in domestic affairs than in foreign relations. Lack of interest, geographic and cultural distance, American reluctance to support Barre who had been so recently closely allied with Moscow, and Carter's commitment to diplomacy as a primary instrument of foreign policy contributed to U.S. pragmatism on the Horn of Africa.

Ten years after the Soviets and Cubans intervened on the Horn the basic problems of the region have remained essentially unchanged. Despite Ethiopia's adoption of an official Communist party, there is no evidence of the emergence of another Cuba in Africa, or the spread of communism to neighboring countries. More importantly, U.S. interests have not been seriously affected, and its Western European allies continue to enjoy economic and diplomatic relations with both Ethiopia and Somalia. U.S. allies in East Africa, particularly Kenya, have also benefitted from the moderate, pragmatic U.S. policy on the Horn. In fact, without risking American prestige, Somalia, Ethiopia, and Kenya have made significant progress in creating an improved climate for the resolution of conflict. And by allowing the Organization of African Unity to exercise primary responsibility for solving African boundary conflicts, the United States continued to experience close ties with moderate African states and did not antagonize the others.

Given Africa's serious economic problems, the judicious U.S. response to the military aspect of the conflict and its provision of humanitarian assistance to Ethiopia and the Sudan, especially in the absence of a similar Soviet response to starvation, clearly improved its position on the continent. This policy demonstrated U.S. willingness and ability to meet Africa's most pressing needs. Although there is probably no direct connection between this specific policy and Africa's embracing of more free-market practices, it is reasonable to assume that the United States' generosity in Ethiopia's worst food crisis did have an impact on Africa's economic planners. Moscow had nothing to offer its starving allies.

This pragmatic approach to the Horn should serve as a general guide to policy making with respect to specific areas in which there is Soviet-Cuban involvement. As indicated earlier, each situation must be carefully analyzed, U.S. interests carefully assessed, and various strategies for their achievement carefully evaluated. The Horn demonstrates that military action or direct confrontation with Moscow and Havana is not appropriate where the causes of the conflict are indigenous to the region and where no important U.S. interests are at stake. Although the situation in Afghanistan is more complex because of Soviet occupation of that country, some lessons from the Horn can be applied. The United States must carefully evaluate its interests there, consider the costs of getting the Soviets to leave, and the impact of the conflict on broader U.S. interests in the region.

AFGHANISTAN

3

Afghanistan: Define Interests and Recognize Limits of Power

Afghanistan is a clear example of the limits of Soviet-Cuban convergence. It demonstrates Soviet determination to protect perceived national interests without Cuban assistance. In fact, involving the Cubans would have been an admission by Moscow that it was unable to deal with problems within its own sphere of influence. Perhaps more significantly, the Soviet invasion seems to have occurred without much consideration of its impact on Cuba's foreign policy objectives. Indeed, a strong case can be made that Soviet involvement did serious damage to Cuba's foreign policy interests.

Soviet military aggression in Afghanistan in 1979 could not have been more ill-timed as far as Cuba's interests were concerned. After managing to establish its credibility with Third World countries as a relatively independent actor in international affairs, Cuba was enjoying its position as leader of the Nonaligned Movement when Moscow invaded a member of that organization. Castro's problem was that the invasion was clearly a case where a superpower was imposing its will on an impoverished Third World country through the use of brutal military force. It was therefore humiliating for Cuba to vote (with eight other nonaligned states) against the UN resolution condemning the Soviet Union. Cuba's UN ambassador, Raul Roa, was careful not to endorse Soviet intervention, but voted against the resolution "because to condemn Moscow would be the same as endorsing U.S. imperialism."[1]

Although Cuba voted with the USSR, partly because of bloc loyalty, Castro was dismayed and frustrated over Soviet policies in Afghanistan.

No effort was made to support or defend the Soviet rationale for occupying a neutral country and, privately, Cuban diplomats asserted that the invasion was unfortunate and a mistake, one that would seriously undermine the international prestige of Moscow and its allies.[2] The impact on Cuba was immediate. It engendered strong anti-Cuban sentiments in the Third World, precluded any possibility of Cuba, as head of the Nonaligned Movement, taking the lead in extending military assistance to groups approved by that organization, destroyed Cuba's bid for membership on the UN Security Council, and gave Reagan another justification to go to the source of Central America's problem, an obvious reference to military action against Cuba.[3]

In an effort to reduce the negative impact of Soviet occupation in Afghanistan on Cuba's foreign policy objectives, Castro deemphasized military action and focused instead on providing developmental assistance. He also attempted to mediate a settlement to the Afghan situation, which he undertook in his capacity as head of the Nonaligned Movement. In March 1980 he sent his foreign minister, Isidora Malmierca, to try to resolve the crisis through shuttle diplomacy between the Soviet Union, Afghanistan, and Pakistan.[4] Castro's failure to convince the Soviets to withdraw seriously diminished his influence in the Third World, and demonstrated Cuban-Soviet differences on foreign policy issues. The conflict between Havana and Moscow over Afghanistan provided an opportunity for the United States to drive a wedge between these two allies and to improve its chances of moderating Cuba's international behavior. However, American foreign policymakers overlooked this opportunity and focused solely on Moscow.

Having declared the Soviet invasion of Afghanistan to be the most serious threat to world peace since World War II, American policymakers initially reacted with a series of punitive measures designed to force the Soviets out. A country to which little attention was previously given was now regarded as vital to U.S. security interests in the Persian Gulf and South Asia. Eight years later Afghanistan had virtually disappeared from the front pages of leading newspapers in the United States and, despite his harsh anticommunist rhetoric, Reagan did not go beyond occasional rhetorical statements of support for the "freedom loving Afghans" who were being decimated by increased Soviet military power until 1986, when Stinger anti-aircraft missiles were given to the Afghan resistance to improve its defensive capabilities against helicopter gunships and MiG jets.[5] The invasion was also costly for Moscow. Not only did the Soviets pay a heavy price in terms of lives and military equipment; they also seriously damaged their reputation in Asia, the Third World, and among Soviet Asians.[6] Afghanistan demonstrates that even the superpowers must recognize the limits of power and search for alternatives to military force to achieve their objectives.

Afghanistan provides an excellent example of how not to deal with Soviet aggression in an area in which U.S. interests are vague and its power is seriously limited. Failure to clearly define our interests and recognize the limits of our power contributed to the deterioration of overall U.S.-Soviet relations, highlighted U.S. foreign policy failures, and diminished the negative consequences of aggression for the Soviet Union. Carter's actions, partly designed to disprove domestic critics who viewed him as indecisive and soft on communism, were hastily contrived, and exaggerated concern about a problem over which the U.S. could exercise very little control. He assumed that the Soviets would do what he feared and confused their purported aspirations with their ability to actually achieve them. While Carter saw the invasion in terms of the historic Russian goal of access to a warm-water port and eventual denial of U.S. access to Persian Gulf oil, the Soviets' stated objective was to prevent Afghanistan from becoming a hostile, weak, unstable neighbor and not retain the country as a strategic ally or a model socialist state. Blind acceptance of the Soviet statement or, as was the case, rejection of it, was inappropriate and even dangerous. By 1987 the Soviets had consolidated their control over major cities in Afghanistan, and U.S. policy remained essentially unchanged from what it was in 1979.

Afghanistan also shows that a reactive foreign policy is generally counterproductive because it seldom takes into consideration the fact that local actors or less conspicuous third parties may be better suited to solve problems in a particular region. The situation is compounded when preoccupation with our objectives causes us to exclude the interests of those with whom we must cooperate to achieve our goals. To be successful our foreign policy must be consistent with their aspirations. Furthermore, emphasizing military solutions in the context of anticommunism may exacerbate problems in the region and inadvertently contribute to further Soviet gains in areas vitally important to us by not addressing the internal problems which weaken areas such as Pakistan and the Persian Gulf countries. Less American anxiety could help countries to take more seriously the problems which create an environment conducive to Soviet involvement and are ultimately detrimental to U.S. security. This is especially true for Pakistan under Zia's authoritarian rule. By stressing the danger of the invasion to U.S. interests, the United States allowed Pakistan to strengthen its bargaining position *vis-à-vis* the United States. U.S. fear of communism resulted in committing American power and prestige to an internally weak Pakistan and further alienating India to the benefit of the Soviet Union.

An excessively anticommunist foreign policy is likely to be disastrous because it usually prevents the attempt to understand Soviet reality and thus reduces our effectiveness in world affairs. By putting ourselves in the Soviets' shoes we would have realized the futility of harsh rhetoric, and that the continued presence of the Soviets in Afghanistan was an attempt to protect their interests. Given their view of reality, it was unrealistic for the United States to expect the Soviets to meet its demand that they withdraw from Afghanistan, respect the Afghans' right to self-determination and nonalignment, and the right of refugees to return safely without some guarantees for Soviet security and appreciation of their interest in having a strong, friendly, stable neighbor. Furthermore, given the lack of any major U.S. commitment to the Afghan guerrillas until Stinger missiles were given in 1986, did the Soviets perceive the United States as being serious about Afghanistan? Not only did Reagan lift the grain embargo imposed by Carter, but he shifted attention away from the brutality in Afghanistan by highlighting what he perceived as a communist threat in Central America. Indeed, Reagan's arguments for U.S. involvement in El Salvador and Nicaragua allowed the Soviets to justify their occupation of Afghanistan on the grounds that because they shared a 1,000 mile common border with Afghanistan they faced more immediate threats to their security than did the U.S. from the relatively distant Central American turmoil. To condemn the Soviets for their actions in Afghanistan, while stressing U.S. commitment to the restoration of democratic regimes friendly to the United States, appeared hypocritical. The invasion of Grenada further reduced U.S. leverage *vis-à-vis* the Soviet Union and focused world public opinion away from Afghanistan to American militarism at least for a short time.

In the meantime the Soviets, whose aggressive behavior was due partly to their fear of appearing weak, have been confronted with serious losses and the realization that their power is limited and that they can no longer easily dominate their allies. In light of the Soviets' inability or unwillingness to extricate themselves from Afghanistan for ideological and security reasons, the task of American foreign policymakers is to search for a solution to which the Soviets can respond in the affirmative, that also protects U.S. interests in the Persian Gulf, and provides for the neutrality and stability of countries on the Soviet border.

In addition to dealing with the questions of what we want the Soviets to do, how we can get them to do it, and who is most suitable for performing the task, we must also search for advantages to be gained from continued Soviet military involvement in Afghanistan. In other words, how can we benefit from an undesirable development over which we have little direct influence? There are several opportunities inadvertently created by the Soviet action. The United States should: 1. explore ways of using the invasion to promote greater cooperation between In-

dia, Pakistan, and China and thereby reduce Soviet influence by defus-
ing possible conflicts between them; 2. exert pressure on Pakistan to
respect human rights and address its serious internal divisions in order to
strengthen the country against Soviet expansion; 3. encourage regional
groupings such as the Gulf Cooperative Council; 4. focus less on military
solutions and more on the political and social fragmentation of the Middle East countries; 5. work through third parties to reduce Iran's vulnerability to Soviet aggression; 6. continue to reduce Western dependence
on Gulf oil and develop alternative sources of energy; 7. reduce Soviet influence in the Indian Ocean by supporting efforts to have it declared a
zone of peace, especially because of the obvious vulnerability of Diego
Garcia; and 8. work with the Soviets to create greater stability and
neutrality in the region. Afghanistan is an obvious liability to the USSR
and, despite the unfortunate consequences for the Afghans, could eventually contribute to U.S. security interests in South Asia and the Persian
Gulf and reduce the opportunities for further Soviet expansion by the
strengthening of key countries. Afghanistan's internal chaos was an invitation to the security-paranoid Soviets.

AFGHANISTAN BEFORE THE SOVIET INVASION

The Soviet invasion was partly due to the strategic location of Afghanistan and the internal weakness and instability which have historically
characterized the Afghan political system. This problem was clearly
recognized by many of the Afghan leaders who struggled to safeguard
their own political power while simultaneously attempting to protect national independence and unify the various warring ethnic groups in order
to reduce the country's susceptibility to Soviet aggression. Afghans were
aware of czarist Russia's quest for a boundary well-defined by a strong,
stable neighboring state. Bordering Iran on the West, Pakistan on the
East and South, Russia on the North, and sharing a strip of land with
China on the northeast, Afghanistan was caught between the Russians,
British (before 1947), the Chinese and, later, the Americans. While the
rugged mountains which cover most of the country prevented any meaningful unification of the different ethnic groups and allowed Afghanistan
to remain relatively independent of the Russian and British empires,
Afghans realized their vulnerability. In 1900 Abdur Rahman Khan, also
known as the "Iron Amir," who ruled Afghanistan from 1880-1901 compared his country to a goat standing between two lions and to a grain of
wheat between two millstones.[7] However, the main concern of both
Russia and the British in India appeared to be the neutrality of Afghanistan rather than occupation of it. Consequently, the two great powers
concluded the Anglo-Russian Agreement in 1907 to guarantee Afghan-

istan's independence, and, to emphasize its neutrality, Afghans refused to participate in either of the two world wars. Afghanistan's freedom was safeguarded by the terrain and its people's love of freedom as much as it was by the creative tension between two great powers, Britain and Russia.

British withdrawal from the subcontinent subsequent to granting India independence in 1947 created a power vacuum by removing military support which counteracted Soviet military power. Britain, exhausted militarily by World War II, was now a secondary power, with the United States and the Soviet Union emerging as leading rivals for world power. Logically, Afghanistan turned to the United States, as Britain's successor, to reestablish the balance. The United States saw little reason to become involved in what it regarded as a remote, unfamiliar, primitive, and strategically unimportant country. It was also concerned about getting entangled in the dispute between Pakistan and Afghanistan over the Pushtunistan issue.[8] When the U.S. refused military aid on the grounds that it would not protect the country against a determined Soviet attack, the Afghans reluctantly turned to the Soviet Union.[9] Within four months of Mohammed Daoud's accession to power as prime minister in 1953, an agreement, the first of its kind since the early 1920s, was concluded between Kabul and Moscow which provided that Russia would give Afghanistan $3.5 million credit to build two grain silos, a flour mill, and a bakery.[10] This marked the beginning of increased Soviet involvement in Afghanistan and further fragmentation of the country.

Afghanistan and the USSR experienced an unsteady relationship between 1953 and the time of the 1979 invasion. On the negative side for Moscow, President Eisenhower's visit to Kabul in December 1959 was widely regarded as a success. On the positive side, on September 6, 1961, relations between Pakistan and Afghanistan were terminated over the Pushtunistan problem. Pakistan's decision to close its border with Afghanistan and to isolate it proved beneficial to Moscow. Given the close ties between Pakistan and the United States, the break in relations between the two neighboring countries was used by Moscow to drive a wedge between Afghanistan and the West. By 1963, however, Afghanistan was suffering severely from the loss of customs duties at the Pakistani border which accounted for the largest source of government revenues. The situation having seriously deteriorated, King Zahir asked his brother-in-law, Prime Minister Daoud, to resign and shortly thereafter restored diplomatic relations with Pakistan and the border was reopened.[11]

Given the fact that Daoud's policies were fairly consistent with Moscow's interests, his fall from power was construed as detrimental to Soviet aspirations, despite the fact that the king himself had previously been favorably regarded by Moscow. Traditional and essentially conservative, the king was less likely than Daoud to surrender Afghanistan's neutrality. When Daoud returned to power through a coup d'etat in 1973, the Soviets apparently expected him to fully support them in foreign affairs. When he temporarily abandoned Afghanistan's traditional neutrality it was the beginning of the end of that country's independent, neutral status.[12] His movement away from confrontation with Pakistan and the exchange visits between himself and President Ali Bhutto of Pakistan as a step toward reconciliation only increased Moscow's insecurity. After eliminating some of the friction between the Khalq and Parcham factions of the People's Democratic Party of Afghanistan (PDPA) in the spring of 1977 with the assistance of the USSR, Daoud reversed himself by purging the leftists within the PDPA more drastically in 1978. As Griffiths observed, when Daoud openly expressed the view that Cuba should have been expelled from the nonaligned group for its activities in Africa, his days were numbered.[13] In April 1978 Daoud was overthrown and assassinated by the Armed Forces Revolutionary Council led by Nur Muhammed Taraki and hardliner Hafizulla Amin. Approximately 2,000 people died during the violence in which the Soviets were implicated.

Internal divisiveness in the PDPA created serious problems for both Afghanistan and Moscow, eventually leading to the downfall of Taraki and Soviet military occupation. The Khalq faction to which Taraki belonged clashed with the Parcham led by Babrak Karmal. Karmal was forced to leave Afghanistan to become Ambassador to Czechoslovakia only to return on the eve of the Soviet invasion. In the meantime, the Soviets provided significant amounts of economic and military aid to the new regime, signing no less than seventy-five new economic assistance agreements between April 1978 and March 1979. These were accompanied by about 4,500 Soviet advisors.[14]

Ignoring Afghan realities, Taraki began implementing far-reaching social and economic reforms which alienated a wide cross-section of the Afghan population. For example, despite Afghanistan's strong adherence to Islam and traditional neutrality, Taraki replaced the green Islamic flag with a red flag resembling that used by the republics of the Soviet Union. Revolt spread quickly throughout the country. The Mujahedeen, or holy warriors, with antiquated weaponry, confronted the well-equipped Afghan army. Many of the revolts were brutally crushed and it was obvious that Taraki's hurried reforms would continue to create additional problems. This realization led Moscow to caution Taraki to reduce pressure for reforms and thereby prevent further alienation of many Afghans. Despite Moscow's concern over rapid reform, Taraki's visit to Moscow in December 1978 culminated in the signing of a twenty-five year treaty of friendship, neighborliness, and cooperation, an agreement the Kremlin later used to justify Soviet military intervention and occupation.[15]

On March 27, 1979 Taraki yielded the office of prime minister to the even more radical Hafizullah Amin, but remained titular head of state. Dissatisfied with Amin's ruthlessness toward Moslem rebel groups, Moscow attempted to replace him. Instead, Amin overthrew and killed Taraki on September 16, 1979. Amin then found himself caught between Afghans who associated resistance to his reforms with liberation from Soviet domination, and the Soviets who resented Amin's independence and recalcitrant behavior toward them. His demand that Moscow replace its ambassador in Kabul (because he sheltered Taraki's accomplices after the September shootout) was accompanied by efforts to establish better relations with Pakistan.[16]

Even before Taraki's assassination there were signs that Moscow would sooner or later take decisive action in Afghanistan. Failing to reconcile various communist factions and concerned about mounting military problems, the Soviets sent a delegation, headed by Deputy Defense Minister General Ivan Pavlovski, to study the deteriorating situation in Afghanistan. The delegation remained until October, and allegedly returned to Moscow with an assessment which may have weighed heavily in the Kremlin's decision to invade.[17] However, before the invasion, the Soviet ambassador reportedly met with Amin on December 24, the same day they airlifted approximately 5,000 Soviet troops to Kabul, to persuade him of the necessity of Soviet combat troops inside Afghanistan to restrict rebel activity and to admonish Amin to pursue more modest social and economic changes.[18] While it is difficult to ascertain what transpired during the meeting, the Soviets gave Amin little time to act or to reconsider. On December 27, the same day Amin was overthrown and killed in a coup believed to have been engineered by Moscow, Karmal was placed in control of Kabul as Russian troops poured across the Oxus River and seized the capital.

As Galbraith has observed, nations can act dangerously out of fear of seeming weak. It was this fear that sent Americans into Vietnam and the Soviets into Afghanistan.[19] Although the Soviets have multiple interests in Afghanistan, it is reasonable to conclude that the invasion was one logical result of an incrementalist Soviet policy that came to equate security with control.[20]

SOVIET INTEREST AND ITS OCCUPATION OF AFGHANISTAN

Soviet involvement in Afghanistan was brought about by many of the factors which militarily strong countries take into consideration when they pursue an ideological foreign policy and attempt to dominate regional developments which they perceive as threats to their security. Lost in the controversy and charges of Soviet expansionism is the simple fact that great powers behave very similarly when confronted with what they regard as hostile ideologies or internal chaos in neighboring states. However, when the Soviets occupy a country they stay and try to impose their will by force. Also, there is a substantial difference between being a Soviet ally and U.S. ally. In the latter case one has substantially more latitude for maneuver.[21]

The issue of Afghanistan is therefore relevant for all major countries. It raises the question of how best to safeguard national security without having to invade a smaller country or rely on increased violence by opposition groups within the country. Afghanistan clearly demonstrates that an emphasis on military might to protect a country's interests is not only extremely costly for those directly involved, but also for other states and regions as well. This approach to security generally results in greater insecurity because, in addition to the costs involved, it creates undesirable precedents for the management of international crises.

As mentioned previously, Soviet interests in Afghanistan predate the emergence of the modern Soviet state. Czarist Russia's ambitions are to some extent being pursued by contemporary Soviet leaders. Based on available evidence it appears that despite hostility between Moscow and Kabul, the overriding Soviet objective has long been a stable, neutral, Afghanistan. Several early agreements signed by the two countries, the Russo-Afghan treaty of February 1921, and the Soviet-Afghan Nonaggression Treaty and Neutrality Treaty of 1926, included provisions for neutrality, nonaggression, commerce, and technical assistance.[22] However, a concerted Soviet effort to bring Afghanistan more closely in line with Moscow seems to have emerged during the Cold War period of USSR-U.S. global competition. Nikita Khrushchev sought to undermine U.S. policy that aimed at surrounding the Soviet Union with countries allied to the West by improving relations with Turkey, Iran, and Afghanistan.

The Soviet policy toward Afghanistan also tried to make Afghanistan an economic showcase for Asia and the Third World and to offset Chinese influence.[23] In 1954 Moscow agreed to finance road-building projects earlier turned down by the United States, and Czechoslovakia provided funds for the construction of three cement factories. The Afghans had tried unsuccessfully to obtain resources for these projects from West Germany and the United States for approximately twenty years. But the most significant breakthrough for Moscow came in 1956 when the very cautious King Zahir Khan departed from his traditional neutral position and agreed to purchase modern Soviet military equipment, the complexity of which necessitated the training of

Afghan military personnel in Soviet military academies and the station-ing of Soviet experts at Afghan military bases.[24] Essentially, Afghanistan's quest for economic development and for military security in the Cold War environment, and its preoccupation with territorial disputes with Pakistan paved the way for greater Soviet involvement.

Soviet-American rivalry also caused both superpowers to view the world simply in terms of East and West, communist and anticommunist, and gains and losses. As a global power the Soviet Union played the role traditionally reserved for the militarily strong powers; its interests ex-panded beyond its borders and into the Third World. American failure to understand this reality was first obvious when MacArthur simply told the Soviet representative what American policy was toward post-war Japan rather than consulting and soliciting Soviet advice.[25] Since they had suffered the loss of over 20 million lives and incredible destruction, it was unrealistic to expect the insecure and distrustful Russians to accept the denial of what they considered their legitimate interests.

Afghanistan was of immediate concern because of its shared border with the Soviet Union. As discussed previously, the Russians have historically been preoccupied with Afghanistan's neutrality and stability. A stable communist regime friendly to Moscow is viewed by the Kremlin as highly desirable because it would eliminate the possible emergence of a hostile Afghan government allied with China or the West, provide a buf-fer against U.S.-supported Pakistan, and provide the USSR with oppor-tunities for influencing Iran and Pakistan.[26] Afghanistan was too close for the Soviets to exercise more restraint than they did during the chaotic seventeen-month period before the invasion. In an interview with the West German magazine *Der Speigel* Soviet leader Yuri Andropov asked: "Would the United States not care what kind of government rules in Nicaragua?"[27]

Loosely related to geography are domestic factors which will con-tinue to present serious challenges to Soviet leaders. The major domestic consideration is the ethnic and religious ties between Soviet citizens in Central Asia and the Afghans. A successful anticommunist rebellion nearby could have inspired the already restive 40 – 50 million Muslims to demand greater independence from Soviet control. And in light of the politicization of religion and Iran's revolution, the Soviet Union did not want to be confronted on its southern border with increased Islamic fun-damentalism in Pakistan, Iran, and Afghanistan.

Another major Soviet interest is related to ideology. Soviet ideological commitment to Marxism-Leninism as inevitable for all, com-bined with their insecurity, almost guaranteed that they would invade. By increasing their dependence on Moscow, the Afghan leaders allowed Afghanistan to be embraced by the Kremlin as a socialist state. This meant that the Brezhnev doctrine obliging the Soviet Union to prevent a socialist state from reverting to a noncommunist form of government was now applicable and would have to be implemented to protect Soviet credibility. Nor could the Soviets admit to making a mistake.[28] As is generally the case, they avoided any appearance of weakness by being extremely aggressive. Furthermore, obvious cracks in the communist bloc meant that the Soviets had to act decisively against a weaker neighbor to send a message to Eastern Europe. Failure in a neighboring state would have serious implications for a global Soviet foreign policy which has as its cornerstone military might.

Despite the stated Soviet objective of wanting to prevent Afghanistan from becoming a hostile base on its borders, Soviet expansionism was another reason for military intervention. While not having a blueprint for world domination, it is argued that the Soviet strategy is to move toward greater expansion of its power and influence at a pace and by tactical means that combine maximum prudence with maximum opportunism.[29] From Afghanistan the Soviets could weaken Pakistan by supporting the political autonomy of Pushtunistan and Baluchistan and eventually dominate Pakistan. Moscow could than move toward achieving its long-standing ambition of securing a warm water port on the Indian Ocean. From this perspective, the invasion of Afghanistan, coming at a time when the U.S. was preoccupied with the hostage crisis in Iran, provided the Soviets with a base approximately 200 miles closer to the strategic straits of Hormuz, the entrance to the Persian Gulf through which most of the Western world's oil supplies pass, thereby threatening Western security interests.

THE UNITED STATES AND AFGHANISTAN

U.S. dependence on Persian Gulf oil and its commitment to the containment of communism in South Asia as well as the Middle East following World War II influenced Washington to embrace Pakistan. Although Afghanistan did not receive high priority in the containment effort, the United States provided financial assistance to secure "maximum internal political stability, promote friendly economic relations with Afghanistan's Free World neighbors, and minimize any possibility that Afghanistan might be a victim of, or pathway for, Soviet domination in South Asia."[30] However, between 1950 and 1959, the Soviets were more actively involved economically and militarily than the U.S. in Afghanistan. Furthermore, the polarization of the world between East and West and the formation of regional security alliances could only result in increased competition between the superpowers for the hearts and territory of neighboring states. This ideological struggle is perceived as a zero-sum game. Thus, when U.S. Ambassador Adolph Dubs was kidnapped on February 14, 1979 and later murdered by Afghan security police in the presence of Soviet advisors, and Washington responded by terminating its fairly insignificant aid program, it essentially gave the Soviets unrestrained dominance in Afghanistan.[31] When the Soviets invaded later that year, the U.S. assumed that they intended to establish a strong foothold in Afghanistan and subsequently push through Pakistan to the Persian Gulf. Consequently, both Carter and Reagan believed that Pakistan should be strengthened militarily. What both failed to realize is that emphasizing the military option without being willing to commit significant resources to the resistance, would not only exacerbate Pakistani-Indian problems but would eliminate all chances of Soviet withdrawal from Afghanistan,[32] without solving the problems in the Gulf.

Moscow's invasion of Afghanistan brought into clearer focus the Soviet threat to Western, particularly U.S., interests in the Persian Gulf and, to a large extent, influenced the American response. During the Cold War the Gulf became extremely important in the U.S. effort to prevent Soviet expansion of communist control. The Truman administration, in articulating the Truman Doctrine, which pledged support for free people resisting outside pressure or armed internal minorities, instituted the United States' policy of containment and rendered diplomatic assistance to both Turkey and Iran in their struggle against Soviet pressure. The United States operated on the assumption that countries in the region would be best protected through the maintenance of their integrity and independence.[33] Truman's policy was continued by President Eisenhower who viewed the Persian Gulf as extremely important strategically and, in 1956, pledged U.S. cooperation with the Central Treaty Organization (CENTO), formerly the Baghdad Pact, established for the defense of the Middle East against Soviet encroachment.

Despite good intentions embodied in the policy of containing communism, it suffered from the fact that most Arab states did not share U.S. ideological anticommunist fervor to the extent that it would override their preoccupation with Israel and the Palestinians. Furthermore, the East-versus-West approach failed to take into consideration that for many in the Middle East, the United States itself was more threatening than the Soviet Union. Its support of Israel against the Arabs only served to unite domestic Arab forces committed to a national homeland for Palestinians and influenced them to rely increasingly on Moscow and its allies for assistance. As Campbell suggests, it was partly the U.S. policy of containment that opened the doors to a larger role for the Soviet Union in the Middle East.[34] Inevitably, the United States became embroiled in Middle Eastern domestic disputes, such as the Iranian crisis, which had global ramifications.

The Iranian Revolution and hostage crisis, which demonstrated U.S. weakness and may have influenced the Soviets to invade Afghanistan, pointed out another flaw of containment as a foreign policy; it overlooked the internal weakness of various Gulf States as the main contributing factor to instability and Soviet involvement. Largely divided politically and fragmented into different ethnic and religious groups, many Gulf States are governed by elites whose rule is not based on a deep historical consensus. Their relations with other states are therefore subject to rapid fluctuations.[35] Furthermore, even the staunchest U.S. ally, Saudi Arabia, had studiously avoided any appearance of being dominated by the United States in order to avoid further domestic and intra-Arab conflict.

Soviet liabilities and assets in the Gulf seem to be fairly balanced. Its proximity is both an advantage and a disadvantage; its military support is limited by communism's atheistic component; and its support of the Palestinian issue is undermined by its inability to replace the United States, and the West in general, as a reliable source of technical assistance and economic development. However the Soviets do stand to benefit from social and political instability concomitant with economic and political development. According to Chubin these elements of instability include:

1. weak or noninstitutionalized means of succession;
2. increasingly politically mobilized populations;
3. heavy and growing demands on weak administrative structures;
4. societies fractured in differing degrees along religious, ethnic, and linguistic lines vulnerable to sectarian feuds; and
5. the vulnerability of most states to transnational appeals.[26]

Developments in Lebanon in 1984 illustrated how domestic forces and the Palestinian issue worked to the benefit of Syria and Moscow to the detriment of U.S. policy in the region.

THE AMERICAN RESPONSE TO THE INVASION

Carter's extreme response to the Soviet invasion of Afghanistan was predictable, in light of U.S. dependence on petroleum from the Persian Gulf countries and his susceptibility during the 1980 presidential election to charges that he was indecisive and essentially soft on communism.

Carter dramatically denounced the invasion as the gravest threat to international peace since World War II and proclaimed the Carter doctrine, which committed American forces to defending the Persian Gulf against external threats. While U.S. interests in the Gulf were clearly defined, not much attention was paid to Soviet activities in Afghanistan prior to the invasion. Therefore, from the Soviet point of view, the U.S. did not have any significant interest in Afghanistan. Although the Carter administration had issued warnings before the invasion, given the fact there was no clear focus on the problem or on how to implement actions against the Soviets if they ignored the threats, it is difficult to believe that the Soviets took the U.S. seriously.

Following the invasion, Carter announced specific American actions that would be taken against the Soviets. Some of them were counterproductive or far more detrimental to the United States than to Moscow, although the Soviets did lose more than they gained. Carter called for a boycott of the Summer Olympics in 1980; the Soviets responded by boycotting the Olympics in 1984. An embargo was imposed on 17 million tons of grain originally destined for the Soviet Union. This seems to have caused greater hardships for the American farmer than for Soviet consumers because other countries such as Argentina supplied grain, but at higher prices. A year later, Reagan lifted the embargo as the Soviets consolidated their grip on Afghanistan. Other responses included delaying the ratification of SALT II, severe restrictions on trade, curtailment of Soviet fishing privileges in U.S. waters, postponing new cultural and economic exchanges between the two countries, and delaying the opening of new consular facilities in Kiev and New York City. While the U.S. lost its seven-person Kiev outpost, the USSR continued to have access to New York through its representatives at the United Nations. The deferment of cultural exchanges proved more damaging to American scholars than to the Soviet Union because many Soviet researchers already had access to outstanding U.S. technological institutes and universities and scientific meetings.[37]

In addition to diplomatic and economic pressure, the United States responded by giving approximately $30 million in military aid to Afghan resistance movements. The basic objective in supplying weapons to the Afghans was to perpetuate resistance to Soviet occupation. The dilemma Washington confronted was how to keep the Afghans strong enough to increase the costs for the Soviets but not so strong as to cause an escalation of the conflict and involve Pakistan. However, by 1987 more than 150 Pakistanis had died in Soviet air raids against suspected targets in Pakistan.[38] Reluctance to provide sophisticated weapons in the face of escalating brutal air and ground attacks prior to 1986 when Stinger missiles were given to the resistance presented serious problems for a policy designed to bleed the Soviets. Although Reagan increased military assistance to about $280 million in 1986,[39] the guerrilla movements, already fragmented and fighting among themselves, could not mount a serious challenge to determined Soviet military action.

Since bleeding the Soviets also involves bleeding the Afghans, Washington's policy of limited military aid could prove counterproductive if not accompanied by serious diplomatic efforts. This is not to deny that the Soviets have paid an extremely high price. Indeed, they have been in Afghanistan longer than they were engaged in fighting in World War II. However, few in Washington seriously consider that limited military supplies to the resistance will force them out of Afghanistan. The U.S. dilemma is that its "clear view of the desirable in Afghanistan is not matched by equally clear policy options."[40] Part of the problem is that what is desirable and what can be done are two different things. A pragmatic foreign policy attempts to reconcile the two. The effectiveness of U.S. policy also depends on the response of other nations to Soviet aggression.

Following Carter's pronouncement that the Soviet invasion was a serious threat to world peace, the United Nations' General Assembly passed a resolution condemning Soviet behavior as being inconsistent with the fundamental principle of the organization's charter and called for the immediate, unconditional, and total withdrawal of foreign troops from Afghanistan. Subsequent resolutions were equally ineffective, partly because the United States, preoccupied with Iran and presidential elections, exerted little effort to mobilize Third World opposition to Soviet occupation of a neighboring, developing country. Iranian officials were also distracted from Soviet involvement in Afghanistan by their internal problems with the Shah and Khomeini's rise to power prior to the invasion. Nevertheless, by June 1979, Soviet military actions in Afghanistan prompted Khomeini to warn Soviet Ambassador Vindgradov against interfering in Afghanistan or fomenting unrest in the Kurdish or Baluchi areas of Iran.[41] However, seizure of the American embassy personnel created opportunities for the Soviet Union to serve as a counterweight to the United States by supporting Iran, while simultaneolusly diverting Iranian attention away from the occupation of Afghanistan. By December 1982, when Iran marked the third year of Soviet occupation of Afghanistan and condemned Moscow for its brutal destruction of Afghan lives and property and its "hegemonistic move against the oppressed Moslem people of Afghanistan,"[42] the Soviets were so deeply entrenched that Iranian protests were virtually ignored.

The Europeans did not respond enthusiastically to America's call for sanctions against the Soviets. Indeed, Washington's failure to consult its European allies on a number of important policy decisions, which required their cooperation for successful implementation, has alienated many allies. Although strongly condemning Soviet aggression, Europeans favored political and economic measures over a military response. Essentially, their decision not to follow the U.S. wholeheartedly was quite pragmatic. They felt that Eastern Europe would eventually pay the price for Soviet actions and that complete endorsement of American initiatives would lead to further strains in East-West relations. Furthermore, European officials generally believe that since each European nation is unique in its economic ties with Moscow, the adoption of a uniform policy toward Soviet intervention is extremely unlikely. West Germans, for example, reacted calmly to the invasion because it wants to maintain communication with the Soviet Union as it improves relations with East Germany; to reduce the number of nuclear weapons through negotiations with the Soviets to receive about 40 percent of its natural gas supplies from the Soviet Union; and to continue other trade with Eastern Europe and Moscow.[43] The Soviet Union has taken advantage of differences among NATO allies and of Washington's tendency to implement hastily-made policies which ignore the interests of those whose cooperation is needed. However, as U.S. ties with Pakistan illustrate, doing what we think is in our allies' short-term interests may be detrimental for the United States and its allies in the long run.

U.S. TIES WITH PAKISTAN

U.S. policy toward Afghanistan is complicated by regional rivalries and alliances, the conflict between India on one side and Pakistan and China on the other, the Sino-Soviet competition in Asia, and by Indian-Soviet relations. For example, despite their common adherence to communism, the Chinese and Russians have been historically antagonistic and continue to be distrustful of each other. So pervasive is the view of the world in terms of East versus West that what is frequently overlooked is that the Soviets and Chinese concentrate most of their military resources along their common border. Soviets are constantly reminded by China of their expansionism and China's lost territories gained through unequal treaties concluded in the nineteenth century. The Soviets exhibit a basic fear of China. A similar fear exists between India and Pakistan. Here religion has been a key factor in the most savage religious war in history.

The Indian Hindus and Pakistani Moslems base their contemporary hatred of each other on deep, historic, religious and social differences. Despite Mahatma Gandhi's effectiveness as a nonviolent charismatic leader, he was unable to lead a united India to independence. Indeed, during the same year the British ended control of India (1947), Pakistan and India were locked in deadly combat over the disputed Kashmir province, regarded by both as essential to their national security interests. Ironically, Pakistan, which fashioned its political system along authoritarian lines, was embraced by the United States while the more democratic India moved closer to the USSR. However, both used their military strength, supplied in part by the U.S., against each other. It was the conflict between them that provided openings for Soviet participation. The Soviets invited both sides to settle their differences through negotiations at Tashkent because Moscow believed that China would be the eventual beneficiary of continued conflict.[44] It is against this background that Afghanistan and U.S. policy in the region must be examined.

By assuming that communism was regarded by other societies as the most immediate threat to their security, the United States set out on the perilous course of providing Pakistan with sufficient military assistance to render it a bulwark against communist expansionism. Truman's decision to arm Pakistan was influenced by: 1) the North Korean invasion of South Korea and Chinese entry into the conflict; 2) growing Soviet nuclear power; and 3) the expectation that Pakistan would fight ground battles against communist troops and guerrillas.[45] Pakistan's instability and its conflict with India did not appear to be of significant concern to the United States. Pakistan's geographic proximity to the Soviet Union was the overriding factor in the Cold War period. Thus, the Pentagon saw Pakistan as a place where bases could be established for U-2 aircraft surveillance flights and electronic monitoring of Soviet missile sites. Pakistan was given $21 million in U.S. military aid in 1954. In September 1954 Pakistan became a member of the South East Asia Treaty Organization (SEATO) and joined CENTO in 1955, thus becoming an important part of the strategy initiated by the U.S. designed to contain communism. But Pakistan's interests did not necessarily coincide with America's. In the India-China border war of 1962 Pakistan moved closer to China and by the mid-1960s Pakistan-Chinese relations were friendly, despite the U.S. view of China. However, it was because of this relationship with China that Pakistan was able to be instrumental in assisting Sino-American rapprochement during the Nixon administration.

Developments in Iran and Afghanistan refocused U.S. military attention on Pakistan. Having depended on Iran to play a pivotal role in U.S. security strategy in the Middle East and South Asia, Khomeini's hostility toward U.S. interests was a devastating setback. The Soviet occupation of Afghanistan only served to underscore U.S. vulnerability in the Persian Gulf. Under these circumstances Pakistan succeeded in persuading the United States to give it $3.2 billion in military and defense-related economic aid over a five-year period. Reagan's predilection for military solutions and his anticommunist emphasis allowed the smaller Pakistan to exercise disproportionate bargaining power *vis-a-vis* the United States to the detriment of both countries. As Harrison put it;

> Examined in the cold light of local realities, the U.S. decision to embrace Pakistani President Zia Ul-Haq emerges as a monumental self-defeating blunder that could enable Moscow to make major diplomatic and political advances in Southwest Asia without any direct military involvement.[46]

This assessment is supported by the fact that Pakistan is weak internally. Given the fact that the F-16 attack aircraft provided by the U.S. are facing India rather than Afghanistan, and the U.S. advanced air-warning planes could be used as effectively against Afghanistan as India, India is likely to continue to allocate more of its scarce resources to protect its security interests from Pakistani aggression, thereby escalating an arms race which could trigger nuclear confrontation between the two countries.[47] Pakistan, even with huge amounts of U.S. military assistance, cannot pose a credible threat to the Soviet Union as long as it remains fragmented and human rights are violated by Zia's authoritarian regime. Indeed, Pakistan's problems have multiplied because of increased U.S. military aid. Soviet planes have escalated bombing inside Pakistani territory and, because of close ties between America and Zia, opposition groups are becoming more anti-American, if not pro-Soviet, as they fight Zia's regime. Failure to address the issues of human rights and ethnic divisions in Pakistan will ultimately work to the benefit of the Soviet Union.[48]

Pakistan, from its inception, has experienced less democracy than India. This was due, in part, to the conflicts between various ethnic groups and the government's inability or unwillingness to unify the country. Today, Pakistan's major ethnic group, the Punjabis, has used U.S. military aid to maintain power without reconciling differences with the Baluch, Sindhi, and Pushtan minorities. Like the regimes of Iran and the Philippines under Ferdinand Marcos, Zia's martial law regime survived by essentially ignoring the 1973 constitution, suspending civil rights and political freedoms, and driving dissidents underground. Like India, Pakistan's religious minorities pose a threat to Zia's regime, and Zia has responded by making it a crime for the four million members of the Ahmadi Moslem religious sect to practice their religion. Zia's attempts to promote Sunni fundamentalism is resented by Shi'ite Moslems. Martial law legislation permits arbitrary arrest and the civilian judiciary has been seriously curtailed. The high courts cannot review decisions of military tribunals and actions of martial law authorities.[49] Despite government repression of opposition groups, in 1984 a coalition called the Movement for the Restoration of Democracy demanded free elections and an end to military rule. Elections held by Zia in 1985 left him fully in control of the country without significantly altering martial law.[50] Given the long history of authoritarian rule and ethnic fragmentation in Pakistan, the human rights situation is unlikely to improve soon without greater U.S. concern for Pakistan's internal stability as an essential aspect of national security.

Pakistan suffers from a common legacy of colonial rule: the drawing of territorial boundaries without much regard for ethnic groups or political entities. As in Nigeria, Ethiopia, and elsewhere, it is extremely difficult to integrate the various ethnic groups into a modern nation-state and to prevent neighboring states, such as Afganistan, from trying to regain lost territory or to prevent areas from attempting secession. The Soviet presence in Afghanistan has helped to encourage the province of Baluchistan to continue its separatist efforts and opposition to Zia's government.[51] Baluchistan comprises approximately 40 percent of the area of Pakistan and stretches across western Pakistan, eastern Iran, and southern Afghanistan. It commands more than 900 miles of the Arabian Sea coastline, including the northern shores of the Strait of Hormuz. Together with Pakistan's Northwest Frontier Province it makes up an area called Pakhtoonistan by the Afghans. Strategically located, it presents a significant challenge to Zia's government.[52] Another province which is strongly opposed to the Punjabi authorities is the Sind, the home of former Pakistani leader, Ali Bhutto. Bhutto's execution by Zia in 1979 added fuel to their discontent. In his effort to consolidate his power, Zia has responded to demands for regional autonomy with military force, especially against the Baluch. But, as Ziring suggests, Zia must work to accommodate the provincial leaders and develop more harmonious relations between the different provinces in order to save Pakistan.[53] U.S. military aid to Pakistan will only exacerbate Pakistan's internal problems and increase anti-American sentiments if the weapons are used against domestic opposition. Equally important is India's perception of Pakistani-U.S. ties as a threat to its security as well as India's relationship with the USSR.

INDIA, AFGHANISTAN, AND THE SOVIET UNION

While the United States regarded Pakistan as a bulwark against Soviet expansionism, India's views of Pakistan differed significantly from Washington's. Not only did the two countries perceive the Soviet threat differently, India saw U.S. military support of Pakistan as instrumental in bringing the Cold War to "the gates of the sub-continent," threatening its policy of nonalignment, and as a continuation of British colonialism under the guide of a worldwide anticommunist crusade.[54] Furthermore, U.S. military aid to Pakistan was perceived as a direct threat to India, not to the Soviet Union. From India's perspective, Pakistan's actions were inseparable from Washington's policy in the region. Consequently, India moved closer to Moscow to counter the perceived Pakistani-U.S. threat. When Pakistan received U.S. military assistance in 1954, India diverted important scarce resources away from much needed projects to augment its military position. The Soviets moved quickly to exploit opportunities created by these developments by sending two Soviet leaders, Khrushchev and Bulgzuin, to India and to the disputed Kashmir territory, and by expressing Soviet support for India on the Kashmir issue. When Nixon decided to side with Pakistan during its war with Bangladesh in 1971 and to send the aircraft carrier Enterprise into the Bay of Bengal as a show of U.S. military might, U.S.-India relations deteriorated while India's ties with Moscow were consolidated.[55] However, the relationship between India and the USSR is only partially related to U.S. backing of Pakistan.

After gaining independence in 1947, India embarked on a course of nonalignment in international relations, a policy that collided with the strong American emphasis on bipolarity and gradually alienated India from the United States. India's prime minister, Nehru, the architect of India's foreign policy in the early 1950s, attempted to develop friendly relations with the Soviet Union and China without endangering India's ties with Britain and the United States. Nehru believed that because of India's geographic proximity to the USSR, it was in India's interest to understand the Soviets and maintain a working relationship with them. This positive view of Moscow was also engendered by the fact that the Soviets were first among Europeans calling for the termination of British control of India.[56]

Both countries share a common interest in the stability of the region. In the pursuit of this objective they have worked to foster stable, friendly, and reliable relations. According to Donaldson, both calculate that their objectives are best served if regional and global rivals know that New Delhi and Moscow can count on each other's support without fear of abandonment or betrayal.[57] Border conflicts with China and Pakistan have helped to reinforce India's view of the Soviet Union. However, India also realizes that ultimately it will have to normalize ties with China and work toward reconciliation with Pakistan to maintain its nonaligned position and guarantee maximum security for itself and the region.[58] Its ties with Moscow do not diminish its interaction with Western Europe and North America. The Soviets, on the other hand, seek to use India's leadership in developing countries in competition with China and the United States. Since China is regarded by Moscow as the greatest threat to its security, the Soviets have endeavored to minimize Chinese influence in Asia, and India is seen as providing a counterweight to China in the Asian "balance of power" game.[59] It is the complexity of South Asian politics that shapes India's position on the Soviet invasion and occupation of Afghanistan.

India has never strongly publicly condemned Moscow for its actions in Afghanistan. India abstained in the UN vote which urged the withdrawal of foreign troops. In fact, the Soviet claim that they were invited to Afghanistan by the government to honor a treaty pledging them to defend the country from external and internal threats was largely accepted by New Delhi.[60] However, it appears that India attempted to influence the Kremlin quietly and privately. According to Horn;

> Indian Foreign Minister Rao journeyed to Moscow for an offical friendly visit. Rao reportedly went to seek 'the unconditional withdrawal' of Soviet troops without waiting for an international guarantee of the security and integrity of Afghanistan. Gromeyko preempted Rao's message . . . by bluntly telling his guest: It must be clear to all that attempts to change the realities existing in Afghanistan are futile.[61]

India's public actions do not demonstrate a serious, concerted effort to persuade the Soviets to leave Afghanistan.

Two factors mitigate the Soviet invasion from India's perspective. First, the Iranian fundamentalist revolution has significant implications not only for Moscow with its large Muslim population, but also for Hindu-dominated India. Sporadic religious conflicts only serve to underscore the serious ramifications of Islamic fundamentalism for India which has approximately 75 million Muslims. Motivated primarily by its need to protect its own security, India has been less sympathetic to the aspirations of the Afghan insurgents than the neighboring Islamic countries.[62] Savage religious wars between Muslim Pakistan and India, and problems between Hindu and Muslim in Kashmir, must be taken into consideration when evaluating India's response to the invasion.

Secondly, India perceives Pakistan and China as the primary threats to its security and cannot risk jeopardizing its friendship with Moscow. Since its independence India has fought three wars with Pakistan and one with China over territory. Consequently, a stronger Pakistan or China, regardless of the circumstances, will be suspected as having hostile intentions. Therefore, when the United States strongly condemned the invasion and Carter's Defense Secretary Brown made a trip to China and worked out an agreement under which China and America would expedite military assistance to Pakistan to counter Soviet expansionism, Indira Gandhi contended that this Chinese-U.S. combination would be dangerous to India and the rest of the Third World.[63]

Not surprisingly, Carter's proposal for a regional security arrangement involving India was rejected as being an invitation to further polarization of the region and inconsistent with India's tradition of nonalignment. When Pakistan's Zia dismissed Carter's offer of $400 million in military and economic aid as "peanuts," India appeared somewhat reassured that, by offering a modest aid package, Carter was sensitive to India's interests and that Pakistan, by refusing, indicated that it realized that no amount of military aid could prevent a determined Soviet effort to invade Pakistan. However, when Reagan gave Pakistan $3.2 billion in military and defense-related economic assistance, India saw this as a direct threat to its security, especially since eleven out of the sixteen Pakistani divisons and their equipment faced not Afghanistan and the USSR, but rather were concentrated along the India-Pakistan border where violent skirmishes frequently occur and where previous wars were fought. On the other hand, India views an unstable and dismembered Pakistan as a danger to its own security and a reasonably strong Pakistan as providing a buffer between India and the Soviet Union.[64]

India's position on Pakistan seems to coincide with the Soviet policy of having stable, nonthreatening countries on its borders. India's fear of China worked to Moscow's advantage by diminishing the possibility of a concerted effort by China, the United States, Pakistan, and India to exert pressure on the Soviets to withdraw.

CHINA, AFGHANISTAN, AND MOSCOW

Unlike India, China's response to the Soviet invasion was predictably strongly negative. Despite common adherence to communism, the Soviets have what Kissinger termed a deep "neuralgic fear" of China, a fear which extends from the leadership to even the dissidents[65] who are alienated from and critical of their government. Apart from historical antagonisms, Moscow's insecurity stems from the vulnerability of Siberia and the far eastern portion of the country to Chinese threats, especially in light of China's stated objective of regaining lost territory. A China which is economically and militarily strong is the greatest threat to the Soviet Union. On the other hand, the Chinese fear Soviet hegemonistic and expansionist policy; and although China realizes that some kind of detente with Moscow is an essential ingredient of Chinese national security strategy, it has deliberately cultivated good relations with the Third World, the United States, Western Europe, and Japan in order to resist Soviet "imperialism and hegemonism."[66] The Soviets, especially under Gorbachev, have responded by trying to improve relations with China, partly to help reduce the amount of Soviet military resources and the number of troops concentrated on the Sino-Soviet border and to prevent close ties between China and the United States.

The Soviet invasion of Afghanistan was condemned by China as part of a master plan for Soviet global expansion and domination. From the Chinese perspective, Moscow's strategy is to gain influence in Asia and Africa in order to achieve its primary goal of controlling Western Europe and menacing the Middle East and Persian Gulf countries where the United States has substantial interests. But China is also concerned about the more immediate threat posed by Soviet intervention in Afghanistan to its northwestern and western border regions where Beijing has experienced difficulties with nationalist-oriented minorities.[67] The presence of Soviet troops along China's very narrow border with Afghanistan was not reassuring.

Following the invasion the Chinese responded by terminating talks with Moscow, demanding the withdrawal of Soviet troops as a precondition for restoring detente, and pledging moral and military aid to Afghani resistance of Soviet occupation. Yet Beijing's aspiration to aid modernization of agriculture, technology, science, and the military distracted China's attention away from Afghanistan because it does not want to antagonize Moscow to the detriment of its economic development. Furthermore, the Soviets have created a quagmire for themselves in Afghanistan and active Chinese opposition is not essential to creating problems for Moscow. They are creating enough difficulties for themselves. As is generally the case in international conflicts, nations have a proclivity to seriously underestimate costs and duration of military operations. This is certainly applicable to the Soviets in Afghanistan.

COSTS OF THE SOVIET INVASION

Although it is uncertain whether Moscow deliberately planned its invasion of Afghanistan or was drawn into the quagmire by its excessive concern with security, the important point is that it is paying an extremely high price for control of a country which may in reality be ungovernable in a manner consistent with the Soviets' perception of security. The instability and fragmentation which characterize developing countries will continue to plague the Soviets in Afghanistan. The lesson for the Soviets is that the use of force to impose a solution on a country as fiercely independent and diverse as Afghanistan is not only costly but is also not very effective in the long run. What is often overlooked by those who believe that Soviet expansion is relatively easy to achieve is the fact that, even if Moscow had the vast resources essential to accomplish this objective, problems accompanying such an endeavor would certainly persuade the Soviets that a global empire might, after all, be more trouble than it is worth.

Afghanistan, like Vietnam, demonstrates that through negotiations and diplomacy the Soviets could have achieved reasonably secure borders without paying such an extraordinarily high price. Even without significant external involvement on the side of the Afghan resistance, Moscow may have created a disaster from which it cannot, for a variety of reasons, extricate itself. Lack of open domestic opposition and the Kremlin's inability to admit mistakes compound Moscow's problems in Afghanistan.[68]

In light of what has transpired over the eight-year period the Soviets have been bogged down in Afghanistan, it seems that they have dangerously miscalculated the limitations of military intervention in a foreign country lacking strong central authority with widespread legitimacy.[69] Even before the invasion, the Afghan religious leaders—the Mullahs—used their influence to spread hostility toward the PDPA which had attacked them and many other segments of Afghan society. Moscow, realizing this major impediment to their control of Afghanistan, encouraged Taraki to reach an accommodation with the traditional power structure by downgrading land reforms, allocating funds for the reconstruction of mosques, shrines, and Moslem educational institutions.[70]

The Najibollah regime continued to be factionalized and conflict-ridden even years after the invasion, a development which only frustrates the Soviets who had hoped to bridge the fundamental schism between the two factions of the ruling party. The Soviets installed the Parcham (Flag) community faction of the PPA when it occupied Kabul. The other faction, the Khalq (Masses) had ruled from 1978 until the invasion. The basic problem is that the latter group is numerically stronger than the Parchem and continues to dominate the Afghan army and security forces[71] upon which the Soviets initally relied to secure the countryside. Because much of the information coming out of Afghanistan is controlled by the Soviets, it is difficult to verify alleged problems Soviets are having with Afghans and to ascertain who is doing more of the actual fighting against Afghan guerrillas. However, given the Soviets' overwhelming military might, it is likely that greater progress toward subjecting the Afghans to Soviet rule would have been made if the Afghan soldiers were cooperating fully. On the contrary, the Soviet presence provided a unifying force for the usually divided Afghans. As Bradsher put it;

It was one thing to organize bureaucrats who could sit at desks in Kabul and shuffle papers to give the appearance of an Afghan administration in front of Soviet control. It was a much different thing to organize Afghan soldiers to go out and fight other Afghans. It even proved difficult to rely on the Afghan army for routine security maintenance because its loyalty was suspect.[72]

Indeed, many Afghans deserted the Soviets to join the resistance and it soon became apparent that some of those who remained with the Soviets provided valuable strategic information to the guerrillas. For example, when the Soviets launched a major offensive against the mujahidin (freedom fighters) in the Panjsher Valley in 1984, it was virtually ineffective because Ahamd Massod, who commanded the guerrillas, had been warned early enough to evacuate approximately 50,000 Panjshes prior to the attack.[73] The Soviets' distrust of the Afghans has influenced them not only to rely more on their own troops but also to engage in limited ground combat with the guerrillas for fear of ambush because of information provided by Afghans from in the Soviet camp. It is also important to note that although there are more than 120,000 Soviet soldiers in Afghanistan, less than 20 percent of them actually take part in military actions against the guerrillas.[74] Nevertheless, partly due to frustration accumulating over the years, the Soviets have waged a brutal war against the people of Afghanistan.

A major Soviet strategy is the systematic destruction of agriculture and livestock in the countryside to deprive the guerrillas of food. The escalation of bombing has coincided with periods when Afghans generally harvest their crops. Indiscriminate bombing of villages and areas suspected to be guerrilla strongholds increased with frustration stemming from military setbacks over eight years of occupation. The disruption of village life is deliberate and no effort is made to protect villages. Soviet troops regularly raze villages, kill the inhabitants, and force those who survive out of the country as refugees.[75] In the process of destroying guerrilla food supplies, the Soviets alienate the Afghan population and make no effort to win their support. Under these circumstances it is difficult to envisage the long-lasting tranquility or neutrality which the Soviets regard as indispensable for their security unless they are willing to engage in genocide. Yet it can be argued that the Soviets have committed "migratory genocide" by making approximately five million Afghans refugees. At the time of the invasion Afghanistan's population was estimated between 15–17 million.

Although the rebels experienced many victories against Soviet troops initially, the early part of 1984 marked a turning point in the war as the Soviets increased the number of troops, escalated bombing, applied the most devastating conventional weapons against mujahidin strongholds, and confronted them directly. Reports from Afghan refugees, Soviet army deserters, and the *Medecins sans Frontiers* (MSF) indicate that the Soviets are merciless. Hospitals have been deliberately bombed, and booby-trapped toys designed to injure children have been dropped by helicopters. Children attracted to the small red trucks and plastic pens have had arms and hands blown off.[76] Given the bonds between various ethnic groups the Soviets know that they will not desert their wounded. The Soviets know that an injured person is more trouble than a dead person for the guerrillas.[77] Given the fact that information about casualties is carefully controlled by the Soviets, it is difficult to estimate the number of Afghans and Soviets killed in combat. However, the general figure given is around 10–15 thousand Soviets killed and as many as one-half million Afghans killed or wounded.[78]

Other general costs include the cessation of agricultural trade between Afghanistan, the Soviet Union, and other countries, the interruption of food supplies from country to urban areas, loss of general revenues from taxation and customs duties, military expenditures, destruction of roads, bridges, and other infrastructure, and disillusionment among young Soviet soldiers and perhaps among the Soviet population, especially the Moslems.[79] All Western aid to the Afghan government has been terminated. This means that the Soviets must supply food, medical supplies, transportation, education (in the Soviet Union), and whatever else is required to maintain a functioning society under military occupation. Whatever the exact figure may be, the important point is that Afghanistan is a drain on Soviet resources, even with exports of gas from Afghanistan to the Soviet Union offsetting some of the costs. Equally serious for the Soviets is the danger of spreading their limited military resources, both human and material, over wide areas. Continued resistance forces Moscow to allocate additional resources to more areas, thus weakening its overall defense capabilities. Moscow, like other great powers, must painfully learn the limitations of power.

Soviet aggression proves costly in other ways. For example, Carter took advantage of the invasion of Afghanistan to garner support for the Rapid Deployment Force and a more visible naval presence in the Persian Gulf and Indian Ocean. Reagan has used it to help secure huge defense appropriations for bigger missiles and more military technology. As expected, the Soviets have had to divert scarce resources away from agriculture and consumer items to the military. Another major cost of Afghanistan for the Soviets is their image as imperialists being reinforced not only in the view of China but also in Third World countries where the Soviets champion antiimperialist causes. Although the Third World has been relatively silent on Afghanistan, there is reason to believe that they identify the struggle being waged by the Afghan resistance as part of a general effort for autonomy from the superpower.[80]

Afghans and Pakistanis are paying an extremely high price for Soviet aggression. Approximately five million Afghans are refugees in both Pakistan and Iran, with Pakistan having between three and four million. As indicated earlier, Afghans suffer immeasurable losses as a result of Soviet helicopter gunships, napalm, and other chemical weapons. Proud and independent farmers and herders must now live as refugees in Pakistan under unfavorable conditions – and depend upon the goodwill of international organizations and the Pakistani government.

Pakistan, too, has been greatly affected by their presence. By taking in refugees, Pakistan has created new problems and exacerbated older ones. With refugees come guns, livestock, and increased competition for firewood, water, food, jobs, grazing land, and government resources. It is estimated that Pakistan spends $1 million each day on the refugees, a factor contributing to growing hostility between the Afghans and their hosts.[81] Social tensions and conflicts arising out of the sudden addition of more than three million people are only part of the problem. During the latter part of 1987 the Soviets appeared unrestrained in their bombing of Pakistani villages on the Afghan border. The influx of refugees and their movement into Afghanistan as guerrilla fighters worried Zia who feared antagonizing the Soviets. Perhaps even more threatening is the fact that the refugees are located in Pakistan's politically most vulnerable areas where resentment against Zia's regime is deeply-rooted.

Furthermore, Zia's opponents have seized the refugee issue, maintaining that since the Afghan guerrillas freely cross the border to conduct raids against the Red Army in Afghanistan with weapons funneled through Pakistan from the United States, Egypt, Saudi Arabia, and China, then Soviet hostility toward Pakistan will escalate proportionately as their casualities climb.[82] Pakistan's dilemma is extremely serious, especially since the Soviets are determined to consolidate their position in Afghanistan and put pressure on Pakistan to accept a Soviet-supported regime in Kabul. There is widespread agreement that they will not withdraw from Afghanistan in the foreseeable future. In fact, the more resources expended on Afghanistan, the tighter Moscow will be wedded to its commitments. Like the United States in Vietnam, Moscow now finds itself entrapped by sunken costs.

TOWARD A PRAGMATIC U.S. POLICY

Afghanistan represents an example of how the lack of clearly defined U.S. foreign policy objectives and our overreaction to communist expansion in an area where our vital interests are not threatened directly can result in the reduction of U.S. credibility and power to the detriment not only of the country in which the Soviets are present but also of countries in the general region, and of overall U.S.-Soviet relations. Afghanistan was not a priority for U.S. policy and little was said or done about the progressive Soviet military buildup prior to the actual invasion. Our failure to clearly demarcate areas of interest may have inadvertently signaled to the Soviet Union that their actions would not be perceived as a major threat to U.S. interests. By giving Pakistan $3.2 billion for defense-related programs, the United States rekindled India's suspicion of Pakistan; and an attempt to play the China card *vis-a-vis* Moscow gave India little choice but to quietly acquiesce to the Soviet position on Afghanistan. Afghanistan clearly demonstrates the dangers of viewing a complex world simplistically in terms of communism. U.S. policy toward Afghanistan should take into consideration that the entire region from India to Iran is wired up together in what Selig Harrison calls "an incendiary network of interacting rivalries."[83]

A pragmatic U.S. foreign policy is achievable if we move beyond ideology and focus on the interests of all parties involved. Not only must we define our interests but also take into consideration the interests of our allies and those we intend to influence. If we want them to appreciate our interests we must evince an appreciation of theirs. A reactive foreign policy is not capable of addressing the various complex interests involved. This does not mean that the United States should discontinue pressure on the Soviets to withdraw from Afghanistan. But pressure exerted by the United States without a reasonable measure of support from our Western European allies and countries in the region which are directly affected by the Soviet invasion will prove ineffective and perhaps costly to overall U.S. interests. The United States' policy on Afghanistan is in accordance with various UN Resolutions which support a settlement embracing total Soviet withdrawal, self-determination for the Afghans, an independent, nonaligned Afghanistan, and the right of the four or five million reguees to return safely to Afghanistan. The U.S. does not accept the legitimization of the Soviet-backed Najibollah regime. However, the question is, are U.S. goals achievable, and if so, how can they be achieved? Given the Soviet reality, are they realistic? Is the United States the most appropriate actor or should another country or group of countries take the leading role in dealing with the Soviets? Given the reality of continued Soviet occupation, how can we take advantage of this situation? How can Soviet miscalculation and aggression be instrumental in the improvement of U.S. policy in the region and elsewhere? How can we use Soviet power against the Soviets?

Understanding Soviet Reality. Afghanistan has shown the limits of Soviet power and Moscow's tendency to make serious political and military mistakes. Soviet miscalculations have proven to be very costly, a factor prolonging their involvement in Afghanistan for a period longer than their participation in World War II. However, despite Carter's sanctions and Reagan's military support of the Afghan freedom fighters, the Soviets are likely to remain in Afghanistan, despite Gorbachev's allusion to Afghanistan as a "bleeding wound," offers of a cease-fire, and withdrawal of some Soviet troops.[84] U.S. policy objectives have not been achieved partly because of failure or unwillingness to deal adequately with the Soviet reality.

The Soviets' perception of security influenced their decision to invade Afghanistan. The chaos in neighboring Afghanistan was viewed as a threat to Soviet security, especially in light of serious challenges to Soviet power in Poland and the growing independence of other Eastern bloc countries. The Soviet view of reality, equating security with control, pushed Moscow to occupy Afghanistan. Related to this is the determination not to appear weak. Failure to control Afghanistan would be an admission of weakness. Soviet credibility and power are at stake in Afghanistan. Their stated reason for invading was to preserve a friendly pro-Soviet-Marxist regime. Because of Soviet casualties and serious resistance from Afghans, Moscow's ideological and military commitments to Kabul have grown over the last seven years. Like America in Vietnam, it has fallen victim to sunken costs. Unlike America, where opposition to Vietnam was openly expressed at all levels of society, the Kremlin is handicapped by its secretiveness and inability or unwillingness to admit mistakes.

Furthermore, the Soviets are sensitive to the rapid increase in the Asian population of the Soviet Union and the fact that many of them share in an Islamic identity with the Moslem world in which Islamic fundamentalism is a potent political force. If the Afghan rebels, 70 percent of whom are fundamentalist Moslems, were successful in forcing the Soviets to withdraw from Afghanistan, the religious fervor could spread to Moslems in Soviet Central Asia, thereby creating a serious challenge to domination of the Asians in the Soviet Union. But another Soviet reality is their dislike of war. The growing financial and military costs of Afghanistan, combined with the Soviet fear of war with China might influence Moscow to accept a political solution.

Find a Face-Saving Way out for the Soviets. Since the Soviets have indicated that they are willing to withdraw from Afghanistan,[55] the United States should not abandon efforts to find ways to give the Soviets an opportunity to leave Afghanistan without appearing to have lost. It is quite probable that the Soviets really don't know how to escape the quagmire they created in Afghanistan. It is in America's long-term interests in the region to help them find a way out. Rather than dismissing Soviet proposals for troop withdrawals, the United States should test Moscow — give them a chance to demonstrate their sincerity and credibility. One could argue that Karmal's replacement (by Najibullah) in 1986, a condition Pakistan has insisted on for its signing any agreement with Kabul, is an indication of Soviet seriousness about reducing its military presence in Afghanistan.[86]

Support Gorbachev's Offer to Work with the Former Afghan King. Gorbachev indicated in 1987 that the former Afghan king, Zahir Shah, who was deposed in 1973, could head an interim regime in Afghanistan.[87] It is important to consider this proposal, especially in light of Moscow's acceptance of the king from 1933 to 1973 and the difficulties involved in establishing a government of reconciliation that would have widespread support among the Afghans. The harsh reality is that the chaos in Afghanistan will make it almost impossible for either the U.S.-backed freedom fighters or the Soviet-backed communists to head a government of reconciliation. In fact, one could argue that the Afghans themselves are making a political solution extremely difficult. This is not to blame the victims; it is reality. The Afghans are deeply divided and time is not necessarily on their side. The leaders of the resistance want an Islamic government, something that might not be in Washington's interest, and the communists want continued control. Both the U.S. and the USSR should downgrade the role of their clients and focus on the 73-year-old king who favors a transitional government composed of both communists and noncommunists, but dominated by the latter.[88] Given the Soviets' perception of their reality and the United States' limited ability to dramatically alter conditions in Afghanistan, U.S. acceptance of this proposal could be beneficial to both Moscow and Washington.

Communication Is Essential. Failure to provide more information on Soviet activities limits the effectiveness of U.S. policy. The United States government must continue to make a serious effort to declassify and distribute pertinent information on major communication centers around the world and to broadcast Soviet actions directly to the Soviet people and the Afghans. Although public opinion in the Soviet Union is not a major force as it is in Western democracies, Soviet citizens are increasingly aware of the war's effects. The younger generation is less likely to tolerate severe sacrifices for a war in Afghanistan — if they get a different version of what is occurring there.

However, if the United States takes the lead in criticizing Soviet involvement in Afghanistan other nations might perceive what is said as part of the usual anti-Soviet rhetoric. Perhaps more neutral countries and those directly affected by the Soviet invasion should lead efforts to mobilize international opinion against the Soviet occupation because they are likely to have greater credibility.

Focus on Objective Standards. U.S. leverage *vis-a-vis* the Soviet Union is significantly reduced when Washington engages in similar behavior for essentially the same reasons given by Moscow for its behavior. This should not be construed as equating U.S. covert actions with Soviet brutality. However, if the United States fails to respect ideological differences and political pluralism in the Western Hemisphere and elsewhere, why should we expect the Soviets not to do the same? If we disregard international law when it is expedient to do so and ignore principles of self-determination and national sovereignty of all states, why should we expect the Soviets to follow a higher standard of international conduct? By strongly endorsing international law as the basic framework for world order and refraining from activities which are contrary to law, the United States will strengthen domestic support for U.S. foreign policy objectives, and improve its credibility with allies and adversaries alike. Gaining the moral high ground is a critical element of a successful foreign policy in the nuclear age, and gives more leverage to counteract Soviet activities which are contrary to generally accepted principles of international law and behavior.

Engcourage Nonalignment. The Soviet effort to dominate Afghanistan resulted in part from Afghanistan's abandonment of its neutral, nonaligned status in world affairs. From its inception, Afghanistan practiced noninvolvement in external conflicts between superpowers in the region, Russia, and Britain. Under these conditions the Soviets could not have invaded on the pretext of rescuing a friendly socialist state that signed a treaty surrendering its neutrality. On the other side of nonalignment is the harsh reality, clearly demonstrated to the Soviets in Afghanistan, that intrusive action on the part of a superpower will generally be detrimental to that particular superpower. The strong commitment by Third World countries to autonomy and independence even in the face of growing interdependence of states imposes restrictions on both superpowers. As Galbraith observed, the closer, more ambitious the superpowers' embrace, the greater will be the adverse reaction and the penalty.[89] Nonalignment in South Asia and the Persian Gulf would reduce the costly U.S.-USSR competition and concomitant instability. Pakistan and India should be encouraged to be neutral and not participate in superpower rivalries.

Strengthen Pakistan Internally. Afghanistan's inability to unite and reconcile conflicting interests of various political factions and of ethnic groups provided the Soviets with an opportunity and justification for military intervention. Soviet reluctance to invade Afghanistan much earlier points to the realization that relatively stable countries on the Soviet border can be deterrents to Soviet involvement. Americans should place less emphasis on military aid to Pakistan and focus more on strengthening the country internally, by encouraging Zia to compromise with the various ethnic groups and opposition factions, to respect fundamental human rights, to move toward greater political and social freedom. The U.S. should also assist in Pakistan's economic development. If Pakistanis have a vested interest in the perpetuation of the system of government in Pakistan, they are less likely to make radical changes when Zia goes or turn to the Soviet Union for support to alter the system, especially if the U.S. is identified solely with Zia.

Reconcile India, Pakistan, and China. Soviet occupation of Afghanistan presents a serious threat to the security of both India and Pakistan. By giving Pakistan increased military aid, the United States not only created greater strains in relations between Pakistan and India, but also made it more difficult for India to condemn the Soviet invasion, or to develop a joint Indo-Pakistani challenge to Soviet activities. It also distracted India's and Pakistan's attention away from the fact that only through attempts to reconcile their differences and a policy of mutual nonaggression can their security be safeguarded against the Soviet threat. It is in India's interest to have a strong, nonthreatening Pakistan on its border to prevent further Soviet expansion. To accomplish this objective both countries must search for common interests and reduce tensions between them. The United States can take advantage of Soviet involvement in Afghanistan to influence both countries to reconcile the very difficult and deep differences and work together to solve the problem in Afghanistan.

It is extremely important that the U.S. not embrace Pakistan and exclude India. Indeed, the U.S. should move aggressively to build stronger ties with India to limit Soviet influence. The Soviets clearly regard India as essential to the achievement of their interests in South Asia and in the Indian Ocean. Conspicuously nonaligned from the beginning of its independence, India would like to maintain relations with East, West, and the Third World. The United States should respect India's position but also encourage better relations between India and China. By settling its border dispute with China, India would become less vulnerable to Soviet pressure. Harrison suggests that the Indo-China border dispute could be settled if the United States could persuade China to return a 2,500 square mile portion of Aksai Chin which India lost in the 1962 war. India would accept the loss of the remaining territory captured by China.[90] Normalization of Sino-India relations would be a serious setback for the Soviet Union and could encourage it to focus more on diplomatic rather than military solutions to problems in South Asia. Improved relations with India would be beneficial to American interests in the Indian Ocean and South Asia.

Recognize India as a Regional Power. An important component of a pragmatic U.S. policy in the region is the recognition that India is more than a minor nonaligned country involved in the superpower competition in Asia. It is concerned about the growing militarization of the area and the introduction of a large number of Soviet troops on the Kashmir border. The United States could facilitate India's role of building a regional consensus on security issues, including an Asian response to the Soviet occupation of Afghanistan.[91]

Secure Interests in the Persian Gulf by Focusing on the Problems, Not the Soviets. The invasion of Afghanistan provided yet another reminder of the explosive nature of the Persian Gulf. Yet many of the problems there are deeply embedded in the social, religious, and political fabric of various countries. Extremes in wealth and poverty, conflicts between traditional and modern values, and the Palestinian issue all contribute to the instability of the region. The United States' policy must go beyond military solutions and address, to whatever extent possible, the causes of instability. However, it must avoid making every instability a cause for involvement or for automatic escalation.[92]

Use Afghanistan to Drive a Wedge between Havana and Moscow. The Afghan crisis provides an opportunity for Washington to drive a wedge between Havana and Moscow. Castro's foreign policy objectives in the Third World were seriously damaged by the Soviet Union's invasion of a member of the Nonaligned Movement headed by Cuba in 1979. Cuba's failure to defend Moscow's actions and its feeble reasoning on the UN vote condemning the invasion were clear indications of serious differences between the two allies and raised new questions about Havana's ability to pursue an independent foreign policy. The United States could have emphasized the costs of the invasion for Cuba and made an attempt to get the Nonaligned Movement to pressure Cuba into taking a clearer position on Soviet occupation of a small Third World country. This approach could have been accompanied by efforts to reduce tensions between Havana and Washington.

Recognize the Limits of Our Power. In order to be effective, U.S. foreign policy objectives must be tailored to fit U.S. power. In situations where our power is limited our objectives should likewise be limited. Making threats that could not be implemented only eroded U.S. credibility and power in relation to Afghanistan. Our policy initiatives were too broad for the resources allocated for their achievement. We strongly condemned the invasion and promised support for the resistance before we could determine how much we were prepared to give. Our bargaining power was limited and the Soviets behaved as though they were aware of it. The lesson of Afghanistan is that America cannot respond to all crises as major threats to U.S. interests. It must define its vital interests and do what is necessary to protect them.

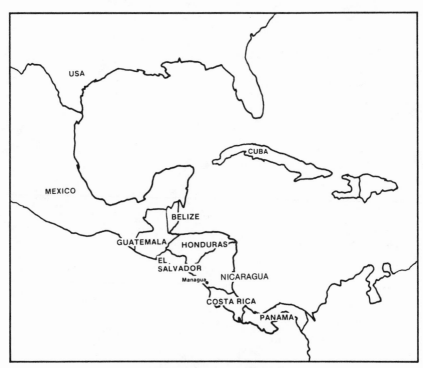

CENTRAL AMERICA

4

Nicaragua: Support the Revolution to Moderate It

Soviet-Cuban activities in Nicaragua and the existence of the Sandinista government quickly became the Reagan administration's major foreign policy concern and, subsequently, the single most important factor contributing to the president's decline in popularity and power. The 1987 Senate hearings on the Iran-Contra affair revealed a general lack of long-term planning in relation to the perceived Soviet-Cuban threat, the absence of clear analysis of policy objectives, the dominance of ideology and emotions over pragmatism, and a general disregard for both U.S. and international law. Reagan's obsession with anticommunism and overthrowing the Sandinistas ultimately resulted in escalating conflicts between Congress and the president, reduced enthusiasm for the secret Contra war, an erosion of U.S. influence over current as well as potential developments in the region and, most importantly, an increase in unnecessary suffering for Central Americans.

U.S. preoccupation with controlling political developments in Central America in general and in Nicaragua in particular inadvertently contributes to a climate of anti-Americanism that is conducive to Soviet-Cuban involvement in the region.[1] Emphasis on stability in the fact of inevitable change and strong opposition to revolutionary movements attempting to implement societal changes have long been hallmarks of U.S. policy toward Central America.[2] However, rather than safeguarding U.S. interests, this approach jeopardizes them and leads to a high-cost policy of self-victimization. By resisting political change, the United States is identified with oppressive regimes that ignore basic economic needs and human rights of their citizens. Consequently, violent change is accelerated by groups with a distinctly anti-American character that find it easy to justify their reliance on Soviet-Cuban support when confronted with opposition from Washington.[3] A pragmatic U.S. foreign policy must begin with a clear definition of U.S. interests in the region, an assessment of costs involved in achieving them, a recognition of the limits of our power to transform societies according to our wishes, a movement away from the ethnocentricism endemic in relations with Central America, and greater appreciation for Central America's economic, social, and political development needs and the changes necessary to satisfy them.

In order to be successful, American policymakers must depart from traditional responses and support revolutionary change in order to exert a moderating influence and deprive the Soviets and Cubans of opportunities to increase their activities in Central America.[4] Instead of focusing on the Soviets and Cubans, American policymakers should emphasize the underlying endemic social, economic, and political problems that cause instability.

The United States' strong reaction to revolution is often perceived as a general disregard for the social and economic causes of the unrest and the sufferings of ordinary people.[5] This antirevolutionary bias appears inconsistent with the founding principles of the United States and its own revolution.[6] But the problem lies at the heart of the American Revolution itself. Unlike the French Revolution, which was concerned with the immediacy of suffering, the American Revolution remained committed to the foundation of freedom and creating institutions to preserve it. The limitations of the American Revolution in relation to revolution throughout Asia, Africa, and Latin America are best articulated by Hannah Arendt who contends that:

> The superior wisdom of the American founders in theory and practice is conspicuous and impressive enough, and yet has never carried with it sufficient persuasiveness and plausibility to prevail in the tradition of revolution. It is as though the American revolution was achieved in a kind of ivory tower into which the fearful spectacle of human misery, the haunting voices of abject poverty, never penetrated.[7]

The essentially conservative American Revolution did not contain the ingredients that would equip foreign policymakers with an understanding of Third World revolutions. More often than not the United States has supported undemocratic governments in rigidly socially stratified societies; U.S. power and prestige were marshalled to support dictators who were obviously despised by their fellow citizens.[8]

Equally important, especially after World War II, radical change became synonymous with communism and Soviet expansion in the minds of American policymakers.[9] This is especially applicable to Central America. The danger of this perception is that by attributing Central Americans' desire to change to Marx and Lenin, ignoring internal dynamics of change, and by identifying with those in power, Washington assumes the role of a counterrevolutionary power and abandons to Cuba and communism the sponsorship of change.[10] By labeling their opposition communists, Latin American dictators have skillfully manipulated Washington into assisting them in their continued repression and corruption. They are also aided by the tactics of revolutionaries such as kidnapping, sabotage, and other violent measures, which shock Americans who, accustomed to an orderly society, are ill-equipped by temperament or historical experience to comprehend the nature of social revolutions.[11]

Revolutionary movements offer the Soviets opportunities for subversion and penetration, but so does a general lack of knowledge on the part of U.S. citizens about Latin America, which expresses itself in the simplistic view of Latin American problems in terms of the East-West rivalry. Coming to office on the heels of the hostage crisis in Iran which followed the revolution against the Shah and Moscow's invasion of Afghanistan, President Reagan was determined to reverse what he perceived as a dangerous decline of U.S. power and prestige under the Carter and Ford administrations. Reagan had long since concluded that the Soviet Union—the evil empire—was the cause of all violent upheavals in the world.[12]

Restoration of U.S. credibility and prestige required not only the absence of nonaligned or Marxist regimes in Central America, but countries unequivocally aligned with the United States. Even their diplomatic ties with Moscow and Havana were perceived as threatening, despite the U.S. diplomatic relations with the Soviet Union. At the heart of Reagan's approach was a return to traditional paternalism toward Central America.[13]

The Monroe Doctrine, current CIA operations, and a Domino Theory that functions automatically assumed a central role in U.S. policy. Assertiveness and nationalism on the part of Nicaraguans would not be tolerated, and the Sandinistas would be forced to say "uncle." Carter's soft policies, viewed as having permitted leftist expansionism in Central America, had to be replaced with a hard-line strategy to reverse it. As Riding put it, the economic, political and historical dynamics of the region were therefore dismissed as largely irrelevant to the basic power play. And the new administration marched confidently toward the quagmire.[14]

THE UNITED STATES POLICY TOWARD NICARAGUA PRIOR TO 1979

Nationalism in contemporary Nicaragua is an outgrowth of that country's lack of control over its internal as well as external affairs since its nominal independence from Spain in 1821. Although sovereign in theory, Nicaragua was dominated by Britain, private individuals, and the United States until the Sandinista Revolution of 1979. Britain's commercial and naval power and its role in Latin America's struggles for independence from Spain gave it a significant foothold in Nicaragua. Throughout the nineteenth century Britain's power was visible in the region, especially in the Miskito area of Nicaragua and Belize, formerly British Honduras.[15] The Monroe Doctrine, proclaiming the emancipation of the Republican New World and its separation from the wars and power-politics of Europe, was virtually meaningless. Its primary objective was to prevent more powerful European nations from seizing former Spanish possessions contiguous to the United States and threatening U.S. vital interests or frustrating its expansion.[16] But as LeFeber notes, the United States could proclaim the Monroe Doctrine but Britannia's fleet and investors wrote their own rules in Central America.[17]

It wasn't until 1848 that the United States, under the leadership of President James K. Polk, took a decisive step in Nicaragua. Following Britain's seizure of part of Nicaragua in 1848, President Polk signed a treaty with Nicaragua which gave the United States rights of the future canal route through Nicaragua in exchange for Washington's guarantee of Nicaraguan sovereignty over its territories.[18] Despite guarantees of sovereignty, American businessmen owned and managed leading mines, railroads, the lumber industry, and banks; and United Fruit and Atlantic Fruit controlled over 300,000 acres of prime agricultural land. With emancipation of slaves gaining increased U.S. support, entrepreneurs saw Nicaragua as a place to expand slavery. The fiction of Nicaraguan sovereignty was demonstrated by free-booter William Walker's control of that country from 1855 to 1857. The United States even granted diplomatic recognition to Walker. His demise came not from actions of Nicaraguans but from competition with Cornelius Vanderbilt who had significant business interests in Nicaragua.[19] Not surprisingly, Nicaraguan nationalism was against not only governments supported by U.S. power but against the United States itself and its business firms.

Direct U.S. involvement in Nicaraguan affairs, influenced by internal political dynamics in that country, was marked by President William Howard Taft's 1909 backing of a Conservative party revolt and the overthrow of Jose Santos Zelaya—whose nationalism threatened Washington—and his replacement with Nicaraguans loyal to U.S. interests. In 1912 U.S. marines landed in Nicaragua and stayed until 1933, with a brief interruption of 18 months between 1925 and 1926, thus giving Nicaragua the dubious distinction of enduring the longest U.S. occupation imposed on any Latin American country during the twentieth century.[20] Protection of U.S. investments, a desire to have a stable, pro-American government in Managua, and establishment of democracy were among the motivating factors for U.S. military involvement. But democracy proved elusive, although elections were held regularly. The manner in which the elections were conducted undermined not only attempts to introduce democracy to Nicaragua, but also set the precedent that the Somozas followed in dealing with opposition and strengthened the erroneous assumption that elections and democracy are synonymous. Marine Corps General Smedley Butler, supervisor of elections in both Nicaragua and Haiti, is quoted as saying that "the opposition candidates were declared bandits, when it became necessary to elect our man to office. . . . Our candidates always win."[21] In reality, Nicaragua never enjoyed democracy.

Armed struggles characterized Nicaraguan politics and elections continued to be veneers legitimizing those in power. In fact, the first fairly democratic elections in 1924 was aborted by Emiliano Chamorro, "the Old Lion," who seized power with the gun after losing at the ballot box. Washington refused to recognize the new government. However, when the deposed president Juan B. Sacassa attempted to regain power with the assistance of revolutionary Mexico, President Calvin Coolidge and his Secretary of State Frank Kellogg responded by dispatching the marines once again to Nicaragua to remove Chamorro and install Alfolfo Diaz as acting president.[22] By so doing, the United States succeeded in effectively neutralizing Sacassa and his army led by General Jose Moncada, but failed to terminate resistance to U.S. intervention. Opposition forces were led by Augusto Cesar Sandino, a privileged Nicaraguan whose experiences with U.S. companies and growing feelings of nationalism strongly influenced his anti-Americanism and his self-perception as an instrument for creating a Nicaragua free of U.S. influences.[23] Sandino's military confrontations with the marines and their inability to destroy his army made him a popular hero among alienated Nicaraguans in the countryside who did not share in the benefits enjoyed by the urban middle class.

Controlling the country was quite an expensive endeavor. Stopping revolutions and suppressing opposition movements required a permanent U.S. presence. However, the United States soon found a solution to this traditional dilemma; native, U.S.-trained forces would be used to safeguard U.S. security interests and protect Nicaragua's leaders from revolutionaries such as Sandino. This led to the creation of the National Guard, led by the strongly pro-American General Anastasio Somoza. In theory, the Guard would be neutral politically and subservient to civilian authorities. In reality, political authority was exercised by the commander of the National Guard. Somoza, shortly after ordering Sandino's assassination, seized power in 1936 and maintained it with military might. Appeals by Diaz, Chamorro, and Sacassa to Washington for assistance went unheeded, giving Somoza free reign in Nicaragua. While one may argue that the United States was not directly involved in Sandino's murder, the overthrow of Sacassa, or the emergence of the Somoza dynasty, ordinary Nicaraguans perceived a direct relationship between Washington and the Somozas. Falcoff is partly correct in stating that the sheer physical and economic dimensions of U.S. power were so overwhelming to Nicaraguans that they viewed Washington as having unlimited power to arrange their political life.[24] Nevertheless, these perceptions were based on their experience with almost twenty years of U.S. occupation and Washington's support of Somoza, especially during World War II. U.S. assistance to Somoza, however, was inconsistent and conditional.

In 1947, Somoza was pressured by the United States into withdrawing from the presidential electoral race. Retaining control of the National Guard, Somoza allowed a puppet candidate, Dr. Leopoldo Arguello, to run, only to overthrow him shortly thereafter.[25] Although U.S. recognition was withheld initially, Washington soon decided that a refusal to grant recognition would be largely ineffective in pressuring Somoza to resign. Somoza's strong anticommunist position earned him continued U.S. assistance until his assassination in 1956.[26] His sons, Luis and Anastasio, inherited control of Nicaragua and American backing.

Luis Somoza, president from 1956 to 1967, attempted to moderate the excessive military dominance in Nicaraguan politics by rebuilding the Liberal party so that it could assist in transferring more authority from the National Guard to civilian leaders. He also utilized highly trained development technicians to assist in economic modernization.

Anastasio (1967–79), on the other hand, was ruthless in his quest for personal enrichment and aggrandizement. He followed the tradition of encouraging corruption and protecting criminals, and unabashedly replaced developmentalist specialists with unqualified supporters.[27] Refusing to seriously negotiate with middle and upper class opposition groups and

amassing more wealth at their expense, Anastasio Somoza eventually significantly contributed to their alliance with the more revolutionary Sandinistas. Skillfully manipulating Washington's fear of communism,
Somoza ultimately succeeded in undermining U.S. interests in Nicaragua
and, paradoxically, assisted in his own demise and the emergence of the
Sandinistas who, once in power in Nicaragua, would turn to Moscow
and Havana to protect their revolution from the perceived threats of
U.S. intervention.

THE RISE OF THE SANDINISTAS

When Anastasio Somoza inherited power from his brother in 1967, the
Sandinistas, who took their name from the anti-American revolutionary,
Sandino, were so ineffectual and nonthreatening that Washington paid
virtually no attention to them, believing that the five-thousand-man National Guard could eradicate them. Founded in Havana in 1962 by exiled
Nicaraguans who regarded Castro and the Cuban Revolution as ex-
emplary, the *Frente Sandinista de Liberacion Nacional* (FSLN) was composed of approximately fifty men who shared a common aversion to the
Somoza dynasty. Trained and supported by Cuba, the FSLN remained
relatively insignificant for over a decade after its creation, claiming only
one hundred members as late as 1974.[28] Clearly, Nicaragua's internal
problems, rather than the Sandinistas, were crucial factors responsible
for the revolution. Somoza's refusals or inability to allow change to occur and his greed assisted the FSLN's growth.

Nicaragua was fast becoming the private property of the Somoza
family and the blood of Nicaraguans was being sold, literally. By the early 1970s they owned the television network, the Mameric Steamship
lines, *Banco de Centroamerica*, the Nicaraguan cigar-making firm, half
the agricultural production of the country, the brick companies which
sold bricks for paving Nicaraguan streets, a half interest in the Inter-
continental Hotel, as well as part of the Lanica Airline. In the process of
amassing his wealth, Somoza made enemies among the independent
businessmen who resented his ruthless acquisition of substantial
holdings, especially in construction and banking.

Since his economic power was based on his political position and
control of the National Guard, Somoza attempted to circumvent restrictions in the constitution which prohibited his reelection by dissolving
Congress and writing a new constitution which would provide for his
return as president. The Independent Liberals, Christian Democrats, the
archbishop of Managua, Miguel Obando y Bravo, and others opposed
the scheme and called for a completely new order.[29] In the aftermath of

the 1972 earthquake which caused the loss of 10,000 lives and devastated Managua, Somoza further contributed to the alienation of poor and middle class Nicaraguans alike by permitting his rapacious National Guard to confiscate materials donated by the United States and international relief agencies, engage in widespread looting of damaged businesses and, despite the people's misery, used his control of government to siphon off international donations for himself. It was at this point that open expression of popular discontent with the Somoza regime began to surface.[30]

Although divided, the Sandinistas were emerging as a major challenge to Somoza. One faction favored a protracted guerrilla war of attrition (*Guerra Prolongada Popular*—GPP) and another, the Proletarios, advocated mass insurrection in the urban centers. A third group, the Terceristas, under the leadership of Victor Manuel Lopez and the Ortega brothers, Daniel and Humberto, favored a more moderate course of action and joined forces with many of Managua's businessmen.[31] Organizational difficulties had been diminished to the point of allowing the FSLN to mount a spectacular and embarrassing attack against Somoza. They seized Somoza's guests at a farewell party in Managua honoring U.S. Ambassador Shelton on December 27, 1974 and held them hostage until Somoza granted them safe conduct out of the country, the release of prisoners, and a substantial sum of money.[32] In response to this and other guerrilla activities, Somoza imposed martial law in 1975 and ordered a National Guard offensive into the countryside where Sandinista fighters had been operating. Unable to locate the Sandinistas, National Guardsmen engaged in general warfare against the peasants, torturing, raping, plundering, and summarily executing hundreds of them. This continued for more than two years. Outraged by widespread atrocities, many Catholic bishops issued a pastoral letter openly denouncing the Guard's shocking brutality. Somoza responded with declaring a state of seige, installing military tribunals, and imposing further restrictions in the process.[33]

Revolutionaries are genereally beneficiaries of state violence against the population because under such circumstances even moderate opposition is perceived as threatening to the regime's survival. By assassinating Pedro Chamorro Cardenal, Somoza sowed the seeds of his own demise. *La Prensa's* coverage of Somoza's commercial blood-plasma operation and Chamorro's advocacy of social justice and freedom could not be tolerated. Chamorro's murder influenced more privileged Nicaraguans to join the growing anti-Somoza opposition. A new revolutionary ferment pervaded the country.[34] Somoza had broken the unwritten rule of the political game. Within the magic circle of old families a certain tolerance was allowed. As Anderson observed, the elite concluded that if

Chamorro could be killed for his political views, then everyone was in danger, and the Somozas would have to go.[35]

Chamorro's assassination was the catalyst for Somoza's demise. Many different political factions, business groups, manufacturing associations, and trade unions united for a general strike to force Somoza's resignation. Anti-Somoza uprisings were spontaneous and more frequent, and the FSLN, supported by Mexico, Costa Rica, Venezuela, Panama, and Cuba, had grown into a major force of 7,000 men and women. In May 1979 they launched their final offensive and were assisted by the brutal murder of ABC-TV newsman, Bill Stewart, who was forced out of a car and shot in the head by the National Guard. Americans viewing this on television were suddenly shocked into realizing what Nicaraguans had endured for several years. Somoza had actually bombed Nicaraguan slums, killing thousands of people. Confronted by well-armed Sandinistas, the National Guard disintegrated and Somoza fled Nicaragua on July 17, 1979 for Florida, leaving behind 50,000 Nicaraguans dead, 100,000 wounded, one-fifth of the population homeless, a destroyed infrastructure, and $1.6 billion in foreign debt.[36]

Creating order out of such chaos would have been difficult under the best circumstances. The Sandinistas were now faced with the challenge of putting together a coalition government and governing the country effectively and responsibly after generations of dictatorships. Reconciliation of competing factions within the FSLN itself was the first major task. In January 1979 a national directorate, composed of representatives of the three factions, had been created. Daniel and Humberto Ortega and Victor Lopez represented the more broadly-based, moderate Terceristas; Jaime Wheelock Roman, Carlos Nunez Telley, and Luis Carrion Cruz represented the Proletarios, and Tomas Borge Martinez, Henry Ruiz Hernandez, and Bayardo Arce Castagno, for the Prolonged People's War.

When the Sandinistas actually seized power they appointed prominent Nicaraguans from different classes in society to serve in the five-member Junta of National Reconstruction. Its membership included Daniel Ortega and Moises Hassan from the Sandinistas, author-educator Sergio Ramirez Mercado, businessman Alfonso Robelo Callejas, and Violeta Barrias de Chamorro from the aristocracy. This representative, pluralistic group aspired to transform Nicaragua into a social democracy which would be politically nonaligned. The armed forces were to be nonpolitical; democratic elections were to be held within a reasonable time; and private property would be protected in a mixed economy.[37]

A number of problems combined to prevent the accomplishment of all of these objectives, many created by the Sandinistas themselves. Rebuilding the economy after a devastating earthquake and civil war and providing ordinary Nicaraguans hope for the future were difficult to achieve simultaneously without alienating members of the fragile anti-Somoza coalition, which supported the revolution, but not necessarily the Sandinistas. Furthermore, Sandinista antiimperialistic rhetoric and Reagan's hostile, inconsistent policies affected Nicaragua's internal as well as international politics.

The Sandinistas proceeded to consolidate power and emphasize unity rather than pluralism or toleration of opposition groups. Reagan perceived the Sandinistas as determined to create another Cuba, a view strengthened by their Marxist ideology and growing ties with Cuba and the Soviet Union. Significant differences between Cuba and Nicaragua were ignored. For example, the Cuban revolutionaries nationalized industries, summarily executed opponents, interfered with religious freedom, and tolerated no political opposition parties. On the other hand, the Sandinistas are not anticlerical, Nicaraguans continue to be very religious, and the church influential; they abolished the death penalty and tolerate a largely ineffective opposition and almost two-thirds of the economy remains in private hands nine years following the revolution.

Millionaires are still in Nicaragua, and large farms produce much of Nicaragua's exports. Of seven million acres of farmland, 4.4 million acres are privately owned and 2.6 million controlled by the government and distributed to approximately sixty thousand farmers. Large farms have not been nationalized without compensation. Under laws enacted in 1983, the state has the right to seize farms larger than 1,200 acres on the more fertile Pacific coast or 2,400 acres on the less fertile Atlantic coast if they are unproductive.[38] When large farms were seized by the government in 1985 for redistribution to small farmers, attempts were made to compensate the individuals involved by offering them land elsewhere; the justification given was that it was easier for one family to move than to relocate fifty families. However, as of 1985, the Pellas family owned 15,000 acres and produced 52 percent of Nicaragua's sugar in its mills.

Despite this, Sandinista rhetoric and restrictions have discouraged private sector investment and impeded production and distribution of basic foodstuffs.[39] Government expenditures on economic development have been insignificant compared to those on military activities, estimated to be 40–60 percent of the budget. Increased military spending and tighter internal controls have been justified by pointing to military threats from the United States. Under these circumstances moderate forces are squashed and repression nourished.

The Miskito Indians are among the main victims of the Sandinistas.[40] Isolated on the Atlantic coast, they were largely ignored by previous regimes. When Indian leaders, such as Brooklyn Rivera and Steadman Muller, expressed their opposition to the Sandinistas by joining forces with the Somocistas in Honduras, the Sandinistas reacted ruthlessly. Many Miskito Indians were evicted from the land or forced to flee to Honduras to escape the Sandinistas' scorched-earth policy of razing villages along the Coco River; approximately three to five thousand were forced into labor camps in the Matagalpa-Jinotega area to pick coffee for the state. It is here that the Contras have been most brutal.[41] Thus the Indians are victimized by both the government and the guerrillas fighting to overthrow it.

The press, particularly *La Prensa*, opposition political parties, and labor unions were all restricted following the declaration of a state of emergency in March 1982 after the Contras bombed two bridges in northern Nicaragua. Influenced by the role of the press in the demise of Allende's government in Chile, the Sandinistas imposed censorship on *La Prensa*. A copy of the paper had to be submitted to the minister of the interior by mid-morning. After examining it and indicating which paragraphs, articles, headlines, and photographs must be omitted, the censors returned the paper, usually three hours later. Although this created delays in publication, the paper published regularly and, on the average, only a quarter of the paper was censored in 1984. However, in 1986 *La Prensa* was closed indefinitely and greater disregard for civil liberties occurred.[42] Complying with the Central American peace plan, the Sandinistas lifted all restrictions on *La Prensa* and moved to restore many civil liberties in late 1987 and early 1988. Opposition parties managed to win 29 seats in the Assembly after the 1984 election in which, despite harassment from the Sandinistas and a boycott by some opposition groups, they won 33 percent of the vote. For the most part, Nicaragua continues to be a relatively pluralistic society, especially when compared with Guatemala and El Salvador.[43]

Nicaragua's foreign policies, closely intertwined with domestic politics, continue to be of great concern to its neighbors, domestic opposition groups, and the United States. Given the strong U.S. presence in Nicaraguan political history, the Sandinistas aspired from the beginning to reduce their dependency on Washington and protect the revolution by obtaining outside technical, economic, political, and military assistance from different countries. The Carter administration, the World Bank, and the Inter-American Development Bank provided Nicaragua with substantial financial support. Between 1979 and 1982, Nicaragua received $1.5 billion in loans, credit extensions, and transfer payments, mostly from Western sources.[44] However, the overriding view in Managua was that the revolution could survive only through acquiring military weapons, especially in light of rumors of military training camps in Miami for opposition groups and possible U.S. military intervention. Their perception of an external threat propelled them closer to Moscow and Cuba while fueling anti-American rhetoric. Excessive preoccupation with antiimperialism in Nicaragua and fear of communism in Washington militated against the moderate Sandinistas who advocated less socialist rhetoric and a foreign policy which took into consideration geographical constraints, Nicaragua's fragile economy, and the revolutionary crisis in Central America.[45] The more militant Sandinistas made little effort to obtain military aid from sources other than the Soviet bloc. From Washington's perspective, this was evidence of Nicaragua's march toward totalitarianism; Nicaragua was regarded as another Cuba, an outpost of Soviet communism in the United States' backyard.

SOVIET-CUBAN INTERESTS AND INVOLVEMENT

Developments in Central America, rather than grand Soviet strategy, have been primarily responsible for increased Soviet-Cuban involvement in the region. By stressing Soviet-U.S. rivalry and seeing the world primarily in terms of East versus West, the United States has inadvertently made the Soviet Union an alternative for Central Americans in particular, and Latin Americans in general, who are determined to gain more economic and political independence from the United States. Economic and social modernization is inevitably antiimperialist and anti-Yankeeist because of pervasive U.S. influence in the area during the last 100 years. Although preferring to work with the United States, most Latin Americans desire to improve their negotiating positions *vis-a-vis* the U.S. by interacting economically and politically with Western Europe. To some extent, Latin American reaction against what they view as "dependent capitalism" promoted by the United States has lent socialism prestige and cast the Soviet Union and Cuba in a favorable light.[46]

Ironically, U.S. responses to change generally help bring about the opposite of desired effects, namely, radical Marxist regimes hostile to the United States. By refusing to acknowledge internal problems which spawn revolutions and then treating those revolutions as Soviet-inspired, the United States shifts attention away from the original problems and compounds the situations with its one-sided political view of the events.

Threats of military intervention work to the advantage of the Soviet Union because they remind Central Americans of previous U.S. interventions on behalf of those relatively rigid and repressive socioeconomic structures.[47] Over time, those interventions created widespread anti-American and powerful nationalist sentiments in various countries. However, this does not mean that Latin American revolutionaries are necessarily pro-Soviet. As Leiken observed, the most important guerrilla groups in El Salvador, the Popular Liberation Forces (FPL), and the Peoples Revolutionary Army (ERP), all have anti-Soviet origins.[48] Furthermore, the Soviets have been more pragmatic and ideologically restrained in Latin America than in areas considered to be of greater national interest. Nevertheless, Soviet involvement in the region is not insignificant or unimportant.

Nicaragua's geographic and cultural proximity to the United States is not ignored by the Soviets. While Moscow realizes that directly confronting the United States in its own backyard would be an extremely costly miscalculation, it is also aware of the political and strategic advantages that can be derived from undermining U.S. influence in an area historically considered to be in its sphere of influence. By forcing the United States to allocate additional time and money to a region so close to its borders, Moscow is free to operate elsewhere without fear of a negative U.S. response. For example, Reagan's preoccupation with militarily assisting the Contras focuses both domestic and international attention on his policy failures rather than on the brutal war in Afghanistan. The Soviets are relatively free to increase their involvement in Nicaragua because of strong American public opinion against military activities in Central America, the disarray within the Contra organization, and congressional investigations of possible violations of the law by the Reagan administration in its efforts to provide military assistance to the Contras.

It is increasingly clear that the Soviet Union realizes that Latin America's authoritarian political cultures, Hispano-Catholic traditions, conservative land-holding classes, its legacy of strong military rule, and opposition from workers and peasants to communism are barriers to direct involvement in the region.[49] However, Moscow's relationship with Cuba provides it with an opportunity to influence political developments in Nicaragua. Although it is generally assumed that Cuba acts as a Soviet proxy in Nicaragua,[50] evidence indicates that Cuba has played the leading role. Cuba's geographic and cultural proximity to Central America, its ability to apply its military capabilities, and its desire to improve its prestige throughout Latin America contribute to its leadership position *vis-a-vis* the Soviet Union. As Duncan observed, the formula for change in local political systems adopted by the Soviets and Cubans distinctly shifted from Soviet to Cuban interpretations by the early 1960s.[51] Prior to that time Moscow had emphasized peaceful state-to-state relations instead of a policy of support for revolutionary change advocated by Havana. Castro's friendship with Nicaragua's Sandinistas, shaped partly by his personal dislike of the Somozas who permitted Nicaragua to be used as a base for the Bay of Pigs operation, strongly influenced him to support their revolution. Similar to the situation in

Angola, Moscow provided military assistance to enable Castro to achieve what could be perceived as mutual interests. His efforts to demonstrate how Cuba could advance these interests in the United States' backyard were rewarded by increased Soviet military aid to Nicaragua during 1985 when he called for stronger backing for the Sandinistas in their fight against the Contras.[52]

Despite continued Soviet support for the Sandinistas, it is apparent that Moscow is reassessing its policy toward radical Third World regimes. No longer is it prepared to give significant amounts of military aid. In fact, a number of political leaders in the Soviet bureaucracy resent the growing burden of military and economic assistance to Third World clients.[53] Economic difficulties in both the Soviet Union and Cuba and these countries' inability to make meaningful contributions to economic development in the region militate against long-term Soviet influence, especially in light of Latin American nationalism and U.S. economic power.

Under these circumstances, Moscow has followed a strategy of turning the weight of the more powerful United States against itself, avoiding aggressive actions, maintaining a low-profile, and waiting to capitalize on Washington's mistakes.[54]

Within this context Moscow pursues several objectives in Central America. A primary objective is to gain recognition and acceptance of its power in world affairs. Normalizing relations with countries considered to be within the U.S. sphere of influence gives Moscow a feeling of equality with its rival and assists Latin American countries to achieve greater political independence from the United States. Moscow is also determined to reduce U.S. influence through support of anti-American regimes to gain facilities for its navy; to widen its presence in the region through educational and cultural ties; and to cooperate with governments interested in implementing socialism in their countries. While promoting communism and undermining U.S. power are important Soviet objectives, they must be placed in the context of maintaining reasonable, peaceful relations with Washington.

Access to raw materials and markets in the region is also important. The Soviets are apparently concerned with shrinking supplies of raw materials and escalating worldwide demand.[55] Perhaps out of economic necessity, they have been extremely pragmatic, trading even with countries strongly anticommunistic. Considering their economic ties with the United States, it should not be surprising that in Latin America economic realities take precedence over ideology. Nowhere in this pragmatism more evident than in Soviet relations with Argentina, even under rightwing military governments. The USSR established commercial offices in Buenos Aires despite Argentina's continued recognition of the czarist representative; in addition, the Soviets refrained from assisting Argentine communists, and limited their propaganda effort to promoting trade rather than spreading communism.[56] Cuba, on the other hand, had traditionally played a greater role in the region, and Moscow appears to favor deferring to Cuba in Nicaragua.

Cuba's initial involvement in Nicaragua and its support for the Sandinistas must be regarded as an issue separate from current Soviet activities and evaluated within the context of Latin American politics. Even before Castro came to power in 1959, Luis Somoza demonstrated his opposition to him by selling Batista weapons to fight Castro's guerrillas. Antagonism characterized relations between Castro and Somoza, each attempting to undermine the other's political power by providing havens and support for exiles from the respective countries. Cuba supported attacks against the Somoza regime, and Somoza volunteered Nicaragua as a forward base of operations during the Bay of Pigs invasion. The FSLN itself was founded in Cuba by Nicaraguan exiles and throughout the 1960s FSLN guerrillas received weapons and training in Cuba.[57] However, it was Somoza himself who created opportunities for Cuba, Mexico, Venezuela, and other Latin American countries to intervene in Nicaragua on behalf of the Sandinistas. When Somoza's downfall was imminent, Castro escalated assistance to the Sandinistas and was instrumental in uniting the various factions in 1979 before the "final offensive." But Castro was cautious and restrained in his support for the Sandinistas.

Having spent much of the 1960s and early 1970s working on restoring relations with Latin American countries, Castro did not want to rekindle regional fears of Cuban intervention or provide a justification for direct U.S. military action against the Sandinistas. It is important to note that Cuban officials did not really believe that revolutionary change could occur in Nicaragua until the September 1978 uprising which was brutally suppressed by the National Guard.[58] That development marked the turning point in Cuban involvement in Nicaragua.

Immediately after the Sandinistas took control, Cuba promised to assist in rebuilding Nicaragua's shattered economy and sent food, construction workers, teachers, nurses, and medical doctors to provide services to poor people in the countryside. Cuban technical and financial assistance escalated. By 1982 there were more than 500 medical personnel and 2,000 teachers from Cuba in Nicaragua. Not only did Castro urge the participation in humanitarian efforts in Nicaragua, he also advised the Sandinistas not to ignore U.S. power and national interests, to preserve economic ties with Western Europe, the United States, and Japan, and not to eliminate private enterprise because, unlike Cuba, they could not rely on substantial Soviet economic aid.[59] In other words, Cuba supported the moderate Sandinistas who advocated modifications rather than a radical transformation of Nicaraguan society.

Former Secretary of State Alexander Haig's statements about Nicaragua's totalitarianism and suggestion of a possible naval blockade as well as other developments in Washington, and Contra activities in Honduras played in the hands of more radical Sandinistas and gave Nicaragua a justification for its increased reliance on military force and, consequently, greater dependence on the Soviet Union and Cuba.[60]

From the beginning, Cuban military and security advisers buttressed the Sandinista regime while aiding in the growing militarization of Nicaragua. By March 1980, Nicaragua's ties with the Soviet Union were consolidated with the conclusion of a number of agreements between Managua and Moscow on trade, technical cooperation, civil aviation, consular ties, and party-to-party cooperation.[61] Between 1981 and 1982 economic, technical communications, and fishery agreements were signed and a number of Sandinista leaders, including Daniel Ortega, Jaime Wheelock, and Bayardo Arce, visited Moscow to attend various state functions.[62]

Relations with other communist states were quickly established and a number of Nicaraguan students left to study in the Soviet Union and Cuba, deepening Soviet influence in Nicaragua. Czechoslovakia provided $30 million dollars in credit, Bulgaria $20 million, East Germany $10 million, and Hungary $20 million. Approximately $28 million worth of Soviet, East German, and Cuban arms were received by Nicaragua between 1981 and 1982.[63] This military buildup was accompanied by an increase of about 1,500 in the number of Cuban military and security advisers, bringing the total number of Cuban military personnel to approximately 3,000. Other communist governments, the PLO (Palestinian Liberation Organization), and Libya provided military technicians, arms, and ammunition. Failure to diversify its sources of arms added credence to the view that Nicaragua was an armed Marxist-Leninist society, an outpost of Soviet-Cuban communism in Central America.

By 1988, nine years after the revolution, Nicaragua was not another Cuba nor totally subservient to Moscow, despite Moscow's pervasive presence. Nevertheless, there were worrisome signs. The Sandinistas had an active duty force of more than 62,000, up from 7,100 in 1977. Their total strength, including all regular, reserve, militia units, and security forces was estimated in excess of 119,000.[64] Nicaragua had amassed approximately 340 tanks and armored vehicles, 70 long-ranged howitzers and rocket launchers, amphibious ferries, and 30 helicopters, including 6 Mi-24/HIND D helicopters. According to the State Department and the Department of Defense, the Mi-24 HIND D is less vulnerable to small arms fire, has a heavy machine gun, can fire antitank missiles and can drop bombs.[65]

Washington maintained that this was evidence of Nicaragua's aggressiveness toward its Central American neighbors. More accurate, however, is the fact that the entire Central American region has become militarized as both Nicaragua and the United States eschew diplomacy and focus primarily on military options. With strong U.S. support, Honduras incrased its active duty armed forces from 14,200 in 1977 to 17,200 in 1984; Guatemala's went from 14,300 in 1977 to 40,000 in 1984; and El Salvador, which experienced great infusions of U.S. military aid, saw its armed forces swell from 7,100 in 1977 to 41,150 in 1984.[66] Not only do Honduras, El Salvador, and Guatemala have five times the population and twice as many regular armed forces as Nicaragua; they also have superior fire power and air forces capable of dominating Nicaragua's. Although Nicaragua is superior in tanks, lack of adequate fuel supplies, domestic economic problems, and the mountainous terrain and abundant rivers deprive it of any real strategic advantage over its neighbors. Furthermore, the U.S. has built tank traps along the northwestern Honduran border with Nicaragua,[67] especially in the Chohiteca Gap, the most obvious avenue of approach for Nicaraguan tanks.

Apart from the strong U.S. military presence in Honduras, superb surveillance equipment, and reconnaisance flights over Nicaraguan airspace, Moscow has informed Washington and the Sandinistas that it will provide "political," not military support, in the event of full-scale U.S. invasion. Cuba, shortly after the Grenada invasion, stated that it will not directly confront overwhelmingly superior U.S. power in the Caribbean or Central America. The Soviets appear to calculate that decisive U.S. action will in fact result in a new gain for their side by escalating anti-Americanism in the region and dividing the Western alliance.[68] From the Soviet point of view, continuation of the ill-defined U.S. policy toward Nicaragua will eventually prove beneficial to communism, the very thing U.S. policy wants to avoid.

THE UNITED STATES AND THE SANDINISTAS: IN SEARCH OF A POLICY

Selective perception, ethnocentrism, ideological blinders, equating strength with the application of military force, and a lack of clear strategies for achieving policy objectives are the key impediments to U.S. efforts to limit Soviet-Cuban involvement in Nicaragua. Profound miscalculations and virulent rhetoric by the United States and Nicaragua will inevitably lead to mutual victimization unless significant steps are taken to realistically assess the interests of both sides and invent mutually beneficial options. By 1985 it was apparent that Reagan's selective perception of the Sandinistas prevented him from seeing improvements in Nicaragua where human rights are generally respected, especially when compared to El Salvador, which he praised for a reduction in death squad activities. It also influenced him to ignore the 1984 elections, in which the Sandinistas won 67 percent of the vote, and to insist on a return to pure democracy which never really existed in Nicaragua.[69]

At the heart of the problem is ethnocentrism. Regarding Latin Americans as culturally, politically, racially, and perhaps even morally inferior, American policymakers have made little effort to understand their reality. Instead, the U.S. generally believes it has the answers to its neighbors' problems.[70] On the other hand, Latin Americans also lack adequate understanding of the United States. This situation is exacerbated by ideological blinders on both sides.

Reagan's political success in the 1980 elections was directly linked to his strong anticommunist rhetoric. Not surprisingly, Nicaraguan leaders were regarded as Marxist totalitarians implacably hostile to the United States, and exporters of terrorism and revolution to other Central American states. They could not be believed; their regime was the Central American outpost of the evil empire and, as such, its very existence was an affront to the United States.[71] Reagan, the crusader, showed no inclination to compromise with the evil Sandinistas, and was determined to overthrow them to rescue Nicaragua from falling into the communist camp.

Virtually declaring war against the Nicaraguan government, Reagan accelerated mililtary pressure on the Sandinistas by funding the Contras, many of them former Somoza guards. The Contras, designated as freedom fighters and equated with Jefferson and Lafayette by Reagan, would, in his view, eventually overthrow the Sandinistas in order to restore democracy. What would happen after the Contras seized power was never really addressed.[72] The fact that the Contras, who cannot militarily defeat the Sandinistas, have violated Nicaraguans' human rights and caused Nicaraguans relentless hardship and suffering was not a major concern.

Encouraging atrocities against ordinary Nicaraguans and prolonging their miseries was not a sign of strength, but an indication of confusion about strategy for achieving stated objectives or reluctance to pay the high price for achieving them. As Dickey put it:

This obviously dangerous lack of definition was exacerbated by the assumption shared on all sides of the debate inside the Administration that what had to be done to get the Sandinistas to negotiate seriously was at any rate exactly what had to be done if one were indeed setting the stage for an invasion. In such circumstances it was impossible to be sure which course one was to follow until the negotiations succeeded or the war had begun.[73]

In the meantime, Nicaraguans, especially the moderates, found it increasingly difficult to openly oppose the Sandinistas or to exert a moderating influence on Nicaraguan politics. And the Sandinistas grew increasingly dependent on Moscow.

The Carter administration had initially pursued a policy of reconciliation with the Sandinista government after failing to persuade Somoza to respect human rights and to allow the moderate opposition led by Chamorro to participate in a meaningful way in Nicaraguan politics in order to deprive the more radical Sandinistas of victory.[74] It was Somoza himself who wrecked Carter's efforts to mediate an end to the violence and bloodshed. Working through the Organization of American States, Carter had managed to enlist widespread Latin American support for a plan calling for internationally supervised elections in Nicaragua, to establish an interim government of reconciliation. This government would provide a transition from politics dominated by Somoza and the National Guard to free elections and competitive party politics. The plan also called for restructuring the National Guard and eliminating its undesirable elements and widespread corruption. Somoza, however, had no intention of voluntarily resigning and played for time to strengthen the foundation of his power, the National Guard.[75]

The Iranian hostage crisis, the Soviet invasion of Afghanistan, and 1980 election politics had a tremendous impact on U.S. policy toward Nicaragua. Despite the fact that Carter viewed economic aid to Nicaragua as the best strategy for countering Soviet-Cuban involvement and supporting democratic forces within Nicaragua, conservative members of Congress and presidential candidate Reagan began to pressure him to take a hardline toward the Sandinistas by accusing him of being soft on communism. Developments in El Salvador and Nicaragua's support for guerrillas there led Carter to delay the projected disbursement of the remaining $15 million of the $75 million U.S. aid program earlier approved by Congress, and to terminate negotiations for the renewal of PL 480 loans for the sale of wheat and cooking oil to Nicaragua.[76] In essence, Carter departed from previous policies which were consistent with those of key Latin American actors, and also pragmatic.

Central America was regarded by Reagan as the testing ground for U.S. power and its resolve to stop Soviet expansionism. The new admin-

istration was strongly supported by extremely conservative anticommunists, and policymakers close to Reagan had to demonstrate unwavering
loyalty to the crusade against the evil empire. When Thomas Enders, the
assistant secretary of state and chief policymaker for Latin America,
disagreed with his colleagues on strategy to achieve what was possible, he
was ousted. His support for the isolation and containment of the
Nicaraguan revolution could not be tolerated by more radical conserva-
tives within the administration who did not want the regime to exist. In
this eyeball-to-eyeball confrontation with Moscow on America's door-
step toughness, not pragmatism, was of crucial importance. As Dickey
notes, even the discussion of options became a test of toughness in which
only the most conservative voices in the administration were found to
measure up.[77]

Another Cuba could not be allowed in Central America nor could
democratic El Salvador be threatened by Nicaragua's assistance to rebels
in that country. Cutting off all economic aid to Nicaragua was the first
step of going "to the source" of El Salvador's problems with guerrillas.
Former Secretary of State Alexander Haig's hostility toward the Sandinistas was obvious from his discussions of possible military action
against Nicaragua to stop its export of revolution to the region.[78] Despite
charges and denials about Nicaragua funneling arms to insurgents in El
Salvador, it should be noted that not a single major cache of weapons
had been interdicted in the eight years (1979–1987) when this was a major
problem.[79] Indeed, evidence indicates that since 1982, virtually no
weapons or ammunition reached El Salvador from Nicaragua.[80] Nevertheless, the administration continued to insist that Nicaragua end its support for guerrilla groups in neighboring countries. Having committed
itself so strongly to ideology, the Reagan administration could not easily
extricate itself from its position that the Sandinistas were totalitarian
Marxist-Leninists. Their close relationship with Cuba and the massive
military aid from Moscow only served to confirm Reagan's views and
deepen the conflict. By 1986, Washington had grown more adamant
about removing the "communist totalitarian" government of Nicaragua
and restoring the original goals of the revolution that Nicaraguans
fought for, even though 75 percent of the American public opposed an
invasion to overthrow the Sandinistas.[81]

Unable or unwilling to directly intervene militarily in Nicaragua
because of public opinion and confusion about what should be done to
achieve stated objectives, the Reagan administration decided to support
armed guerrillas in Nicaragua while simultaneously condemning
Nicaragua for assisting guerrillas attempting to overthrow the government of El Salvador. Although calling on the Sandinistas to hold elections, Reagan actually argued against participation by the leading op-

position candidate, Arturo Cruz, in the 1984 elections because his involvement would legitimize the elections and make it more difficult for the U.S. to continue its opposition to the Sandinistas.[82] Instead, military action continued to be the preferred solution, even if U.S. law had to be violated in order to support the Contras.

Contrary to claims by the Reagan administration that the Sandinistas betrayed the revolution, the fact is that given Reagan's early hostility toward the Sandinistas, and their failure to come to grips with U.S. power in the hemisphere, the revolution wasn't allowed to succeed. Shortly after Reagan's election in 1980, Nicaraguan exiles, many of them former National Guardsmen, were promised military aid and advised by presidential adviser Vernon Walters to unite into a single group.[83] In September 1981 they merged to form the Nicaraguan Democratic Force. However, the Contras could never lead to democracy in Nicaragua. The former guardsmen who had been dedicated to dictatorship during Somoza's rule became collaborators with military death squads in El Salvador and Guatemala, and engaged in criminal activities, such as automobile theft, cattle rustling, and smuggling after the revolution. Indeed, it was their desperateness that facilitated their recruitment by the CIA. It seems ironic that the military regime of Argentina, which had one of the worst human rights records in Latin America, trained the Contras to "restore democracy" to Nicaragua. It wasn't until 1982 that Robelo, Eden Pastora, Brooklyn Rivera, and Fernando Chamorro Rappaccioli formed the Revolutionary Democratic Alliance (ARDE) in Costa Rica to oppose the Sandinistas. Actually military activity by ARDE against the Sandinistas did not occur until April of 1983 following failed negotiations with the Nicaraguan government. Having fought the guardsmen (who killed his father) for more than a decade, Pastora refused to join forces with the larger and better equipped Nicaraguan Democratic Front.[89]

By June 1983, approximately 25–30 CIA agents were advising rebels, and in 1984 a CIA manual for "Psychological Operations in Guerrilla Warfare" surfaced. It instructed the Contras how to shoot innocent Nicaraguan citizens, "neutralize" judges, police, and state security officials, and use general violence to undermine the Nicaraguan government.[85] The Reagan administration reacted calmly to the manual, and continued pressing for "humanitarian" aid for the Contras who were clearly violating human rights. Under the circumstances, it was extremely difficult for moderate Nicaraguans to support Reagan's policy without appearing to support Contra violence. The Sandinistas effectively used these external threats to gain Western European sympathy, succeeded in humiliating the United States before the World Court following the CIA mining of Nicaraguan harbors, and continued to prepare for war.[86]

Armed conflict actually strengthened the more radical Sandinistas, undermined moderate democratic opposition leaders, and escalated the costs for all participants. Honduras, for example, is extremely concerned about almost 15,000 armed and well trained Contras, a force as large as the Honduran army, and their involvement in Honduran affairs, especially when they stop fighting the Sandinistas.[87] The coffee crop, Nicaragua's major foreign exchange earner, dropped from 110 million pounds in 1984, to 80 million pounds in 1985 due to Contra attacks on coffee pickers and their villages.[88] The policy of militarizing the conflict in Nicaragua continued to have negative consequences for the entire Central American region.

Focusing on a negative, worst-case scenario, Reagan perceived El Salvador as the frontline against Soviet-Cuban expansionism and proceeded to prepare for an invasion from Nicaragua, despite the latter's preoccupation with economic problems, social transformation, and protecting its independence from external threats. American policymakers continued to view domestic problems of the region as secondary to the Soviet threat. In 1982 U.S. military aid to Honduras and El Salvador was greatly increased, tripling to over $33 million in the former and rising from $6 million in 1980 to $82 million in 1982 in the latter. Economic aid to El Salvador tripled from $58.5 million in 1980 to $89 million in 1982.[89] Honduras received another $13 million to expand its airstrips to accommodate C-5 and C-130 troop carriers in the event of a war with Nicaragua. In 1983 about 4,500 American troops took part in military exercises in Honduras and over 300 American engineers, radar technicians, and military advisers were stationed in different parts of Honduras. In 1987 approximately 50,000 American troops participated in an exercise, code-named Solid Shield, intended to simulate a U.S. response to a request from Honduras to help fight Nicaraguan forces.[90]

Partly due to these developments, Honduras became increasingly polarized, repressive, and unstable. Furthermore, El Salvador's growing military might continued to be of greater concern to Honduras than an invasion by Nicaragua. Although Honduras cooperated with El Salvador against Salvadoran guerrillas, hostility between the countries over disputed territories continued. In fact, in the process of assisting El Salvador, Honduras occupied the disputed territory which had been demilitarized after the 1969 soccer war. Since El Salvador has made no overtures to resolve the problem, and Hondurans still feel humiliated by their defeat, Honduras not only resents the United States for not pressuring El Salvador to reach a settlement, but also envisions armed conflict with El Salvador to settle the territorial dispute. Consequently, El Salvador's army of 42,000 men is of grave concern to Honduras, which has only 17,000 armed forces.[91] Not surprisingly, Honduras requested more military and economic aid from Washington. The situation was clearly out of control and costly. Responding to growing U.S. military pressure, Ortega announced a moratorium on the acquisition of new arms systems, promised to send 100 Cuban military advisers home, and invited a U.S. congressional delegation to visit Nicaraguan military installations in exchange for U.S. willingness to resume direct negotiations.[92] However, when Congress later rejected military aid to the Contras, and Ortega unwisely visited Moscow the following day, Reagan decided to impose an economic embargo against Nicaragua.

Prior to the 1985 embargo Reagan had ended aid to Nicaragua (1981), refused to disburse a $8.9 million food credit for purchasing wheat, and reduced by 90 percent the amount of Nicaraguan sugar it bought at subsidized prices. By 1984 Nicaraguan dependence on U.S. markets was decreasing, down from $250 million in exports or 40 percent of the total exports in 1978 to $57 million or 17 percent of exports in 1984. The new sanctions denied the Nicaraguan national airline, Aerorica, landing rights in the U.S. and closed the market for spare parts for much of Nicaragua's machinery. Nicaraguan agricultural products, beef, and shellfish were barred from entering the United States, but markets were found in Europe, Canada, Japan, and Latin America. Countries criticizing the embargo included Mexico, Colombia, Venezuela, Ecuador, Bolivia, Argentina, Uruguay, Cuba, Britain, and the Eastern bloc countries. Reagan's actions had clearly isolated the United States, produced tensions in the Western alliance, and generated additional support for the Sandinistas. A confrontational policy against Nicaragua based solely on Soviet-American rivalry ignores regional political realities and the interests of principal actors such as Mexico and Venezuela.

Self-interest, not anticommunism, is the motivating force behind the Mexican and Venezuelan policies toward Nicaragua and their reluctance to have either Cuba or the United States play a dominant role in a region they consider to be within their sphere of influence. From their perspective, U.S. military intervention is no more preferred than Soviet-Cuban involvement in Central America because either would pose a threat to their independence and regional stability. American troops would only serve to remind Mexicans of their own historical experiences with U.S. intervention. Mexico's revolutionary heritage underlies its position that social, economic, and political transformations in the region are long overdue and that forces working to bring them about are now irreversible.[93] Like the United States, it does not favor the Cuban solution, although it does not expect Nicaragua to emerge as democratic as the United States demands. As the July 1985 elections in Mexico demonstrated, Mexico itself is not exactly a model of Western democracy.

Nevertheless its system works and provides the stability essential to U.S. security interests.

Unlike the United States' revolution, the Mexican Revolution could not be isolated from the misery and poverty prevalent in the country in 1910. Consequently, Mexico does not perceive revolutions in the same way as the United States. It actually assisted Castro and the Sandinistas in their struggles against dictators supported by Washington. Rather than taking a strict ideological position, Mexican leaders were flexible enough to coopt and incorporate leftist politicians and their lower class constituents into the political system to ensure compliance with, and acceptance of, ground rules of the political process. Similarly, compromising with Castro, Mexico agreed not to ostracize Cuba in exchange for Cuba's nonintervention in Mexican affairs.[94]

Mexico's desire to play a greater role in world politics by pursuing a more assertive foreign policy further complicated Reagan's approach to Nicaragua. Major steps toward Mexico's new international role commenced during the presidency of Luis Echeverria (1970–76) whose aspirations for Third World leadership were demonstrated by his fervent advocacy for the Charter of Economic Rights and Duties of States that would inaugurate a New International Economic Order.[95] Getting developed countries to redistribute their wealth required Third World support. Mexico not only had to be independent of the United States but also nonaligned. To project its power beyond the region, Mexico decided to build Latin American solidarity by stressing ideological pluralism and Cuba's reacceptance among Latin American States.[96] This policy was strengthened under President Jose Lopez Portillo (1976–82) who was able to exert greater influence in regional and international affairs because of the discovery of vast amounts of petroleum. Proven reserves rose from 6.3 billion barrels in 1976 to 70 billion barrels in 1981. With potential reserves estimated at 300 billion barrels, Mexico was unlikely to continue playing a subordinate role to the United States in Central America. However, by moderating regional revolutions and providing an alternative to Cuba and the Soviet Union, Mexico's policies were ultimately beneficial to Washington.

As early as March 1982, Portillo offered a peace initiative, "the three knots of tension," designed to end hostilities in El Salvador and reduce tensions between the U.S. and Nicaragua. Cuba accepted the Mexican offer. Although the United States representative Vernon Walters met with Castro in Havana in early 1982, the U.S. showed no subsequent interest in later diplomatic efforts.[97]

The Contadora group, composed of Mexico, Venezuela, Colombia, and Panama, was formed in January 1983 in Panama to find a peaceful solution to the crisis in Central America. Under Mexico's leadership the

Contadora countries decided to grapple with the root causes of hostility between Nicaragua and neighboring El Salvador and Honduras.[98] A major objective was to contain the Nicaraguan revolution by reducing military conflict and reaching a negotiated settlement. Washington, on the other hand, embraced the Contadora process because it perceived it as pressuring the Sandinistas to accept U.S. policy objectives. Although the Contadora countries shared U.S. concern about Soviet-Cuban penetration in Central America, they differed significantly on how to reduce and eventually eliminate the communist threat. The crucial misunderstanding between the United States and Contadora group was the fact that the latter feared U.S. intervention in the region and worried about Reagan's designation of Central America as a battleground in the global confrontation between the Soviet Union and the United States. Their concern was that growing militarization of the region and U.S. policies toward Nicaragua would threaten their own countries to a greater extent than the Sandinistas' radical views.[99] Having depicted the Sandinistas as Marxist-Leninists who had betrayed the Nicaraguan revolution, and having committed U.S. prestige and military assistance to overthrow them, Reagan studiously avoided the Contadora process as a vehicle for peacefully resolving the conflict. Furthermore, accepting Contadora would mean that Honduras and Costa Rica could no longer serve as bases for the Contras and would radically curtail U.S. military activities in the region and its support for Honduran and Salvadoran armed forces.

Although calling for negotiations with the Sandinistas, it was quite obvious that the United States was determined not to accept any sort of agreement with Nicaragua, believing instead that stability in Central America could not be achieved while the Sandinistas remained in power. By 1987, there was clear evidence that the Reagan administration had used a variety of tactics, including military and economic aid, to pressure Central American countries to support the Contras, despite the fact that Congress had declared such a linkage illegal.[100] The draft of a treaty proposed by the Contradora group protected U.S. interests by including provisions for the mutual reductions in arms, troops, foreign advisers and the prohibition against foreign military bases. It also called for the establishment of fair judicial systems, respect for human rights, free elections, and the cessation of aid to guerrillas trying to overthrow established governments.[101] Washington declined to agree to the treaty, claiming that it lacked verification mechanisms to guarantee Nicaraguan compliance. It was now obvious that only direct U.S. military intervention to remove the Sandinistas would satisfy Reagan.[102] Diplomacy was never really given a chance to succeed.

The Central American peace plan, proposed by President Oscar Arias Sanchez of Costa Rica in August 1987 and agreed to by the Central

American governments, increased pressure on Washington to emphasize diplomacy and stop funding the Contras. The peace plan requires all countries in the region to broaden political and civil liberties for their citizens; negotiate cease-fires with insurgents; and to prevent cross-border hostilities by denying rebel groups access to their territory. The flexibility demonstrated by the Sandinistas and their compliance with the peace plan presented the U.S. a great opportunity to achieve a negotiated settlement to the conflict.

TOWARD A PRAGMATIC U.S. POLICY

Effectively combating Soviet-Cuban involvement in Nicaragua requires a significant change in the current direction of U.S. policy toward the region. Emotional responses to Soviet-Cuban intrusion in what has long been regarded as U.S. sphere of influence cannot be regarded as policy. Policy includes a set of realistic objectives and appropriate strategies for achieving those objectives.

A pragmatic approach to Soviet-Cuban activities in Nicaragua must begin with a careful assessment of the nature of the threat to our interests and the impact of our response on Nicaragua in particular and Central America in general. What do we want the Nicaraguans to do, how can we get them to do it, and at what costs? What is the most economical and efficient way of achieving our objectives? This requires not only knowing our goals and the price of achieving them, but also knowing what we can reasonably expect from the Nicaraguans. To demand what they cannot give is self-defeating. Since Nicaragua has never really known democracy and currently does not have conditions conducive to its emergence, it is unrealistic to demand a "return" to democracy.

Supporting the Contras, a group united in a marriage of convenience that is even shakier than that arranged between the Sandinistas and Somoza's opponents, cannot bring democracy to Nicaragua. Because of their association with Somoza and widespread violence against innocent civilians, it will be virtually impossible for them to generate a significant following within Nicaragua. We must therefore decide what kind of national involvement, if any, is practical in trying to achieve our objectives in Nicaragua.

The stated objectives of the United States' policy in Central America include the following: 1. An end to Nicaraguan support for guerrilla groups in neighboring countries; 2. severance of Nicaraguan military ties to Cuba and the Soviet bloc; 3. reduction of Nicaragua's military strength to levels that would restore military equilibrium to the region; and 4. fulfillment of the original Sandinista promises to support democratic pluralism and respect human and civil rights.[103] Testimony before the Senate by key participants in the Iran-Contra affair clearly indicates that these objectives were not seriously considered. The overriding interest of the Reagan administration was to overthrow the Sandinista government through funding, training, and arming the Contras, an objective regarded by professionals in the national security bureaucracy as reckless, dangerous, and ineffective.[104] The various tactics used to accomplish this were clearly detrimental to the achievement of the administration's stated objectives.

Major U.S. security interests in Central America are: 1. the prevention of a Soviet military presence; 2. curtailment of Cuban military activities; 3. a peaceful Central America characterized by a reduction in weapons and normal political and economic relations among the various countries; 4. the containment of the Nicaraguan revolution; 5. the protection of the relatively minor U.S. economic interests in the region; 6. the promotion of economic development to diminish hunger, illiteracy, and disease, problems which contribute to political instability and refugees from the area.[105] Several tactics can be utilized to realize these objectives.

Have Realistic Expectations. In order to achieve our objectives in Nicaragua greater effort must be made to improve our knowledge of that country in particular and the region in general. The Iran-Contra hearings indicate a lack of understanding of the area and arrogance nurtured by ignorance. In light of the history of U.S.-Nicaraguan relations, we cannot expect the Sandinistas to embrace Washington or willingly participate in their own demise. An absence of conflict in the region is a realistic expectation.

Return Foreign Policy-Making to the State Department. One of the major causes of the failure of U.S. policy toward Nicaragua is the dominance of foreign policy by right-wing evangelicals and the "band of true believers" who view politics as a struggle between good and evil. Unlike the professionals in the State Department, the private individuals who fashioned U.S. policy toward the Sandinistas could not allow different regimes to co-exist,[106] even if that meant violating the law. The State Department must reassert its control over foreign policy.

Contain the Revolution. Instead of trying to overthrow the Sandinistas, greater emphasis must be placed on containing the revolution. This means that Nicaragua would be allowed to manage its internal affairs but would not be permitted to engage in activities that threaten U.S. security interests or the neighboring countries, including the support for guerrillas in El Salvador. In other words, the U.S. should use the Central American peace plan as a framework for future negotiations.

Remove the Conflict from East-West Rivalry. Regimes which are anti-American are not necessarily pro-Soviet, and groups which oppose radical regimes are not necessarily anticommunist. Although the Soviet-Cuban threat cannot be ignored, it seems self-defeating to perceive the Nicaraguan conflict in East-West terms. As Thornton observed, when we define situations in Central America as a contest between East and West we are defining the Soviets and Cubans directly into the problem along with ourselves.[107] Once perceived as such, it is extremely difficult to think objectively and move toward a pragmatic approach to the problem.

Support the Revolution. The most effective way to diminish Soviet-Cuban involvement in Nicaragua is to support the revolution which we could not prevent because of indigenous social, political, and economic realities. Rather than being pragmatic, our efforts to undermine the Nicaraguan revolution contributed to self-victimization by giving the Sandinistas justification for seeking military assistance from the Soviet Union in order to safeguard the revolution from what they perceive as U.S. aggression. Because Latin Americans are very reluctant to compromise their independence by appealing to extrahemispheric powers for military aid, tolerating the Sandinistas or accepting a *modus vivendi* with them would in fact eliminate Nicaragua's only rational reason for seeking a security relationship with the Soviet bloc and make their decision to avoid such entanglements easier for them to implement.[108]

Supporting the revolution also helps to change Nicaraguan perceptions of the United States as a staunch supporter of oppressive anti-communist military dictatorships and an implacable foe of meaningful social, political, and economic reforms that would alter the status quo. Rather than seeing the revolution as a threat to U.S. interests, it should be regarded as an opportunity to influence the Sandinistas by acting in a manner inconsistent with our past behavior and, consequently, their expectations. Furthermore, accepting social change would have reduced violence on both sides and the seeds of hatred born of bloodshed; and the promise of democracy would have been brighter. American policymakers must carefully consider supporting revolutions that do not threaten our national interests in order to moderate them, thereby reducing opportunities for Soviet-Cuban involvement. Working with the Sandinistas makes it harder for them to work against us.

Relinquish Control Gracefully to Maintain Influence. Nationalism, often detrimental, is pervasive in Third World countries which have been strongly influenced or controlled by an outside power. As the first new nation, U.S. nationalism remains strong. Nicaraguan nationalism must be understood within the context of a new nation struggling for its independence from U.S. control. Just as Indian nationalism was anti-British, Nicaraguan nationalism will be anti-American. Washington must demonstrate vision and be willing to construct a relationship with Nicaragua that reflects political maturity on both sides. It must come to grips with the reality that less direct U.S. involvement may be actually one of the most pragmatic approaches to safeguarding U.S. interests. Britain's experience with its colonies is instructive; by giving them their independence in an honorable way, Britain has maintained its influence with its former colonies through the Commonwealth. Rigid control inevitably leads to resistance. To protect its long-term interest in stability in Central America, the United States must accept change and relinquish control gracefully.

Recognize the Limits of Soviet Power. Reacting to Soviet-Cuban involvement in Nicaragua on the basis of the false assumption that the Soviets know exactly what they are doing or have complete control over events is self-defeating. Evidently, Moscow will continue to undermine U.S. security interests in Latin America and exploit anti-American feelings. However, the Soviets have repeatedly made it clear to Nicaragua that they will not support it against a direct U.S. military threat or subsidize its economy as they do Cuba's. It was the Sandinista regime, rather than the Soviet Union, that advocated closer ties between the two countries. Moscow and Cuba are constrained by the same nationalism with which the United States is confronted. Consequently, the Soviets in particular have been relatively restrained. Their experience in Chile taught them that massive resources, needed at home, are essential to prop up a friendly government in the face of U.S. mililtary and economic power. Recognizing the limitations on Soviet power in Nicaragua will allow the United States to focus on the real problems rather than on anticommunism. Paradoxically, focusing on Soviet expansionism instead of poverty ultimately diminishes U.S. influence while contributing to the improvement of the Soviet image among advocates of social change in the region.

Military Solutions Are Not Effective. Utilizing military force as a substitute for diplomacy is extremely costly to all parties involved. Force is almost by definition the worst way to resolve conflicting interests because an imposed settlement is inherently unstable in the long run.[109] After more than eight years of militarizing the conflict in Nicaragua there are only negative results for all parties. Ordinary Nicaraguans continue to suffer most from violence by both the Contras and the Sandinistas. The Nicaraguan government, by diverting approximately 40–60 percent of its budget to military expenditures and away from concentrating on poverty, undermines its own social objectives, alienates its supporters, and compromises its independence by relying on the Soviet Union and its allies for weapons. U.S. assistance to the Contras divides American society, creates conflicts in the Western alliance, militarizes Central America, and reduces the pressure on the Soviets in Afghanistan while focusing negative world attention on the United States. Anti-Sandinista military operations polarize the Honduran society, create obligations which are becoming increasingly expensive for the U.S., and destroy any chance of moderating the revolution and diminishing the suffering in Nicaragua. The United States should therefore advocate reductions in military forces and a gradual demilitarization of Central America.

Stop Funding the Contras. Negotiations with Sandinistas and efforts being made by Latin American states to end the conflict in Central America cannot be successful as long as Washington views the Contras as part of the solution. The argument that military assistance to the Contras will force the Sandinistas to negotiate is extremely weak and hypocritical. The Reagan administration apparently had no intention of finding a negotiated settlement. Furthermore, the existence of the Contras is part of the problem. It is now obvious that we lack a unifying political vision of society, and are not interested in mobilizing the poor or bringing about democracy. The Contras, widely regarded in Central America as a creation of the CIA, do not have either regional or domestic support and have no chance of military victory.

Seek Amnesty for All Combatants. Halting aid to the Contras could be accompanied by direct negotiations with the Sandinistas to implement constitutional provisions, and to allow all unarmed opposition groups to return to Nicaragua. While removing the United States from direct involvement in the conflict, this strategy would allow Washington to begin a constructive dialogue with and gain access to the Nicaraguan government to protect our interests.

Assume a Nonthreatening Role. Given the great disparity in size, resources, and power between Nicaragua and the United States, Nicaraguans tend to perceive any antagonistic action or statement by Washington as a serious threat. Reducing military aid to Honduras, stopping overflights of Nicaraguan territory by American spy planes, and ending U.S. military exercises in the region would contribute to easing tensions. Nicaragua would be expected to significantly reduce its military expenditures as well as the number of Cuban military personnel in the country.

Encourage the Creation of a Nonpartisan Group to Monitor the Transition. A lesser degree of U.S. involvement in the region is probably the easiest way to allay the fears and insecurity of the Sandinistas. Since they have persistently sought closer ties with Spain, Canada, Western Europe, and other Latin American states, perhaps our allies would be in a better position to work with them. These countries are likely to be perceived as being less threatening and more objective by both Nicaragua and the United States.

Respect International Law. By observing the rules of international behavior the United States strengthens its position not only in Central America but around the world. Serious setbacks suffered by Washington in the World Court have implications beyond the Nicaraguan conflict. More important national interests are threatened when we fail to uphold standards of international conduct essential for world order.

Encourage Economic Integration. The Kissinger Commission Report strongly endorsed economic development in Central America and the reinvigoration of the Central American Common Market.[110] This recommendation was based on evidence that the trend toward more pluralistic political systems in the region was reversed with the pernicious effects of worldwide recession in the early 1970s. Since poverty breeds conditions conducive to Soviet-Cuban involvement, pursuing a strategy of economic development would at least reduce their opportunities and simultaneously allow moderate Nicaraguans to be more significant participants in the transformation of Nicaraguan society. However, economic development in the region is virtually impossible as long as the Nicaraguan conflict continues. Various aid programs are less likely to be successful while military solutions are emphasized.[111]

Regional economic integration would be beneficial to the entire region and help to moderate the Sandinista regime by reducing antagonism toward the United States and creating webs of interdependence among Central American states. Despite hostilities among them, Nicaragua, Costa Rica, El Salvador, Guatemala, and Honduras (members of the Central American Common Market) realize that their economies are closely linked and structured to benefit each other. For example, Costa Rica sells about $1.3 million worth of electricity to Nicaragua each month. There is also trade in food, textiles, and construction materials. Due to conflict and increasing militarization, regional trade dropped from $1.3 billion in 1981 to under $750 million in 1983. Furthermore, the flight of private capital meant a loss of $4.5 billion from 1979 to 1983 in investments. Focusing on economic development would change the game from military confrontation, which is beneficial to Cuba and Moscow, to economic prosperity, which is a U.S. strength.

Lift Economic Sanctions. Making the Nicaraguan people suffer will neither eliminate the Sandinistas nor improve U.S. image in Nicaragua. Imposing economic hardship is counterproductive because it destroys economic progress (the engine of political development) and it allows the Sandinistas to justify repressive policies. Political solutions are more likely to flow from economic growth than economic decay.[112]

Encourage Private Groups to Assist Nicaraguans. Many Americans, including Benjamin Linder who was killed by the Contras in May 1987, are already helping the Nicaraguans with rural development projects. Private American groups and organizations such as Habitat for Humanity and Catholic Relief Services, which play a constructive role in economic and social development at the grassroots level are well equipped to serve as a bridge between the United States and Nicaragua and to facilitate the restoration of good relations between the two countries. They would also help to reduce Nicaragua's need for Cuban workers and, consequently, diminish Cuban as well as Soviet influence.

Focus on Positive Developments in Nicaragua. The Sandinistas have made tremendous progress toward eliminating illiteracy; providing medical care for people who never had access to it; redistributing farmland to destitute peasants; removing many of the brutalities of the Somoza regime; respecting basic human rights (especially when compared to our major allies, El Salvador and Guatemala); and, perhaps most important, they have given many ordinary Nicaraguans hope for the future. Focusing on positive developments reduces hostility and unnecessary suffering, diminishes the power of more Marxist-oriented Sandinistas, enhances prospects for opposition parties to play a meaningful role, and improves U.S. maneuverability. A policy of hostility perpetuates anti-Americanism, beneficial to Moscow and Havana, isolates the United States rather than Nicaragua, and influences opposition groups to adopt the "politics of catastrophe," waiting for American marines to rescue them. Unless the United States is prepared to invade Nicaragua, a negative policy is self-defeating.

Shift the Focus from Havana to Mexico City and Elsewhere in Latin America. Cuba is neither the cause of the problem in Nicaragua nor its solution. Focusing on Cuba makes the United States appear insensitive to much needed reforms and puts it in opposition to the Contadora group and its efforts to peacefully resolve the problem. Mexico's fear of instability in Central America is no less than America's. Mexico, however, realizes that change is an inevitable part of Nicaragua's political development. Given Mexico's proximity to Nicaragua, its ability to effectively communicate with the Sandinistas, its understanding of the region, and its interests in peace, stability, and a Nicaragua free of Soviet-Cuban or U.S. domination, Washington must involve Mexico in the process of finding a solution. In light of U.S. historical experiences in Nicaragua, policymakers must consider the advantages of Washington deferring to Costa Rica, Mexico, Venezuela, Panama, and Colombia. This requires a lower U.S. profile and acceptance of the fact that cooperation, rather than control, is the most pragmatic strategy for achieving U.S. objectives.

Work with Latin American Writers and the Church. Understanding Nicaraguans, their culture, and their hopes is vital to our ability to influence their behavior. By dismissing poets and intellectuals as idealists, policymakers in Washington deprive themselves of an opportunity to achieve some of their foreign policy goals. They also contribute to our cultural chauvinism which prevents us from understanding Nicaragua's reality. Nicaragua has long been a land of poets, a fact not changed by the revolution. Writers, respected and influential throughout Latin America, are generally deeply involved in articulating social grievances and advocating social reform. Consequently, they identify with leaders of change. American hostility toward Cuba and Nicaragua serves to insure intellectuals' protectiveness and loyalty to Havana and Managua, despite their private criticisms of Castro and Ortega. As Riding observes, their solidarity with the Sandinista revolution has grown in direct proportion to the rise of U.S. hostility toward the Managua regime.[113]

Unlike Cuba, Nicaragua enjoys considerable religious freedom and the Catholic Church exercises tremendous power over ordinary Nicaraguans as well as some Sandinista leaders, some of whom are also religious leaders. The Church's attacks against Marxism continue to be a moderating influence on the Sandinistas. Unlike Castro, Ortega baptized his children, met privately with various bishops, established a dialogue between the Sandinista Directorate and the bishop's conference, and appointed Cardinal Obando y Bravo as head of the National Reconciliation Commission. These positive aspects should be highlighted and encouraged.

Support Human Rights. Emphasizing human rights in Central America is both moral and pragmatic. U.S. power ultimately rests upon its ability to give hope to the downtrodden, to provide a positive example of respect for those fundamental rights which elude the vast majority of humanity, and to identify with those who struggle to bring about greater observance of human dignity. The assumption that U.S. security interests are best safeguarded by dictators who torture and kill their own citizens has been extremely costly, ultimately depriving the United States of the very security it sought. Financing groups to violate human rights undermines U.S. interests abroad and destroys the consensus at home that is vital to a successful foreign policy. Focusing on human rights benefits both Central America and the interests of the United States while frustrating Soviet-Cuban ambitions in the region.

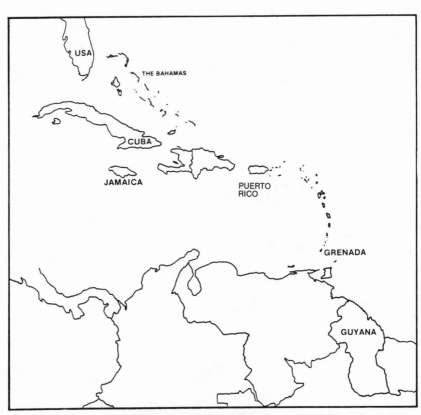

THE COMMONWEALTH CARIBBEAN

5

The Commonwealth Caribbean: Exercise Economic and Diplomatic Options

Preventing Cuban-Soviet involvement in the Caribbean and Latin America emerged as a principal objective of President Reagan's foreign policy. Former U.S. Ambassador to the United Nations, Jeane Kirkpatrick, gave the intellectual justification for Reagan's preoccupation with communist expansionism, contending that the deterioration of America's position in the hemisphere had created serious vulnerabilities where none previously existed. The United States, in her view, was confronted with the unprecedented need to defend itself against a ring of Soviet bases on and around its southern and eastern borders.[1]

Given this perception, Reagan's anticommunist record, the strident antiimperialist rhetoric of Grenada's revolutionary leaders, and their close ties to Cuba and the Soviet Union, the U.S. invasion of Grenada was not unexpected. The rigid commitment of the Bernard Coard faction to the ideological principles of Marxism-Leninism, and the ruthlessness with which they were being implemented, made U.S. military involvement almost inevitable.

Although this unprecedented U.S. military intervention in the Commonwealth Caribbean may have demonstrated U.S. resolve and resulted in a serious setback for Cuba, the underlying causes of instability have by no means disappeared. Indeed, the dangers for U.S. foreign policy in the region may escalate and outweigh the positive aspects of the invasion if preoccupation with Soviet-Cuban activities divert attention away from the economic and social problems confronting all Commonwealth Caribbean leaders. By viewing Caribbean problems in an East-West context and focusing on Cuban activities as part of Soviet global ambitions, the United States may inadvertently encourage Caribbean leaders to perceive opposition movements as being communist inspired and create a dangerous situation in a region where it can least afford to have an increase in Soviet-Cuban influence and activity. As the aftermath of the Grenada invasion shows, addressing economic problems and demilitarizing the Caribbean is the most appropriate strategy for safeguarding both U.S. and Commonwealth Caribbean security interests. It also demonstrates the extraordinarily high price of military solutions compared to sound diplomacy.

Safeguarding U.S. national security interests requires a foreign policy consistent with basic American social, economic, and political values and the shaping of an external environment where these values can survive and flourish. The Commonwealth Caribbean islands, like the majority of developing countries, are newly independent and nationalistic. They require a peaceful international environment to consolidate their political independence and economic development. However, because they are essentially transitional societies, a certain amount of disorder and social conflict is inevitable, a condition conducive to Cuban-Soviet intervention. While it is tempting to use military force to prevent revolution, the real challenge is the creation of stability out of revolution. If the United States and its anti-Soviet and Cuban policies are equated with support for reactionary anti-Sovietism, the U.S. will suffer,[2] primarily because revolutionary movements generally reflect the struggle of poor people, usually a majority of a country's citizens, against poverty, oppression, and backwardness. Rather than distinguishing between national security and economic and political development, they must be seen as inseparable, especially in relation to Soviet-Cuban expansionism. As Anthony Lake observes:

> The United States competes best with the Soviets in most Third World nations by deemphasizing global competition. Treating such nations as pawns in a larger game, interpreting "socialist" domestic institutions as allegiance to the Soviets, and insisting on alignment with either the United States or the Soviet Union offends Third World nationalism and thus limits American influence. The United States competes best in the Third World by pursuing policies that respond primarily to Third World concerns: economic development and national independence.[3]

Focusing on the aspirations of Commonwealth Caribbean countries rather than on Soviet-Cuban activities is beneficial to the United States in the long run. However, U.S. policy toward the Caribbean is complicated by a strong emotional attachment to the region and an insistence on isolating Cuba diplomatically and economically. It also demonstrates the failure of successive administrations to deal with Cuba realistically. Castro's decision to align Cuba with the Soviet Union deprived the United States of its traditional ability to dictate the terms of U.S.-Cuban relations.[4] Despite this significant development, initial attitudes, formed in the atmosphere of intense hostility of the early 1960s, have changed little. When it comes to Cuba, the U.S. seems to be locked in a time warp.[5] Consequently, American leaders resort to a more confrontational approach which, ultimately, results in an even greater decline in influence and prestige each time Castro calls Washington's bluff.

Because of its geographical, political, and cultural proximity to the United States, the nature of its problems, the increasing international prominence of its leaders, and the fact that it essentially represents a microcosm of the world, the Caribbean demands a successful U.S. foreign policy. Not only is it a litmus test of the attitudes and policies that Washington will adopt toward the Third World countries generally,[6] but far more significant, failure in the Caribbean will overshadow success elsewhere, and will have direct consequences for the United States as a superpower with global interests and responsibilities, especially in relation to its attempts to frustrate Soviet objectives.

By examining the Commonwealth Caribbean it becomes increasingly obvious that the traditional status quo—anti-Soviet approach to foreign policy toward the Third World—is not only unsuited for a time of unrest and instability, but will ultimately assist in the self-victimization which characterizes contemporary U.S. foreign policy.

The Commonwealth Caribbean demonstrates that instead of focusing primarily on Cuban-Soviet expansionism, more attention should be paid to the economic vulnerability of the islands, which has a significant impact on political developments. The Soviets view the Caribbean as an important region primarily because of its geographic location and its special relationship with the United States. As Robert Leiken of the Georgetown Center for International and Strategic Studies points out, Soviet military leaders perceive U.S. strategic freedom in other parts of the world as dependent on stability in the Caribbean.[7] From Moscow's point of view, the Caribbean lies in North America's strategic rear; to weaken the grip of imperialism in the region would shift the correlation of forces between imperialism and socialism to the advantage of the latter, or more directly, diminish Washington's power and increase Moscow's. Developments in the Caribbean are regarded as part of "a global pattern"—a view consistent with the Soviet ideology and reinforced by Cuba's Revolution.[8]

Events in Grenada before the invasion served to support the pragmatic as well as ideological aspects of Soviet foreign policy, and challenged the U.S. on how to deal with small, irritating, but nonthreatening regimes which advocate an adherence to Marxist-Leninist principles. The invasion itself proved that because the United States enjoys an overwhelming military advantage in the Caribbean area, neither the Soviet Union nor Cuba will offer much assistance to countries that are confronted with direct U.S. military intervention.

In addition to the crucial factor of geography, the islands are important because of their general adherence to deeply rooted democratic traditions. Relatively stable societies, they help to enhance and promote American values and traditions and create an external environment conducive to the protection of U.S. security interests. Therefore, substantial Cuban achievements there promote Soviet goals and ideology, to the extent these accomplishments undermine the democratic traditions of Commonwealth Caribbean countries. Again, Grenada shows that Cuba's success resulted largely from that island's endemic poverty.

U.S INTERESTS AND ECONOMIC AND POLITICAL CONDITIONS

Politically, the Caribbean has always been considered to be in the American sphere of influence, a view intertwined with both domestic and foreign policy. As Crassweller observes, among the general public the historic concern with maintaining the Caribbean free from any hostile incursions from abroad has resulted in the importance that the concept of space has always held in American thought. Safety and freedom have traditionally been associated with space, with serene waters washing against every seacoast.[9] The Monroe Doctrine flowed from fear of European encroachment, the Spanish-American War from U.S. expansion toward world power, the Good Neighbor policy in part from FDR's need for hemispheric power against the Axis powers, and the Alliance for Progress in part from the struggle with communism.[10] Today, renewed American interest in the Caribbean is directly related to Soviet-Cuban involvement.

The United States has significant military and economic interests in the region. Approximately 45 percent of U.S. shipping and oil tankers move through the Caribbean. Much of the supertanker traffic also passes through the Caribbean on the way to Europe, and a significant proportion of petroleum eventually consumed in the United States is refined in Trinidad, Puerto Rico, St. Croix, and Aruba. American military presence is visible throughout the area, especially in Puerto Rico. There are undersea surveillance systems and oceanographic research stations. So effective and omnipresent is the U.S. Coast Guard that many Caribbean islands rely heavily on it. Economic ties and the movement of people are other obvious examples of the irrevocable link between the Caribbean islands and the United States.

Historical U.S. ties with the area and an awareness throughout the world of its concern with the Caribbean make the region a testing ground for U.S. power and global leadership ability. So well known and so accepted a reality is this concern that its weakening would hardly be consistent with an assertion of continuing concern and involvement elsewhere.[11]

Overwhelming advantages enjoyed by the United States in the area should assist in diminishing external threats and strengthening America's image in the Third World and elsewhere. Like the United States, the Commonwealth Caribbean has a democratic tradition. It is only when this fact is understood that one can move on to a realistic appraisal of current problems in the area, especially those relating to Soviet-Cuban involvement and a movement toward the left. Barbados, for example, was under uninterrupted British control from 1627 to 1966. Its House of Assembly, which began meeting in 1639, is the third oldest legislative body in the Western Hemisphere—preceeded only by Bermuda's legislature and the Virginia House of Burgess. In Barbados, Jamaica, Trinidad and Tobago and, to a lesser extent, in Guyana, an essential stability has developed. The two party system is an integral part of political life and a tradition of civility and accommodation is well established. It is generally accepted that the political affairs of the Commonwealth Caribbean are run with competence and restraint.[12] The vast majority of island states enjoy the political and civil freedoms emphasized in the United States. Grenada, of course, was the exception.

The movement to the left in the Commonwealth Caribbean countries is deeply rooted in persistent economic and social problems confronting them. Leftist sentiments are generated by the very intensity of the search for solutions to these problems, a crucial fact to take into consideration when analyzing Soviet-Cuban interest in the region.[13] Domestic pressures, prior to independence, influenced leaders to advocate what could be regarded as leftist policies. This is not surprising. The Commonwealth Caribbean, with one of the highest literacy rates in the world, high unemployment, and a large number of British and American-trained intellectuals, adopted policies similar to those in Britain where most of the older elite were educated.

Norman Manley, for example, advocated socialist views quite similar to those being advocated by the Fabian Socialists in Britain. His son, Michael Manley, was influenced by the British socialist theoretician, Harold Laski. Guyana's Burnham was educated at Oxford, as were Sir

Grantley Adams of Barbados and Norman Manley of Jamaica. All advocated "colonial socialism" patterned after the British example. As O'Flaherty observed, even in practice, Jamaican socialism evokes Britain in 1946 and 1947, with gradual nationalization of key enterprises, such as utilities and urban transportation, and tighter government control of imports.[14]

Difficult domestic economic and social conditions rather than external factors are influencing contemporary Caribbean leftism. President Reagan acknowledged that economic disaster in the Caribbean "is consuming our neighbors' money reserves and credit, forcing thousands of people to leave for the United States, often illegally, and shaking even the most established democracies. And economic disaster has provided a fresh opening to the enemies of freedom, national independence, and peaceful development."[15] These problems emanate from overpopulation, agricultural decline, high oil prices, and dependence on one or two sources of income.

Until quite recently overpopulation was not as severe as it is currently, largely because there were escape valves abroad for those who could not secure employment at home as well as for those who saw Britain, Canada, and the United States as providing opportunities for upward mobility. With increased demand for labor in Britain subsequent to World War II, many citizens of Commonwealth Caribbean countries settled there permanently or returned home after a very long stay overseas. By the early 1960s there was a decline in Britain's demand for immigrant workers, a development which posed no serious difficulty to the Caribbean because by that time the United States and Canada needed workers and found West Indians most suitable due to their adaptation to production processes in an industrial society, common cultural characteristics, and language.

Following the passage of the U.S. Immigration Act of 1965, the number of immigrant visas issued to citizens of the Commonwealth Caribbean increased from 2,961 in 1965 to 14,537 in 1969, to 27,354 in 1976. From 1962 to 1976 a total of over 245,000 immigrants were admitted from Jamaica, Trinidad and Tobago, Guyana, and Barbados. This translated into a reduction in the natural increase in population by 36.9 percent for Jamaica, 34.4 percent for Trinidad and Tobago, 25.5 percent for Guyana, and 49 percent for Barbados.[16] By 1980, 50,000 Barbadians—about one of every six Barbadians alive anywhere—and approximately one-half million or one out of five Jamaicans lived in the United States.

This approach to controlling the size of population in Caribbean states is no longer feasible in light of restrictive and sometimes hostile policies toward immigrants in Britain, the United States, and, to a lesser extent, Canada. Furthermore, the population is expected to continue to grow rapidly because those between the ages of 15 and 25 make up about two-thirds of the population on many islands. They have an unemployment rate of 40 percent. In light of this, economic problems are likely to be severe and social unrest and discontent widespread—regardless of who is in power.

Although agriculture continues to play a dominant role in the economies of all Caribbean countries, migration of rural residents to urban areas, uncertain land tenure, inexperience with more efficient and economic agronomic practices, and higher costs for energy and fertilizers have contributed to the decline of agriculture. In several islands sugar production is down, partly because of bad weather, cane fires, strikes, and the lack of chemicals and proper machinery. In addition, world prices worked against exporters, with production costs in many countries above market prices. Banana exports also declined in 1982 compared to 1981.[17]

In addition to the problem of the agricultural sector facing the Caribbean states, higher oil prices have had a devastating effect on all of them, with the exception of the only major oil producer, Trinidad and Tobago. Because the islands are heavily dependent on imports from industrial countries and on tourism, economic growth continues to be elusive and the standard of living, high by Third World standards, is in serious jeopardy. Even Trinidad and Tobago experienced a decline in economic growth because petroleum output fell by 6 percent between January and June of 1982, compared with the first half of 1981. Bauxite exporters, severly affected by the recession in the United States and elsewhere, experienced a 29 percent decrease in production in 1982 compared with 1981.[18]

Although per capita income for the Commonwealth Caribbean is high (ranging from roughly $6,850 U.S. in Trinidad and Tobago to $600 in Guyana) compared to other Third World countries, bitter poverty is widespread. In Jamaica, for example, one-third of the population receives an annual income of under $200. This poverty is highlighted, and its psychological effects aggravated, by the juxtaposition—through migration, tourism, and the media—with American affluence.[19] The islands' small size makes these disparities very visible. Consequently, greater pressure is exerted on governments to provide high standards of living and a redistribution of incomes. Unfortunately, poverty is likely to persist, unemployment is expected to increase and deteriorating payments deficits and soaring debts are almost inevitable. This reality, and growing nationalism combine to produce an environment which was conducive to Soviet-Cuban involvement in Grenada, Guyana, and Jamaica.

SOVIET-CUBAN ACTIVITIES IN THE
COMMONWEALTH CARIBBEAN

Soviet-Cuban activities in the Commonwealth Caribbean are far more complex than the overwhelming preoccupation with East-West confrontation would suggest. The Caribbean itself has always defied simplistic analysis, despite great temptation to do so. Several factors must be considered simultaneously in any attempt to evaluate Soviet-Cuban involvement in the region. In addition to economic development issues, one must include the political and cultural diversity of the area, the influence of European rather than U.S. colonialism, the islands' desire to be autonomous and nonaligned and, despite their disinterest in the East-West conflict and dislike of militarism, their willingness to utilize the Cuban threat to obtain U.S. attention and economic assistance.

The Soviet-Cuban alliance in the Caribbean is quite different from their relationship in Ethiopia, for example. Contrary to the view that Cuba is a mere front for the USSR, Cuba has long pursued its own foreign policy interests aimed more at avoiding U.S. attempts to isolate it than at carrying out Soviet policy objectives. While Moscow recognizes the Caribbean as a "special preserve of the United States" and believes that we will defend it against any external threat,[20] Cuba regards the region quite differently. For Castro, the Caribbean has a special significance, apart from his ties to Moscow. Many of the region's leaders have interacted with Castro, and Grenada's Maurice Bishop and Jamaica's Michael Manley enjoyed friendships with him. What is easily overlooked is that Cuba is part of the Caribbean, not only in terms of geography, but also historically and culturally. Not surprisingly, Cuba's interests are paramount in the Caribbean, an area of less direct strategic importance to the Soviet Union.[21] Consequently, it is Cuba that initiates activities there and is able to gain Soviet support.

Prior to the 1980s, distinct differences existed between Havana and Moscow as to how to bring about change in the region. While the Soviet Union favored peaceful state-to-state relations and advocated united fronts against capitalism and imperialism, Cuba actively assisted leftist movements, including those engaged in armed struggle.[22] And while Cuba viewed Grenada and Nicaragua as close allies, the Kremlin was extremely reluctant to acknowledge them as "socialist path" states.[23] Castro's support of radical regimes in the Caribbean allows him to project his influence in an area close to the United States. However, although Castro ultimately pursues his own policies, his success in the Caribbean also benefits Moscow by advancing Soviet objectives in America's backyard.

Most Commonwealth Caribbean countries recognized Cuba as part of the region and accepted its Spanish authoritarian tradition. As is generally the case, there has been a dynamic interaction of people between democratic and authoritarian islands to cut sugar cane or to trade. Thousands of Jamaicans migrated to Cuba before the Castro Revolution. Current relations between Cuba and the other islands are also influenced by the desire of these newly independent countries to determine their own foreign policies despite, or perhaps because of the reality of their inextricable ties to the United States.

Contemporary Commonwealth Caribbean leaders aspire not only to stand more firmly in the ranks of the Third World but to lead in international forums where such issues as nonalignment and the New International Economic Order are being discussed. Burnham of Guyana, as early as 1959, denounced apartheid in South Africa and moved into the nonaligned camp. Manley envisioned the Caribbean as acting as a sophisticated leader in the development of relevant Third World policies. Movement in this direction preceded Manley's administration and was continued more vigorously by him. Jamaica was merely an observer at the Heads of States Conference of the Nonaligned countries in Cairo in 1964. By 1968 it was a full member, and in 1973 Jamaica sent high level officials to Algiers with Manley himself attending, traveling with Castro.[24] By supporting Cuban military action in Africa, Manley attempted not only to respond to domestic feelings of solidarity with Africa but also to improve his credibility as an antiimperialist spokesman and an advocate of a distribution of wealth between rich and poor countries.

Somewhat paradoxically, Commonwealth Caribbean countries, while wanting a new economic order which inevitably leads to greater interdependence, advocate national autonomy. Jamaica, Barbados, Guyana, and Trinidad and Tobago demonstrated their independence from the United States by establishing diplomatic ties with Cuba. In defiance of superpower rivalry, in 1965 Jamaica disagreed with the United States on the issue of admission of Red China to the UN by abstaining from voting. In 1971, Jamaica voted for China's admission. Although these actions can be construed as leftism, they more accurately reflect the sentiment of most developing countries and in particular, reflect rejection of traditional U.S. domination of the Caribbean and Latin America.[25]

Another consideration overlooked in relation to Cuban activities in the Caribbean is that, as a result of the United States' inexorable fear of communism, Cuba is somewhat trapped into the role of granting assistance when the United States refuses. This is one of the few effective methods of getting the United States to pay attention to very small island-states. Caribbean leaders have tried to obtain aid from the United

States and have used the possibility of turning to Cuba as bait. For example, in March 1980, Manley went to Cuba immediately after a particularly difficult series of negotiations with the IMF had been unproductive.[26] But Cuba also gains from assisting Caribbean countries. An examination of Cuban involvement in Jamaica and Grenada reveals that the activities were relatively inexpensive and their impact immediate and tangible.

There is little evidence to demonstrate a strong connection between developments in Guyana and Jamaica and Soviet-Cuban activities. The State Department indicated, for example, that in 1982 there were only 300 students from the Eastern Caribbean studying technical and academic subjects in Cuba and that the study of Marxism-Leninism is compulsory in many courses. According to the report, local Marxist-Leninist groups with ties to Cuba played a key role in selecting the students.[27] In Guyana, movement toward the left seems unrelated to Cuba or the Soviet Union. State Department reports do not show any significant communist involvement in Guyana, apart from the establishment of diplomatic ties, and the stationing of 200 Cuban technicians, advisers, and medical personnel. Indeed, the government expelled five Cuban diplomats in 1978. It is alleged that Cuban military advisers have provided guerrilla training outside Guyana to members of a small radical Guyanese opposition party, the Working People's Alliance.[28]

Manley's willingness to openly support Castro's stationing of Cuban troops in Angola, and closer ties between Jamaica and Cuba were of serious concern to the United States. According to the official U.S. view, Jamaica had become a special Cuban target, with Cuban security personnel training Jamaican security officers in Jamaica and Cuba, including members of the security force of the office of the prime minister. Cuba also trained about 1,400 Jamaicans in Cuba as construction workers, simultaneously providing political indoctrination and instruction in revolutionary tactics and use of arms.[29] The students who were recalled by Seaga do not appear to have any meaningful political influence in Jamaica. Basic economic problems remained the primary source of difficulty for Seaga's government.

Cuba's success in developing better relations with Jamaica would seem to be tied to its provision of appropriate technology and services which impressed Manley. Cuba assisted in the construction of housing, schools, mini-dams, and the improvement of Kingston's water supplies. Partly because of Manley's policies, which influenced medical personnel to leave in large numbers, Cuba provided doctors, nurses, and others to staff Jamaican hospitals. Perhaps more importantly, in the long run, Cuban emphasis on fisheries and fish-processing operations focused the attention of Caribbean leaders on the economic potential of the oceans.[30] These relatively inexpensive projects are appealing to developing societies. Seaga, however, as part of his election campaign strategy, decided to "halt the expansionist movement of Communist imperialism" in the Caribbean. When he assumed office he expelled Cuban Ambassador Ulises Estrada. Unlike Manley, Seaga did not entertain ambitions of becoming a Third World spokesman. Instead, alignment with the West and a corresponding hostility to Soviet and Cuban influence became the touchstones of his foreign policy.[31]

BACKGROUND TO DEVELOPMENTS IN JAMAICA AND GUYANA

The leftward movement in Guyana seems to have been spawned out of political expediency. Accused by the opposition headed by Jagan that he was a U.S. puppet, former prime minister Burnham moved further to the left, declaring his country a socialist and a nationalist state determined to create an egalitarian society, and labeling his party as Marxist-Leninist in order to reach an accommodation with Jagan. Similarly, Burnham's nationalization of the bauxite industry was motivated more by Guyana's desperate need for revenues and his desire to remain in office than by any commitment to socialist principles. However, socialist rhetoric which was used as an *ex post facto* justification of nationalization later on assumed a determinative role in economic policy.[32]

Jamaica, the largest of the Commonwealth Caribbean islands, faced severe economic problems, social change, and increasing nationalism which eventually influenced Manley to move further to the left than previous Jamaican governments. Success in Caribbean politics, as in other democratic societies, is dependent upon politicians' abilities to improve economic conditions for the upwardly mobile middle class who are the main participants in the political process. Failure to provide employment opportunities has serious consequences for the party in power.

Jamaican leftism or socialism under Manley was part of the platform of the People's National Party (PNP) from its formation in 1940. By the 1950s, however, the PNP retreated from its commitment to socialism and expelled a left-wing group from its ranks.[33] The popular perception of socialism and communism as being identical prevents the growth of leftism. Although socialism may have been regarded as a solution to Jamaica's endemic problems, what was overlooked was the strong influence of the church, deeply rooted capitalism, the general conservativeness of Jamaicans, and the island's irrevocable link to the United States, Canada, and England. By 1974, however, new demands influenced a return to democratic socialism.

Like Burnham in Guyana, Manley's concern with equal distribution of wealth both at the domestic and global levels emanated from serious domestic pressures. Comprising the vast majority of the population, many black Jamaicans escalated their emphasis on disparities between themselves and the small white and racially mixed elite that dominated the economic and political life of the country. Manley attempted to contain the growing Black Power movement by advocating socialism and egalitarianism in a society that inherited obvious class distinctions from its British experience. These demands could have been met more successfully if wealthy Jamaicans were protected by a growing economy. In fact, the Jamaican economy did experience rapid growth between the early 1960s and 1970s, largely due to expansion of the bauxite and tourist industries, and substantial private investment. In order to maintain a high level of growth and development, Manley's government increased the deficit from 4 percent to 19 percent betwen 1972 and 1976, much of the money being borrowed from foreign commercial banks. Consequently, Jamaica's external debt quadrupled by the end of 1976 to about $830 million and net official reserves fell by $350 million to minus $230 million.[34]

Jamaica's indebtedness was partly the result of OPEC's quadrupling of oil prices, which could not be offset by the controversial bauxite levy. In 1972, just before the Arab-Israeli War, which sparked OPEC's action, Jamaica spent $49 million on imported oil, or roughly 9 percent of total imports in that year; in 1979, the figures escalated to around $200 million or, 25 percent of the total import bill.[35] Because the industrialized countries were also seriously affected by oil prices, the costs of imported manufactured goods rose while tourism declined. To make matters worse, floods devastated agriculture. Attempts at land reform were also a fundamental cause of agricultural decline. Manley's democratic socialism, which began in 1974, was an indication of a democratic government being responsive to demands by assertive segments of the population for satisfaction of material needs and greater control of Jamaica's natural resources. Government attempts to enhance its extractive and distributive capabilities were impeded by the slowness of the U.S. State Department in granting a loan to Jamaica after Alcoa's lobby indicated its displeasure with Jamaica's proposal to gain a controlling interest in bauxite companies and to relate the price of bauxite to the price of finished aluminum ingots.[36] Business confidence evaporated causing a dramatic decline in private investments. Between 1975 and 1978 investments dropped by two thirds, despite a relaxation in 1977 of the terms on which foreign investment would operate and very little nationalization.[37]

Overall, Manley's proposals for resolving economic difficulties led to an even further deterioration in Jamaica's economy. Private lending institutions were reluctant to grant additional credit and, simultaneously, professional and technical personnel, as well as those in the upper middle class, left the island in large numbers. Van Horn summarizes the problem:

> In 1972, Manley inherited an island with 710 doctors, 6,960 general nurses, and 4,584 midwives, but by 1976 there was only 390 doctors, and by 1978 the number of general nurses and midwives had declined to 305 and 144 respectively. The unemployment rate in 1974 was 21 percent, but by 1979 it had risen to 31 percent. In 1972 the Jamaican Labour Party government left the incoming one J.$179 million in foreign exchange reserves and an exchange rate of J1.00 v. U.S. $1.14 but by July, 1980, the island's foreign exchange reserves had plummeted to −J $902 million, and the exchange rate was J.$1.76 v. U.S. $1.00.[38]

By 1977, Jamaica had turned increasingly to the IMF for loans. As part of the agreement to grant the loan, the IMF stipulated that budget deficits had to be brought in line with projected real resources (that is, without bank credit) and that foreign funds should be attracted in order to have a more gradual adjustment in the balance of payments than Jamaica was currently being forced to adopt, and Jamaica's difficulties only multiplied when negotiations with the IMF were not respectful of Jamaica's sovereignty. Jamaican officials charged that the IMF expected massive and sudden adjustments in deflating the economy without allowing sufficient time and money to keep the humanity of the poorest people intact.[39] These economic hardships eventually defeated Manley in the election and provided Seaga with an opportunity to improve economic conditions.

Despite his strong anti-Cuban and anti-Soviet rhetoric, Seaga was quite aware of the fact that his government had to be responsive to demands by registered voters. Indeed, this position, which satisfied Washington, was soon followed by calls for a Caribbean Marshall Plan to which the United States, Western Europe, Japan, and Canada would contribute $2 billion, and oil producing Mexico, Venezuela, and Trinidad and Tobago would give $800 million in oil rebates.[40] The unfortunate reality is that despite Seaga's program of deregulation, which involved the transfer of uneconomic state enterprises to private ownership, and the dismantling of import controls, the economy's performance has not been satisfactory. These actions only exposed deeply entrenched inefficiencies in local industries.

Bauxite production, which accounts for approximately 75 percent of Jamaica's export earnings, fell by 30 percent in 1982 compared with 1981 because of continuing weak demand.[41] Consequently, Seaga was forced to impose new taxes to raise revenues which would offset this decline. There were layoffs in mining and other sectors and unemployment rose to 27.9 percent in 1983, from 25.8 percent in 1981. The trade deficit stood at J$1.1 billion and the net external debt increased to J$2.498 billion in 1983, from J$1.959 billion at the end of 1981.[42] These mounting economic problems were exacerbated by strikes by civil servants. The political consequences were obvious. Public opinion polls conducted in 1983 showed that in an election, Michael Manley would receive 41 percent of the vote, compared to 38 percent for Seaga's Labor party and 1 percent for the Marxist Workers party of Jamaica. Approximately 44 percent of Jamaicans surveyed believed that economic conditions had worsened since Seaga came to power, while 32 percent said that things had improved, and 24 percent didn't see any significant change.[43]

In addition to regarding socialism as a solution to Jamaica's economic problem, Manley decided to champion Third World causes. This movement toward the Third World bloc repudiated Alexander Bustamante's view that Jamaica was irrevocably tied to the West, the United States and Britain in particular. Writing in *Foreign Affairs*, Manley stated that "in the long run it may yet transpire that differences between stages of economic development, as between various nations and regions of the world, are more important determinants of history than differences in ideology or systems of government."[44] Manley contended that the Caribbean must be understood within the Third World context. Emphasizing the nature of this new relationship, he writes:

> The ability of the Caribbean to achieve progress goes beyond regionalism to the necessity for the developing world as a whole to evolve a common strategy with regards to its economic dealings with the metropolitan nations. The extent to which the Caribbean must act as a sophisticated leader in the development of relevant third world policies, to that extent can it help to underwrite its own survival.[45]

Any U.S. policy that attempts to permanently reduce Cuban-Soviet influence in the Commonwealth Caribbean must take into consideration the fact that the movement toward the left is complicated by North-South issues, the desire for economic growth and development, political and economic autonomy, and increasing nationalism. Preoccupation with Soviet-American rivalry can obscure these realities and militate against a successful U.S. policy in the region and elsewhere.

GRENADA: THE DANGERS OF IDEOLOGY

The 1979 political coup in Grenada, led by Maurice Bishop, a London-trained lawyer from a fairly wealthy family, was the first in Common-wealth Caribbean history and signified a new and threatening development in the politics of the English-speaking island democracies. The subsequent assassination of Bishop and other Grenadians, the emergence of Bernard Coard as leader of the revolution, and the invasion by American and Caribbean troops clearly demonstrated the dangers of ideology. Both Grenada and the United States became prisoners of rhetoric and victims of rigid adherence to ideological principles. Both Reagan and the leaders of Grenada's New Jewel Movement (NJM) refused to come to grips with economic and political realities of the Common-wealth Caribbean, choosing instead to sacrifice human beings on the altar of abstractions.

The leftward movement in Grenada, as in Jamaica, emanated from economic stagnation and gross violations of political and social freedoms of Grenadians by Prime Minister Eric Gairy. With a per capita income of $630 in 1982, Grenada ranked with Haiti as one of the poorest countries in the Caribbean. Although its population is around 110,000, approximately 500,000 Grenadians are scattered among Trinidad and Tobago, Canada, the United States and Britain. At the time of the 1979 coup, almost 50 percent of Grenada's work force was unemployed, the trade deficit was roughly $18 million; and the standard of living, rather than improving, was deteriorating. The hospitals had too few sheets, hardly any medicines, and no qualified nurses. Schools were virtually on the verge of collapse and had few books. Despite these harsh conditions, Eric Gairy continued to illegally elect himself and to violently suppress all opposition. It is under these circumstances that the NJM emerged and seized power in Grenada.

Grenada's method of acquiring independence contained the seeds of rebellion. Unlike the orderly transition from colonialism to independence enjoyed by the other islands, Grenada's new political status was preceded by demonstrations and strikes against Gairy's venality and brutality. Gairy responded to the unrest by imprisoning the opposition, which included Maurice Bishop and Unison Whiteman, and murdering Bishop's father, Rupert Bishop. Despite this violence, Britain, anxious to unload its expensive possessions, decided to grant Grenada independence.

Even before independence, the NJM was emerging as a serious rival for political power. Its leaders were middle-class intellectuals and businessmen who were frustrated and disillusioned with parliamentary democracy as a process by which Gairy could be defeated or corruption controlled. The NJM was a combination of various groups sharing a common dislike for the Gairy regime. In 1972 Unison Whiteman formed Jewel (The Joint Endeavor for the Welfare, Education and Liberation of the People) to mobilize farm workers. Bishop founded the Movement for the Advancement of Community Effort (MACE), an organization which stressed the concept of participatory democracy, based on the failed Ujamaa Villages philosophy of Tanzania's Julius Nyerere, as an alternative to the Westminster model. The committee of Concerned Citizens, led by Bernard Coard, joined with MACE to form the Movement for Assemblies of the People (MAP). Eventually, MAP and Jewel merged in 1973 to create the NJM as a united front against Gairy and to reduce Grenada's traditional dependency on Western Europe and the United States. Gairy's persecution of the NJM was accomplished by the denial of functioning legitimate political opposition and the utilization of the infamous Mongoose Gang, later renamed the Defense of Fundamental Human Liberties, to intimidate and injure NJM members. The lack of effective political choice indicated a failure of constitutional government which, in large measure, led to the 1979 coup.

On March 13, 1979 the first violent unconstitutional acquisition of political power in Commonwealth Caribbean history occurred, representing a radical departure from the constitutional democratic tradition which had been firmly established in the islands. Approximately forty-five NJM members, led by Hudson Austin, a corporal in Gairy's army who first met Bishop in 1973 when he was guarding the then detained Bishop, attacked the army headquarters located at True Blue. Twelve hours later, Grenada was controlled by the NJM. Only two of Gairy's soldiers were killed in the essentially bloodless confrontations.[46]

Reaction from neighboring states immediately following the coup was generally negative, despite the overwhelming disapproval of Gairy's abuses. Their primary concern related to the legitimization of Bishop's unconstitutional acquisition of power as well as revolutionary activities in their own countries. At an emergency meeting of the council of ministers of the West Indian Associated States the revolution was condemned and the new government was not granted recognition by those legally qualified to do so. The prime minister of St. Lucia, John Compton, requested British intervention and the WIAS proposed the establishment of a regional security force to prevent revolutionary seizure of power in the islands.[47] It was exceedingly clear that democratic principles could not be violated with impunity.

Bishop initially did very little to reassure Commonwealth Caribbean leaders that "participatory democracy at the grassroots level" would eventually lead to free elections, legitimate opposition parties, a free press and a return to basic democratic processes. Instead, Bishop and the new leaders of Dominica and St. Lucia later met and issued the 'Declaration of St. Georges' which contained more leftist ideas. This rigid adherence to ideology and rapidly developing ties with Cuba raised serious questions in the minds of the moderate leaders about the broader implications for the Commonwealth Caribbean.

In his March 13, 1980 speech, "Forward Ever," Bishop tried to allay his neighbors' fears by pointing out that:

> . . . .some people are under the mistaken impression that we are trying to make enemies with some governments in the region and internationally. Some people are under the mistaken impression that the revolution in Grenada is anxious to get everybody in the region to act like we do. . . .This is not correct. We recognize and respect the right of all people in the region and outside the region to determine for themselves what kind of process they want to build for their own country.[48]

By June 1981, many Commonwealth Caribbean leaders seemed to believe that Bishop did not intend to destabililze the region by exporting revolution. Consequently, they decided to work on Caribbean unity, hoping that through cooperation they could modify extremist tendencies within the NJM. Therefore, when the United States attempted to exclude Grenada from participating in a grant to the Caribbean Development Bank, the bank's directors unanimously agreed to reject the grant on the grounds that Grenada's exclusion would have violated the stipulation in the bank's charter against interference in the affairs of a member-state.[49] This trend toward accommodation was strengthened at the 1982 CARICOM (Caribbean Common Market) meeting at Ocho Rios in Jamaica.

GRENADA'S TIES WITH CUBA AND THE SOVIET UNION

Shortly after the coup, Cuban activities in Grenada escalated and Grenada moved quickly to support both Cuba and the Soviet Union on a number of international issues. While the vast majority of UN members voted to condemn Soviet aggression in Afghanistan, Grenada voted against the resolutions with the Soviet Union — a step which marked a radical departure from Commonwealth Caribbean practice. This highly unusual alliance may be explained by Grenada's strong desire to reduce its traditional dependency on the West, its heavy reliance on Cuban military, technical, economic, and security assistance as well as a significant amount of economic aid from the Soviet Union and other eastern

European countries and their allies. Perhaps an even more important explanation was the fact that the NJM leaders, blinded by ideology, misconstrued middle-class Grenadian opposition to Gairy as support for a radical transformation of their society. Furthermore, close friendship ties between Bishop and Castro and the personalization of politics, common in the Caribbean, served to push Grenada closer to Cuba and the Soviet Union. Finally, perceived hostility from neighboring states, and especially the possibility of Gairy using mercenaries to regain power, influenced the NJM leadership to rely on Cuba for military assistance. Approximately 30 days following the unprecedented coup, a Cuban freighter with 1,000 tons of cement docked in Grenada and also unloaded wooden crates containing weapons.[50] Given the process by which Bishop acquired power, it is not surprising that his regime became increasingly dependent on force and countries willing to supply the instruments of coercion, especially in the face of threats from the United States and the refusal of Britain, Canada, and others to respond positively to requests for security assistance. Cuba was inadvertently given an initial monopoly on influence in Grenada.

Boersner, for example, contends that Cuba's success in developing close ties with Grenada was due in part to Venezuela's failure to act on requests from the NJM immediately after the coup. Cuba and Venezuela had discreetly agreed on mutual noninterference in areas of geographic proximity to one or the other. When Venezuela continued to neglect its interests in its "sphere of influence," Cuba felt free to move in.[51]

Although there was general respect for private property, the NJM looked to Cuba as a model, and became increasingly tied to socialist principles. Maurice Bishop intimidated and imprisoned opponents without charges being brought against them, suppressed opposition newspapers, suspended elections and the constitution, seized several privately-owned farms of more than 100 acres, and continued to militarize Grenada. By the time of the invasion, Grenada had an army of about 1,000 soldiers, equivalent in size to that of Trinidad and Tobago, with a population at least ten times larger than Grenada's 110,000.

Documents and weapons found during the invasion support the view that Grenada was becoming an armed island, a development worrisome to neighboring states. Agreements with the Soviet Union provided for military training for twenty junior officers and five senior officers for up to one year and the provision of an assortment of various weapons. At least 9,000 rifles and machine guns were delivered to Grenada between 1979 and October 1983.[52]

As the NJM leaders became more imprisoned by ideology and alienated from the masses they claimed to represent, Cuba became more attractive as a model of revolutionary success. In "Progress Report of

Commissions #5," the idea of National Service and Labor Army was discussed. Despite the obvious admiration for Cuba's achievements in this area, the NJM recognized severe limitations on such an approach in Grenada and postponed its introduction until the fifth anniversary of the revolution. Among the obstacles cited to the creation of a National Service and Labor Army were: the reaction of neighboring states; the lack of a military tradition in Grenada; lack of interest on the part of Grenadians who were more interested in making money than protecting the revolution; the difficulty in applying restrictions to people wanting to leave, especially in light of their "visa mentality"; the openness of Grenada to outside imperialist influences; and the inability of Grenadians to understand why their children had to serve in the military rather than follow the tradition of contributing to the family finances.[53] The realities of Grenada and the alien nature of socialist ideology eventually clashed, dividing the NJM leadership and contributing to the demise of the revolution.

Before Bishop's assassination and the U.S. Caribbean invasion, the most controversial project involving the Cubans was the construction of a major international airport at Point Salines on the southern tip of the island, a project subsequently completed by the United States at a cost of $19 million. The overall cost is estimated at $80 million. About 65 percent of the project was done by the Cubans. The United States saw the Cuban presence and the airport as a clear indication of Soviet-Cuban expansionism and military interest in the Caribbean, despite the fact that Bishop emphasized the importance of an all-weather airport that could handle international flights to improve tourism on the island. Point Salines, a relatively useless area for agriculture, was selected as the most appropriate site for an airport by the British as early as 1926, but the costs were prohibitive.

Overlooking this historical fact, the dangers of the airport at Pearls, the difficulties involved in getting to Grenada, and contributions many countries made to the project, the United States focused on the idea that the 9,800 foot runway was of military significance, contending that it would allow operations of every aircraft in the Soviet-Cuban inventory and give Cuba a guaranteed refuelling stop for military flights to Africa.[54] In addition to Cuba, which was responsible for over half the expense of the project and was overseeing construction, Libya contributed the eight-year interest free loan of $4 million; Mexico, Canada, Venezuela, and Algeria also provided assistance. The U.S. company, Morrision-Knudson of Boise, Idaho, put down the final two inches of asphalt on the runway, a Finnish company installed airport lighting and set up fire and rescue equipment, and the British company, Plessey Airports, Ltd., received a $10 million contact to supply wiring, furniture, finishing materials, and air conditioning. The Soviets gave 1 million rubles to purchase steel and other materials, plus a 10-year credit of 5.5 million rubles.[55] In May 1983, Grenada signed agreements with Venezuela for two flights a week between the two countries, and tourism offices were set up in Trinidad and Tobago and Venezuela. The European Economic Community (EEC) was also considering a request for $1.7 million in funding for training and technical assistance for the airport.[56]

Other communist countries' activities included: North Korean assistance in the construction of a sports stadium, and the development of fisheries and agriculture; East Germany's provision of a $6 million line of credit for modernizing the telephone system and for agricultural equipment purchases; Soviet purchase of Grenadian nutmeg and cocoa at stable prices under a five-year agreement; Cuban and Bulgarian help with a fisheries training school; and the construction of a fish-packing complex and ice plant. Grenada established an embassy in Moscow and the Soviets had an embassy in Grenada.

Documents captured during the invasion reveal Soviet interest in Grenada and Grenada's efforts to convince Moscow of its importance and ability to influence regional events. Rather than the Soviet Union trying to expand its influence, what the documents show is a small Caribbean island trying very hard to get Moscow's support and approval.

The letter by the Grenadian ambassador in Moscow, W. Richard Jacobs, to Bishop and others clearly indicates that Grenada's small size and distance from Russia "would mean that we would figure in a very minute way in the USSR's global relationships.[57] Grenada's revolution would have to be seen as being rooted in the Great October Revolution and Grenada would have to sponsor revolutionary activity in the region. Suriname and Belize were the most likely candidates for such attention because of their instability. By the time this letter was written on July 11, 1983, there were clear divisions within the NJM as well as attempts by Bishop, who had visited Washington, to moderate the anti-American rhetoric. These schisms, resulting primarily from the quest for ideological purity, marked the beginning of the demise of the Grenadian revolution, the destruction of many of its architects as well as innocent civilians, and culminated in the U.S.-Caribbean invasion. Ironically, in a letter from Vincent Noel to the Central Committee, Bishop was reportedly concerned about an Afghanistan solution in Grenada, especially in light of Moscow's support for Bernard Coard.[58] He evidently was aware of the bloodshed and disaster that would terminate a Revolution whose leaders had earlier supported the Soviet invasion of Afghanistan.

U.S. COMMONWEALTH CARIBBEAN POLICY

The invasion of Grenada focused attention of Reagan's policy toward the Commonwealth Caribbean and its failure to address the serious problems of the region. Grenada also demonstrates that Caribbean tranquility and adherence to parliamentary democracy is usually a liability in that the islands are taken for granted until what are regarded as vital U.S. interests are perceived to be seriously challenged by communist activity.

The turning point for contemporary U.S. policy was the Cuban revolution and growing Soviet relations with Castro. Following the Bay of Pigs fiasco of April 1961, a permanent sense of frustration and irritation developed in response to the survival of an anti-American regime and what was viewed as Soviet beach head just 90 miles from Florida. Subsequently, any major response to Caribbean problems has been prompted by fear of Cuban advancement. This applies to Kennedy's Alliance for Progress, Johnson's invasion of the Dominican Republic, Carter's increased economic and military aid package, Reagan's Caribbean Basin Initiative (CBI) and the U.S. military intervention in Grenada.

Preoccupation with communism in Cuba draws a negative reaction from Commonwealth Caribbean leaders who, because of the region's historical diversity and common geographical space, think of Castro as only one of several Caribbean actors rather than solely an instrument of Soviet policy. As Lowenthal observed before the Grenada invasion:

> The activist approach to the Caribbean carries the risk that Washington will become too interventionist. Active or covert U.S. pursuit of political goals could stifle local initiative or promote nationalist reactions. And, to the extent that U.S. interest appears to be merely expedient, not really concerned with the region's people but rather only with potential threats to the United States, the chances increase that an active U.S. presence in the Caribbean will backfire.[59]

Short-term success in Grenada should not influence American policymakers to overlook this point. Carter's policy was reasonably successful because he initially focused on Caribbean problems and stressed that an inordinate fear of communism was detrimental to U.S. interests, although toward the end of his administration and prior to the 1980 election, his actual policies on communism were indistinguishable from those of his predecessors. Andrew Young, Carter's United Nations ambassador, was instrumental in formulating a more realistic foreign policy toward the Commonwealth Caribbean in particular and the Third World in general. As a leader in the Civil Rights Movement, Young understood that poverty breeds destructive tendencies which threaten the fabric of society. In addition to recognizing the serious economic problems as fundamental causes of vulnerability to Cuban-Soviet involvement, Young was apparently cognizant of the strong democratic traditions, high level of education and political sophistication, and special positive sentiments toward the United States in the Commonwealth Caribbean, despite its acceptance of ideological pluralism.

One of Carter's contributions was making the United States the leading participant in organizations such as the Caribbean Group for Economic Cooperation and Development, the Inter-American Bank, and the Caribbean Group for Economic Development, which works under the direction of the World Bank and is composed of about thirty-one countries and sixteen financial institutions. Since 1978 the Group has channeled approximately $300 million to the Caribbean. Economic assistance from all sources almost tripled between 1977 and 1979, from $220 million to $612 million. The United States alone doubled development aid during the 1977–80 period. With Food for Peace shipments included, it provided $155 million in fiscal 1980.[60] Carter also launched a private sector entity, the Caribbean/Central American Action, supported by U.S. corporations and Foreign Service personnel on leave to ameliorate and augment relations with the region. U.S. Peace Corps volunteers are actively involved in the Commonwealth Caribbean, including the tiny island of Anguilla. Among them are agronomists, mechanical engineers, nurses, teacher trainers, veterinarians, food technologists, and many other technical personnel. There were about 160 volunteers in the Eastern Caribbean and 120 in Jamaica in 1985.

A more controversial aspect of U.S. assistance deals with Carter's decision to supply a limited amount of military equipment and training to the area, an action based partly on the assumption that if the United States does not fill the vacuum created by Britain's steady withdrawal through granting independence to the islands, the Cubans will. In Barbados there is a small international military education program for the Coast Guard. The Carter administration requested $5 million in military sales credits for Barbados to purchase communications and navigational equipment, with the view that this would strengthen the entire eastern Caribbean. Smaller military education and training programs were proposed for Jamaica and Guyana, again to eliminate or reduce Cuban activities.

Given the fact that Caribbean leaders knew that the Soviet troops had been in Cuba from the time of the missile crisis, it is not surprising that they did not share Carter's concern for the Soviet brigade in Cuba. In fact, Carter's emphasis on this issue during his reelection campaign against Reagan, who accused him of being soft on communism, dangerously backfired. It demonstrated U.S. inability to dictate Cuban behavior and diminished U.S. credibility. Furthermore, Carter's reaction influenced Jamaica, Guyana, Grenada, and St. Lucia to issue a joint statement critical of Carter's plans for a greater U.S. military presence in the Caribbean. To demonstrate U.S. naval power and visibility, warships made approximately 125 calls in 29 Caribbean ports, and the Voice of America constructed on Antigua in the Eastern Caribbean a transmitter powerful enough to reach all the islands.

The Reagan administration continued to evince serious concern about Cuban-Soviet involvement in the Caribbean—America's "soft underbelly"—a feeling which culminated in the invasion of Grenada. In addition to strident anticommunist rhetoric and bolstering U.S. military might near Cuba and the rest of the Caribbean, the president proposed and Congress approved a broad economic plan for assisting development in the so-called Caribbean Basin. In general, for completely different reasons, Reagan focused attention on Jamaica and Grenada.

Seaga's stunning electoral victory over Manley in October 1980 was greeted in Washington as a defeat for leftism and Cuban-Soviet involvement in Jamaica. Reagan's Caribbean Basin Initiative is an endorsement of Seaga's contention that Cuban-Soviet advances in the Caribbean are directly related to the almost intractable economic difficulties that are undermining political stability throughout the region. Seaga, unlike Manley, advocated private enterprise, increased foreign investment, placed less emphasis on Third World issues, and was militantly anticommunist. As a showcase for Reagan's philosophy of private enterprise, Jamaica received support for a $600 million loan from the IMF. Reagan also appointed a U.S. Business Committee on Jamaica, chaired by David Rockefeller, to encourage foreign investment in Jamaica. The administration's aid request almost doubled to $90 million.[61]

In February 1982, a U.S.-Jamaican Barter agreement that allowed the United States to procure 1.6 million tons of Jamaican bauxite for U.S. strategic stockpiles was concluded in order to stimulate the Jamaican economy. Jamaica, in return for its bauxite, received approximately $39 million in foreign exchange, 7,000 metric tons of nonfat dry milk and 1,900 metric tons of anhydrous milk fat valued at $13 million. This represented the first agricultural barter to acquire strategic raw material in almost 15 years.[62] Despite these efforts, widespread violence against police officers and protests against the Seaga government's inability to improve economic conditions were common problems in 1987.

Grenada experienced a very negative reaction from the Reagan administration from the beginning. The United States attempted to punish Grenada by encouraging European countries to withhold financial support for the Grenadian airport, terminating the existing aid program to Grenada and trying to prevent Grenada from participating in the Caribbean Development Bank. Furthermore, Reagan tried to persuade several Caribbean leaders, including Adams and Seaga, to change the treaty governing the Caribbean Community and Common Market (Caricom) in order to commit its members to the principles of parliamentary democracy and human rights.

In order to demonstrate tolerance for ideological pluralism and Caribbean unity, the Caribbean leaders decided not to significantly amend the treaty and called only for a commitment to the international covenant on economic, social and cultural rights. This should not be construed as an endorsement of Bishop's rule, but rather as an indication that Grenada was regarded as less of a threat by most Caribbean leaders than by Reagan.

In March, 1983, Reagan declared that Grenada was a threat to U.S. security. This statement, made on the opening day of a month long Caribbean exercise by 77 U.S. and allied warships, influenced Bishop to return to Grenada from a nonaligned summit in India. Subsequently, Bishop accused the CIA of plotting to overthrow his regime.[63] By June 7, 1983, there was a step toward improved relations between Grenada and the United States. Bishop was granted a meeting with National Security Advisor William Clark and Deputy Secretary of State Kenneth Dam, due partly to congressional pressure. Developments in Grenada, however, led not only to the demise of the revolution but also to the U.S.-Caribbean invasion on October 25, 1983. Violence and bloodshed in Grenada provided Reagan with an opportunity to confront and contain the perceived communist threat with a minimum number of casualties and guaranteed victory. Grenada was a low-cost foreign policy victory which renewed American patriotism, humiliated Castro, cast doubts on the reliability of the Soviet Union as an ally, served as a warning to left-wing groups throughout the Caribbean and Central America and, perhaps most importantly, diverted attention from the Beirut disaster which resulted, in part, from an inept Mideast policy.

THE INVASION: THE PRICE OF IDEOLOGY

Imprisoned by ideologically-based foreign policies, both Bishop and Reagan contributed to the chaos in Grenada which finally led to the invasion. Reagan continued to punish Grenada even when Bishop took the unprecedented risk of visiting the United States at a time when the moderate faction of the NJM clearly opposed those who wanted to implement a set of undiluted Marxist-Leninist principles in Grenada. Bishop's previous statements against imperialism, his close alliance with Eastern bloc countries, Nicaragua, and Cuba, and his disregard for democracy in Grenada limited his ability to moderate the revolution which was now devouring its architects.

The assassinations of Bishop, other Cabinet members, and a number of civilians served as a catalyst for the close-knit Caribbean states and the United States to act. Bishop, who had been placed under house arrest by Hudson Austin because of displeasure with his departure from the Party line, was rescued by an estimated three thousand Grenadians, forty of whom later died with him. Although it may be convincingly argued that Reagan took advantage of developments in Grenada to implement his invasion plan, there is also significant evidence supporting the view that the initiative was taken by the English-speaking Caribbean States, the majority of which had demonstrated strong opposition to Grenada's leaders' excessive preoccupation with implementing Marxist-Leninist ideology. Not surprisingly, shortly after Bishop's death the 13 members of the Caribbean Community and Common Market, meeting in Trinidad to discuss possible action in Grenada, agreed to reverse a situation they considered threatening to regional peace and security by deciding to sever diplommatic ties, impose economic sanctions, and take military action to restore "normalcy" in Grenada.[64] Eventually, they invoked an unregistered treaty of mutual assistance designed to protect member states (including Grenada) from external threats in order to justify the invasion of Grenada.

Whether the invasion was the most appropriate action is questionable. Labeled a "rescue operation" to prevent a reoccurrence of the Iranian hostage crisis by the Reagan administration, it was opposed by Prime Minister Thatcher and Fidel Castro, both of whom, for different reasons, asked Reagan not to invade after learning that an invasion was underway. The necessity of a "rescue operation" is certainly debatable, especially in light of the fact that on October 22, U.S. and British representatives in St. George's had spoken with Hudson Austin and the newly established provisional military government members and were assured that there was no threat to American medical students attending St. George's medical school. This was confirmed by the administration of the American medical school. Furthermore, they were informed that the students could be evacuated. A day before the invasion, Canada successfully evacuated its nationals without any interference from the new leaders.[65]

Despite earlier restrictions on Grenadians, the curfew was being lifted and there was evidence that the leaders were increasingly isolated at home and ignored by Castro whose friendship with Bishop influenced him to refuse calls for assistance and strongly condemn the assassination. Surrounded by a hostile crowd loyal to Bishop, the leaders of the assassinations were obviously frightened by their own behavior and appeared willing to give Grenadian civilians greater control. It is obvious that the "rescue operation" could have been executed without complete control of Grenada and the stationing of U.S. military personnel on the island until June 1985, two years after the invasion. It took the "rescue force" approximately thirty-six hours after landing to reach a sizable number of Americans. Clearly, using the analogy of the Iran hostage situation was an extreme case of misperception or exaggeration. The Cubans and Grenadians had much time and opportunity to hold Americans in Grenada hostage; they did not.

Concern about Cuban military involvement also seemed distorted in view of the relatively low level of resistance and the fact that the island was under complete American-Caribbean control within four days. Fewer than 500 Cubans were involved, many of them construction workers with only militia training. Castro had apparently instructed the Cubans to take only defensive action. The fact that Army Rangers were "surprised" to find six Soviet-made 23 millimeter automatic anti-aircraft cannons on a ridge overlooking the Point Salines airport where they landed contradicts Reagan's argument that strong Cuban resistance was anticipated.[66]

Intraservice rivalry, poor coordination and communication, surprisingly inadequate intelligence information, and accidents were the major obstacles to invading Grenada and resulted in many unnecessary casualties. Confusion over who should do what emanated from competition for glory between army and navy commanders. The army units were hesitant to call in navy attack planes to suppress Grenadian and Cuban resistance, relying instead on helicopters and gunships which were more vulnerable to being shot down. Lack of advance planning resulted in costly problems. The two squadron commanders, whose job consisted of providing air cover for army and marine ground forces, complained that navy aviators had not previously discussed attack plans, and that once the landing commenced air and ground forces found it difficult to coordinate activities.[67] Under such circumstances there was a very high percentage of mishaps for a relatively simple operation. Three helicopters plowed into each other during an assault on an unoccupied Cuban barracks, killing three soldiers, two marine gunships were shot down; and a soldier was killed by a navy fighter bomber.

Out of approximately 6,400 U.S. military personnel involved in the invasion, twenty of them died, one hundred and fifteen were wounded;

twenty-four Cubans and forty-four Grenadians were killed. Many of the Grenadians died when a mental hospital was accidentally bombed by U.S. planes. Another 337 Grenadians were wounded. There were additional costs. The invasion gave Moscow an opportunity to justify its own invasion of Afghanistan, rightly or wrongly, and rendered it more hypocritical for Washington to denounce Moscow for using force to settle problems in neighboring states. It rekindled the bellicose image of the U.S. throughout Europe, gave South Africa comfort in southern Angola, reminded Latin Americans of gunboat diplomacy and eroded institutional checks in executive branch relations with Congress and the press.

Significantly, the invasion reinforces the dependency psychology common among Grenadians, from which the U.S. will find it extremely difficult to extricate itself. It was this dependency that contributed to the emergence of the New Jewel Movement and its antiimperialist rhetoric as well as its Marxist-Leninist ideology. The almost euphoric 91 percent of Grenadians who supported the invasion expected the richest and most powerful country in the world to build the island's infrastructure and create employment opportunities; in short, to take care of the liberated Grenadians. The new leader, Herbert Blaize, publicly stated that Grenada needed $500 million to ensure economic development and democratic government,[68] far more than the $54 million allocated between 1983 and 1985. Congress is unlikely to appropriate large sums of money for Grenada, given economic and political realities in the United States. This presents a dilemma, especially since the Grenadian economy under Bishop had showed definite signs of improvement.

Under Bishop, the unemployment rate stood at 14 percent; in 1985 it was between 20 and 30 percent. Just before the invasion the IMF —despite strong U.S. opposition—agreed to a standby loan of $14 million for Grenada and did not attach conditions similar to those applied to Jamaica. Between 1978 and 1983 per capita income had risen from $450 to $870.[69] Unless the economy continues to improve, the Grenada invasion will emerge as a serious liability for U.S. foreign policy in the Commonwealth Caribbean and elsewhere. Even before the Grenada invasion much emphasis was placed on the Caribbean Basin Initiative as an instrument of economic development and as a way to simultaneously reduce Soviet-Cuban influence in the region. However, Grenada was excluded as a recipient of economic assistance.

THE CARIBBEAN BASIN INITIATIVE

One of the outstanding features of this program is its broad definition of the Caribbean Basin, which included the Caribbean islands and Central

America. The Caribbean Basin Initiative (CBI) represents a very pragmatic and innovative step toward resolving regional conflicts and protecting U.S. security interests. It demonstrates an awareness of the centrality of economic factors in political stability and the perpetuation of democracy, especially in the Commonwealth Caribbean. President Reagan articulated the seriousness of the economic problems and how they provide opportunities for Cuban-Soviet subversive activities. The CBI is based on the premise that aid must be complemented by trade and investment in order to ensure self-sustained growth of Caribbean economies.

The centerpiece of the CBI is free trade for exports to the United States from Caribbean Basin countries. Although approximately 87 percent of these exports entered U.S. markets prior to CBI, under the Generalized System of Preferences, they covered only a limited range of products—not the wide variety of potential products capable of being produced in the various countries. Under the free-trade arrangement, Caribbean exports will receive duty free treatment for twelve years, allowing new investors to have confidence that their investments would be made under favorable conditions. Excluded from the free-trade concept are textiles and apparel products which are regulated by other international agreements. Noting that this economic proposal was as unprecedented as the current Caribbean crisis, Reagan asserted that such a commitment makes U.S. determination to help its neighbors grow strong unmistakably clear.[70] Simultaneously, new markets for U.S. exports will be created.

This broad objective is supported by the other components of the CBI. In order to attract additional investment in the Caribbean Basin, significant tax incentives are being offered. Recognizing that trade and investments would be more effective if supplemented by economic aid, Reagan asked Congress for $350 million to assist those countries which are particularly devastated economically. Consistent with his free enterprise philosophy, the president indicated that much of the aid would be concentrated on the private sector. Technical assistance and training are included to enable the private sector to benefit from opportunities provided by the program. Both the business community and the Peace Corps would actively participate in developing local enterprise. Another aspect of CBI is cooperation with Mexico, Canada, and Venezuela and the encouragement of increased assistance to the region from European allies, Japan, and multilateral development institutions. Finally, the CBI emphasizes the necessity of military assistance.

The shift from an economic to a military emphasis is predicated on the assumption that if prompt and decisive action is not taken in defense of freedom, new Cubas will emerge from the ruins of current conflicts, and that free and peaceful development requires the U.S. to help governments confronted by external aggression. Based on this assessment, the president requested increased security assistance "to help friendly countries hold off those who would destroy their chances for economic and social progress and political democracy."[71]

Of the additional $350 million in economic aid most went to El Salvador ($75 million), Costa Rica ($70 million), Jamaica ($50 million), the Dominican Republic ($40 million), Honduras ($35 million), Belize ($10 million), Haiti ($5 million), and the Caribbean ministates ($10 million). This uneven distribution has been widely criticized. Several congressional committees and members of Congress asserted that the CBI represented an attempt by the administration to secure additional aid to El Salvador at a time when regular foreign and military aid for it was challenged by strong opposition in Congress. In light of this, Congress voted to prevent any one country from receiving more than $75 million and insisted that one-fourth of the funds be allocated to traditional economic development purposes such as health, education, and infrastructures.[72]

In relation to the Commonwealth Caribbean, a major criticism of CBI is that Jamaica has been singled out for favored treatment, a development which could result in the alienation of smaller Eastern Caribbean islands. The tax deduction for attending meetings and conventions is regarded as being less favorable to the smaller islands whose economic survival depends to a large extent on tourism. Given the nature of the investment package proposed by Reagan, they also argued that larger islands with greater productive capacity would attract industry. Several of the islands lack the infrastructure—roads, electricity and water—to encourage the private development which is the cornerstone of the program. Expectedly, Seaga praised CBI, citing Jamaica as an example of what it could accomplish. He saw it as "a new window of opportunity for hard-pressed Caribbean countries to create the new employment and improved standards of living which are essential to all democratic systems of government."[73] Although CBI will assist in this endeavor, its emphasis on the private sector may discourage the development of the infrastructure essential to private sector activities. Furthermore, by providing a credit for new investments in plants and equipment, it encourages capital-intensive investment desperately needed by an overpopulated region. Because CBI rewards friendly governments, and initially punished Grenada, instead of promoting regional economic integration, it could contribute to further intra-Caribbean competition and polarization. This deficiency is partly due to an underlying flaw in CBI; namely, the Reagan administration's preoccupation with anticommunism and Cuban expansionism in Central America and the Caribbean.

A careful reading of the President's CBI speech reveals that anticommunism is the basis of U.S. foreign policy in the Caribbean. An East-West focus distorts many aspects of the CBI, including the concept itself, the Caribbean Basin concept distorts reality by lumping the Caribbean islands and Central American countries together. The Caribbean islands have established democratic traditions and political institutions which manage the allocation of values and the transfer of political power, whereas Central America's experience is with military rule and civil wars. The islands are very closely tied to the United States through extensive economic, cultural, and demographic interaction. They share historical relationships with the United States and Western Europe that differ significantly from those in Central America.

The Caribbean Basin is a politically expedient concept that allows aid to be channelled to Central American countries, El Salvador in particular, to be used against insurgent activities supported by Cuba. Perhaps even more disturbing is the fact that the very nature of the U.S. political system may make it almost impossible to secure the necessary resources for Commonwealth Caribbean development without stressing threats to U.S. security.[74] Therefore, anticommunist rhetoric is a convenient method utilized by countries seeking aid and those in Congress and the administration wanting to grant it. Extending this strategy to the Commonwealth Caribbean sets a dangerous precedent, and may ultimately destroy democracy by allowing leaders to stifle opposition in the name of anticommunism.

Some of the positive aspects of CBI encountered opposition. Representatives from Hawaii and Puerto Rico expressed concern that the duty-free treatment of Caribbean imports and encouragement of exports to the United States could adversely affect sugar and pineapple sales. Domestic sugar producers voiced similar concern. Most Commonwealth Caribbean countries exported sugar to the U.S. duty free prior to CBI under the generalized system of preferences. Furthermore, there is a complex web of legislation to protect domestic sugar producers. With declining sugar consumption in the United States, sugar imports have been dropping steadily, from approximately five milion tons in 1981 to three million tons in 1982. In May 1982, Reagan raised the domestic price of sugar by establishing a global quota system with no preference for the so-called Caribbean Basin. This action reduced the amount of sugar Caribbean countries could sell to the United States by about one-third, rendering many sugar producers considerably poorer than before CBI.[75]

The investment component of CBI was challenged by Puerto Rico. According to Hernandez-Colon, the departure of old industries from Puerto Rico outpaces the opening of new ones, thereby creating a net loss of jobs and a 5 percent decline in real investment per year.[76] High unemployment, hovering around 22 percent and federal budget reductions combine to make Puerto Rico vulnerable to CBI-related industrial development in the Caribbean countries. As far as Puerto Rico is concerned, CBI translates into increased competition for U.S. markets. Arguing against CBI, Hernandez-Colon contends that Marxist-Leninist groups have had only minimal success because of Puerto Rico's economic growth and stability. However, if CBI's effects are added to current problems, that country will also undergo social upheavals that will provide opportunities for the advocates of violent change.[77] Despite opposition from various groups, Congress approved a scale-down version of the trade portion of the president's proposed CBI as well as $350 million in aid. The tax proposals designed to stimulate investments have not been considered. Despite its negative aspects, the CBI is a positive beginning toward addressing the serious economic problems in the Commonwealth Caribbean, Jamaica in particular, which undermine democratic practice as well as U.S. regional and global security interests. It demonstrates an awareness of the relationship between Caribbean economic viability and U.S. national interests.

Unlike Central America, the Commonwealth Caribbean conflict is relatively nonviolent and primarily concerned with economic change and development. Of the four so-called "mutually supportive elements" upon which U.S. policy toward the Caribbean and Central America is based only one is really applicable to the Commonwealth Caribbean: addressing on an urgent basis the economic and social problems of the region by providing economic assistance to stimulate growth, create opportunity, and improve the quality of life for the people. The other three, assisting in the development of democratic institutions, providing security assistance to enable countries to defend themselves against the Soviet bloc and Cuba, and promoting peaceful solutions through negotiations, are perhaps more appropriate for Central America.[78]

Soviet-Cuban penetration in Jamaica and Grenada seemed to be largely due to the islands' frustrations over the economic system most appropriate for the mobilization of human and material resources. As Grenada shows, failure to deal with this reality and projecting American fear of communism onto developments in a region where U.S. interests are most secure and easily protected, is costly and dangerous. When the United States is preoccupied with Soviet-Cuban activities it loses sight of the economic and social problems with which Caribbean leaders are preoccupied and misses opportunities to remove the conditions conducive to outside intervention. The emphasis on the status quo rather than controlled change is ultimately harmful to U.S. interests in the Commonwealth Caribbean.

Toward a Pragmatic U.S. Policy

Exercise the Economic Option. The key challenge to the Commonwealth Caribbean and U.S. interests there is not Cuban-Soviet activities, but rather the ability of governments to provide a decent livelihood for their citizens. Seaga's victory in Jamaica, the invasion of Grenada, and Herbert Blaize's electoral landslide have not altered this reality. In both cases the Cubans were sent home, albeit under different circumstances, but unemployment remains dangerously high, especially in Jamaica.

Available evidence suggests that despite CBI the economic crisis in Jamaica, a major target of the program, is likely to deteriorate. Although approximately 7,000 jobs were created in the Jamaican garment industry and winter vegetable production increased significantly, the overall economy declined. By 1985, the bauxite industry, the island's main source of foreign exchange, was only half of what it was in the 1970s.[79]

Overall results of the CBI were disappointing. Expectations were not matched by performance because interest in the region declined following Cuba's departure from Grenada and Jamaica. Tax incentives designed to attract private investment to the Caribbean were cut and economic assistance reduced. Furthermore, restrictive quotas on sugar were imposed in 1985, throwing about 100,000 Caribbean Laborers out of work.[80] The General Accounting Office estimated that CBI county exports actually decreased by 19 percent from 1984 to 1985. Only the Eastern Caribbean states with the smallest economies showed an improvement. Between 1983 and 1985 their exports to the U.S. rose 19 percent.[82] There is obviously a need for significant increases in U.S. economic assistance, greater incentives for companies to invest, and the removal of trade barriers.

The invasion and its aftermath show that economic assistance is the most effective and least costly long-term solution to Commonwealth Caribbean problems. A major step toward economic development is the improvement of the islands' infrastructure. Much of the money allocated to Grenada between 1983 and 1987 was spent on repairing roads, improving electric and water utilities, and finishing the airport. Foreign investment will not be attracted to an island without good transportation and communications systems.

In the process of encouraging foreign investment, the interests of Caribbean people must take precedence over those of foreign investors. In this connection, appropriate technology should be provided and emphasis placed on labor-intensive industries to reduce high levels of unemployment. A significant decline in population growth should be an integral component of economic development programs.

The Peace Corps is the Most Effective Army in the Struggle against Poverty. Because of the small size of the islands and their close cultural, economic, political, geographic, and demographic ties with the United States, Peace Corp volunteers can be extremely effective. Greater use should be made of U.S. specialists in areas such as tropical agriculture, solar energy, and general health care. American students should be encouraged to participate in work-study programs in the Caribbean and summer programs for Caribbean students should be implemented. This exchange could prove invaluable not only for economic development, but also in augmenting U.S.-Caribbean relations at the grassroots level. Cuba's successful use of technical and medical personnel in both Grenada and Jamaica is illustrative of the positive impact that providing assistance in such areas as health, construction, and agriculture has on individual citizens. Instead of pointing out how many Grenadians or Jamaicans are studying in Cuba, the United States should do more to encourage West Indians and Americans to engage in cooperative endeavors.

Support Regional Economic Integration. One of the most effective ways of reducing poverty is to eliminate duplication of products and economic competition among the islands. Rather than excluding islands because of their ideology and attempting to divide the region, efforts should be made to construct bridges among the islands. Accomplishing this goal should not be difficult in light of serious efforts by Caribbean leaders to unify the region economically, monetarily, and politically. Countries which are interdependent obviously find it more problematic to ignore the views of those with whom they interact.

Involve Caribbean Governments as Partners. The Grenada invasion was widely supported by Caribbean people not only because of their revulsion at the assassinations but also because the United States included them in the invasion plans. Although their people may be poor by U.S. standards, Caribbean leaders are extremely sophisticated and politically independent. It is therefore wise for American foreign policymakers to enlist their views and suggestions on how to address their problems. The United States must be sensitive to the desire of Caribbean governments to remain in control of their economic policies. Too great a U.S. influence is likely to lead to increased Caribbean nationalism.

Try to Understand Caribbean Reality. An effective U.S. policy is also dependent on the realization that Caribbean states are generally considered part of the so-called Third World and, as such, their interests do not always coincide with U.S. interests. The United States should therefore respect their relative independence, in light of the reality that the islands are inextricably linked to it. Caribbean nationalism, leftism, and nonalignment are not primarily communist-inspired developments but emanate from domestic weaknesses and a desire to reduce economic and psychological dependency.

Deemphasize the East-West Rivalry in the Caribbean. To diminish the real or perceived dangers of the Soviet-Cuban activities the distinctiveness of the Commonwealth Caribbean should be recognized. For example, linking the Caribbean to Central America to support the view that U.S. security interests are threatened in the former is politically expedient, and dangerous. As a careful reading of the Grenada Papers reveals, Grenada attempted to take advantage of Soviet-American rivalry. Similary, Seaga's focus on Cuban activities is an effective short-range strategy for getting U.S. attention, but dangerous to Caribbean stability in the long run. Rather than stressing the communist threat, the strong, deeply-rooted democratic institutions should be highlighted. Seaga's victory in Jamaica is evidence of democracy, not a victory over communism. In other words, emphasize the positive aspects of Caribbean societies.

Coordinate Policies with Canada. Canada enjoys much influence in the Commonwealth Caribbean because of its association with Britain. Many West Indians live in Canada, further cementing Canadian-Caribbean ties. Where there is a genuine threat to U.S.-Caribbean interests Canada may be in an excellent position to work with the United States to diffuse that threat.

Exercise the Diplomatic Option. Military solutions are generally costly to all involved and the price continues to be paid long after the actual operation ends. Military threats force others to make military preparations to respond to them, as evidenced by developments in Grenada prior to the invasion. Under such circumstances, the Soviets and Cubans are given a greater opportunity to increase their influence in countries which perceive themselves as extremely vulnerable in the face of U.S. military might. American foreign policymakers must be more confident that U.S. military presence in the region is sufficient to defend both Caribbean and U.S. interests against external threats. Grenada demonstrated that neither the Soviets nor Cubans will engage in direct confrontations with the United States in the Caribbean. Consequently, a general demilitarization of the region is a low-cost strategy for protecting U.S. interests.

Talk with Castro. Finally, the U.S. must move in the direction of safe-guarding its interests by reducing Soviet influence in Cuba itself. A less emotional approach to Cuba, increased communication, and providing Cuba with options that will eventually lessen its dependence on the Soviet Union should be hallmarks of U.S. policy. The Cuban-Soviet alliance should not be regarded as unchangeable or one that excludes improved U.S.-Cuban relations. Attempts to isolate Cuba will be generally unsuccessful in the Commonwealth Caribbean because of a long tradition of toleration of differences in a region characterized by unusual cultural and political diversity. Establishing diplomatic ties with Cuba would give the United States a better chance of influencing Cuba as well as reduce opportunities for groups such as the New Jewel Movement to exploit Cuban-American antagonism.

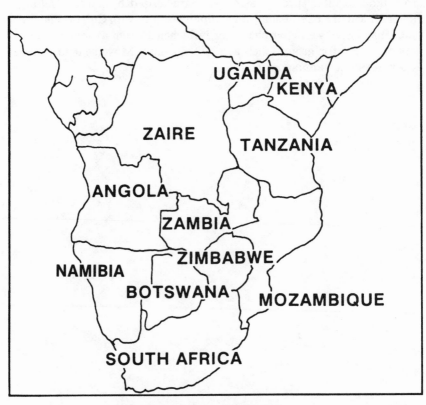

SOUTHERN AFRICA

6

Southern Africa: Focus on the Problems, Not Moscow

An anticommunist confrontationist U.S. policy in southern Africa is essentially self-defeating and inadvertently beneficial to the Soviet Union. By focusing on communist expansionism rather than the conditions which are conducive to Soviet-Cuban involvement in southern Africa, we run the danger of escalating the conflict and contributing to the continuing cycle of violence which is ideal for the accomplishment of Soviet objectives and detrimental to U.S. interests not only in southern Africa but elsewhere on the continent and throughout the world. It is increasingly obvious that the Soviets clearly benefit from violent conflicts in the Third World, whereas peaceful solutions are generally beneficial to the United States.

Southern Africa in general, and South Africa in particular, provide the Soviets with what could be considered a unique opportunity to force the United States onto the side of minority rule and racial segregation and against its own fundamental principles of human rights and individual freedom. Several factors combine to make developments in southern Africa ideal for the advancement of Soviet foreign policy objectives and disadvantageous to U.S. interests if the conventional East-West approach is applied to the region.

Perhaps the most important factor contributing to Soviet success is, paradoxically, South Africa's extremely broad definition of communism. The Communism Act of 1950 actually includes any protest against apartheid or attempts to bring about sociopolitical and economic change by promoting disorder or encouraging hostilities between the white minority and the overwhelming nonwhite majority. Since changing apartheid is viewed as communism, by being against communism in southern Africa, the United States is perceived as supportive of apartheid. Ironically, the Soviets and communism are thus viewed as opponents of apartheid and champions of social, political, and economic justice. Rather than being a bulwark against communism, South Africa encourages communism. Furthermore, within both the African and international context, the problem of racial supremacy assumes special importance. As Hedley Bull put it:

> It is a political fact that opposition to oppression of blacks by whites unites the world in a way in which other violations of human rights, including other kinds of racial oppression, do not. There is not a world consensus against communist oppression, or of one Asian or African group by another, comparable to that which exists against this surviving symbol of a white supremacism that all other societies of the world, to different degrees and in different ways, have repudiated over the last three decades.[1]

By assisting groups challenging apartheid, the Soviet Union is supported by world public opinion, including that of the general public in the United States.

Another factor favoring the Soviets is the extent to which conditions in South Africa fit Soviet perceptions of U.S. policy in the Third World. Moscow's basic argument is that the United States is determined to crush any political threat to "American monopoly capital" and that by preserving its influence, Washington is attempting to guarantee its continued access to raw materials, inexpensive labor, and to maintain strategic strongholds for the struggle against socialism and the liberation movements.[2] U.S. support for South Africa demonstrates, in the Soviet view, that human rights and individual freedoms are secondary to the protection of business interests. Unfortunately, this position is widely supported throughout Africa and around the world.

Finally, the general economic and political instability in southern Africa provides opportunities for Soviet involvement. It is generally agreed that poor economic performance renders even the most democratically inclined governments vulnerable to instability which, in turn, influences them to adopt harsh measures to prevent violence, an endeavor which may eventually take precedence over economic development. This situation presents an opportunity for Moscow to offer military aid, especially if the particular African government fails to get assistance from the United States or Western European countries.

Similarly, when liberation movements are unable to obtain Western support, they generally appeal to anti-Western forces for military, economic, and political backing.[3]

SOVIET OBJECTIVES IN SOUTHERN AFRICA

Historically, the Soviet Union has advocated ending colonialism in Asia and Africa and is committed to supporting liberation movements fighting colonial governments. Following World War II, European colonial powers relinquished control over their Asian and African possessions in an orderly manner, with only few exceptions. By providing for a peaceful transition from colonial rule to independence, European powers removed opportunities for prolonged Soviet involvement with liberation groups. However, in southern Africa, given the intractability of minority rule and its association with capitalism, the Soviet policy of Marxism-Leninism still makes sense; and the Soviets, it is argued, are the natural ally of the oppressed.[4] By clearly identifying with anticolonial groups, Moscow's objective is to expand its influence in southern Africa. Other motives that have been advanced for Soviet interest in southern Africa include the following: 1. diverting U.S. attention from more important areas, such as the Middle East and the war in Afghanistan; 2. the eventual elimination of both Chinese and U.S. competition; 3. weakening Western economic and political influence in the region; 4. staking out a role for itself in the ultimate outcome of racial conflict in South Africa, thereby reinforcing its claims to status as a global power; and 5. access to strategic minerals. Not only is Moscow attempting to deny the West access to minerals critical to its security, but also to reduce southern Africa's competition with the Soviet Union for supplying various minerals. Another related argument is that the Soviet Union is seeking to procure additional supplies of minerals to meet rising demands by Eastern bloc countries.[5]

Despite the fact that conditions in southern Africa are conducive to the achievement of Soviet objectives, several factors combine to limit long-term, permanent Soviet influence there. Among them are African nationalism, the instability which characterizes many African governments, a general commitment to nonalignment in foreign policy, black consciousness, the social, religious, and eclectic political values of Africans, and the serious inability of the Soviet Union to make a significant contribution to southern Africa's economic development.

The importance of African nationalism is underestimated by the United States as well as the Soviet Union. Both countries appear to be operating on misperceptions of African realities. For example, the

Soviets may be blinded by their Leninist ideology which oversimplifies world developments and assumes that communism will grow in Africa, overlooking that nationalism is much too strong to allow either the East or West to dominate African politics. Alliances with the Soviet Union have generally been transient, primarily because they are intended to achieve essentially short-term objectives. Although African countries welcome assistance from both East and West in pursuit of their national interests, it is inconceivable that they would deliberately allow Soviets and Cubans to establish a new form of colonialism. Historical evidence and current trends in Angola, Mozambique, and Zimbabwe indicate that a return to colonialism or external domination is unlikely. Although there is a tendency to overemphasize the extent to which a major world power, either the Soviet Union or the United States, can exercise meaningful control over countries not contiguous to its own military area,[6] the Soviets will have some impact on the politics of those countries in which they are involved.

Soviet-Cuban gains in Africa may be limited by the internal dynamism which characterizes African politics. The relative instability of African governments means that permanent gains by outside powers are not easily achieved. In Angola, for example, Soviet-Cuban support is needed just to keep the MPLA in power. Assuming that UNITA should manage to weaken the existing regime significantly and later on gain control over the country, gains made by the Soviets and Cubans would be diminished, but not totally eliminated. Soviet-supported groups within these countries, though not in control, could pose serious threats to their economic and political stability.

Another limitation on the ability of the Soviets to have a significant amount of influence in southern Africa is their "innate racism." Unlike the United States, the Soviet Union does not have black issues and is therefore more inclined to be less sensitive in the area of race-relations. Africans who have studied in Moscow and worked with Soviet military advisers resent the Soviets' racist attitudes. Like nationalism, racism is a widespread concern among Africans. This difficulty has been partly avoided through widespread use of Cuban troops and advisers in Angola. Although President Carter charged the Soviets with racism, little attention was given to how it will eventually be a hindrance to them in southern Africa.

Perhaps the most important obstacle to continued significant Soviet influence in Africa is its inability and unwillingness to play a significant role in economic development. Western technology is far superior to what the Soviets have to offer, and private multinational corporations provide access to technology, capital, managerial know-how, markets, etc. Africans realize that although the Soviet Union has made tremendous economic gains since 1917, they cannot solve many basic economic problems confronting them today. Their agricultural productivity is far behind that of the United States, and the distribution and availability of consumer goods continue to be a problem. The recent crisis in Poland, the fundamental cause of which was the inability of communism to provide enough food, further underlined this weakness. As Adelman observed, the Soviets have serious handicaps that limit their effectiveness in Africa during quiet times. They have little to offer except weapons and military advisors. No African development official wants to emulate the Soviet economic system.[7] But the issue in southern Africa is minority rule and oppression. As Angola demonstrates, U.S. ties with South Africa and excessive concern with communism provided the Soviets an ideal opportunity to be portrayed as champions of freedom pursuing policies consistent with African aspirations, struggles for human dignity, and the general principles of the Organization of African Unity (OAU). In Angola Moscow's policy of not resisting change worked. Because Moscow does not have any overt economic or political ties with the South African white supremacist regime or stake in its survival, it has little to lose by backing movements advocating change and much to gain by forcing the United States to take the position of an ally of racial and political oppression.

SOVIET-CUBAN ACTIVITIES IN ANGOLA: LESSONS FOR WASHINGTON

Prior to the unprecedented massive Soviet-Cuban military assistance to the Popular Movement for the Liberation of Angola in 1975, the Cubans pursued what was clearly an independent African foreign policy. Although there has obviously been a convergence of Soviet and Cuban policies toward Angola, it is important to distinguish early Cuban involvement in Angola from developments in 1974 and subsequently.

The first significant interaction between Cuba and Africa was in March, 1959, when representatives of the Algerian National Liberation Front stopped in Havana to congratulate Castro shortly after he assumed power. As an indication of its commitment to Third World countries, and a reaffirmation of its own independence, Cuba sent Che Guevara to confer with Nasser in Cairo. By 1962 Castro and Algeria's Ben Bella had agreed to establish more formal relations. Cuba provided approximately fifty physicians to assist Algerians.[8] In return, Castro obtained much needed recognition as an independent actor in foreign policy, as well as political leverage *vis-a-vis* both Washington and Moscow following his humiliation during the October 1962 missile crisis when Khrushchev withdrew the missiles without consulting him. Cuba's African policy developed precisely because of Castro's desire to demonstrate Cuba's independence. As Halperin pointed out, an active African role would repair his injured pride, demonstrate his renewed determination to conduct his own foreign policy, interfere with U.S. interests outside the Western Hemisphere, and help to develop his bargaining power with the Soviets.[9]

Indeed, rather than being an integral part of the Soviet Union's global strategy, as is generally assumed, Cuba's southern African policy emerged precisely because of Castro's distrust of the Soviets, fear of the United States, and his commitment to African liberation movements; all three were interrelated. Che Guevara visited southern Africa in 1964, and Cuba became militarily involved in the Congo Crisis on behalf of Tshombe who was later overthrown by Mobutu in November, 1965. Subsequently, Cuba's Congolese allies asked the Cubans to leave so that they could negotiate a peaceful settlement of the civil war with the new regime. Although Che Guevara left for Bolivia, where he later died, many of his troops remained in Africa as military advisors to the MPLA in particular.[10] In addition to his genuine concern about colonialism, Castro had other reasons for being involved in southern Africa. Soviet-American relations had improved to the point where Moscow and Washington agreed on peaceful coexistence, at a time when the United States expressed overt hostility toward Cuba. The growing Sino-Soviet schism shattered the unity of the socialist camp which Castro regarded as essential for Cuban security. Furthermore, when escalating U.S. bombing raids in Vietnam in 1964 did not meet with Soviet or Chinese retaliation, Castro concluded that neither the Soviet commitment to defend Cuba nor the rhetoric of Marxist-Leninist international solidarity was sufficient guarantee against military attack.[11] Solidarity with the Third World became increasingly important for Cuba.

Although the Soviets had competed with the United States for influence in Africa during the first half of the 1960s, by 1966 there was clearly a shift in Soviet policy away from supporting liberation movements and greater emphasis on geopolitical considerations to safeguard Soviet security interests in Iran, Turkey, and India. The intensity of commitment to Africa by both Moscow and Havana was indicated by their different reactions to setbacks there. After an unsuccessful effort in the Belgian Congo and the fall of Kwame Nkrumah of Ghana in 1966, the Soviets saw little hope of any significant revolutionary transformation in Africa and decided to give the area lower priority. Cuba, on the other hand, responded to the downfall of Ben Bella and Nkrumah by supplying military missions to friendly countries to protect the regimes against coups d'etat. The provision of palace guards marked a new development in Cuba's African policy.[12] For approximately eight years this divergence between Soviet and Cuban policies remained. Two developments in 1974 contributed to their coordination of policies in Angola: increased Chinese support for the rival National Front for the Liberation of Angola (NFLA) and the U.S. decision to commence arms shipments to the NFLA through Zaire.[13] Prior to 1974, the United States had paid very little attention to Cuba's involvement in Angola.

American policy toward southern Africa was intertwined with its relationship toward its European allies. Other areas, such as Southeast Asia and the Middle East, became priorities of U.S. foreign policy while African aspirations and problems were relegated to the bottom of the list because Africa was omitted from the balance-of-power equation.

U.S. indifference—and sometimes hostile opposition—to African liberation movements has been shaped by its overriding concern with communism and its alliance with Western Europe rather than the value of majority rule. For example, concern over landing rights in the Portuguese Azores influenced the U.S. position on the liberation struggles in Angola and Mozambique. The now infamous National Security Council Memorandum 39 clearly indicated a dramatic shift away from the Kennedy-Johnson concern for a gradual peaceful transition to majority rule in southern Africa to intensified de facto support for continued white domination. The memorandum stated that the liberation groups were ineffective and, as a consequence, white minority governments were entrenched for the foreseeable future. Therefore, accommodation was sought with the minority governments in Zimbabwe (Rhodesia), Mozambique, Angola, and South Africa in order to foster political stability, economic security, and above all, the strategic balance of power.[14] The strength of the liberation movements and widespread African support for them were seriously underestimated, and Washington sought to maintain the equilibrium by supporting the status quo. By so doing, U.S. policy was consistent with its perception of developments in southern Africa in terms of superpower rivalry. Change was viewed as beneficial to the Soviet Union. Consequently, U.S. counterrevolutionary strategy inevitably corresponded to that of South Africa and inadvertently assisted Soviet-Cuban success in Angola.[15]

Preoccupation with the balance of power between East and West influenced Washington to regard Angola as a battleground between communism and anticommunism, rather than a struggle for independence which had enlisted an assortment of external powers in support of three rival groups which spent more time fighting each other than they did fighting the Portuguese. This complex, three-sided affair was reduced into a simplisitc East-West confrontation by Washington. The MPLA, labeled pro-Soviet, was assisted by Moscow, Cuba, Yugoslavia, Sweden,

Denmark and Nigeria; the NFLA and UNITA (The National Union for the Total Independence of Angola), seen as pro-Western, were actually supported by the United States, China, Zaire, North Korea, Rumania, and India.[16] These ideological designations may have been the major impediments to a negotiated settlement of the Angolan civil war and key contributors to increased violence which ultimately worked to the advantage of the Soviet Union.

The United States and the Soviet Union had an opportunity at the inchoate stages of the Angolan conflict to agree on a mutually acceptable formula for arranging a transition from Portuguese control to independence. The formula was the coalition government, the People's Republic of Angola, comprising UNITA, NFLA, and the MPLA. The OAU had succeeded in pressuring the leaders of the three groups, Neto (MPLA), Roberto (NFLA) and Savimbi (UNITA), to meet in Portugal to negotiate a peaceful settlement. The negotiations resulted in the Alvor Agreements which endorsed the tripartite transitional government, called for a single national party, and set November 11, 1975 as the date for Angolan independence.[17] Both the Soviet Union and the United States, in pursuit of their own particular objectives, were partly responsible for the demise of the Alvor Agreements and the internationalization of the conflict. While the Soviet Union encouraged recognition of the People's Republic of Angola (PRA) and supported the Alvor Agreements, its support of the MPLA indicated that it was deliberately sending out contradictory signals simultaneously in order to play both sides of the fence. The Soviet naval force sailing for Angola was clearly a signal to pro-MPLA hardliners that they could be assured of continued Soviet military assistance.[18] In the meantime, Washington responded in a perfunctory, lukewarm manner to the Alvor Agreements after having tried to discourage Savimbi from participation in the conference which formulated them. The CIA not only rejected the possibility of a negotiated settlement but after Savimbi had ignored CIA pressure not to attend the meeting, the CIA made clear to Savimbi that the U.S. wanted no soft allies in its war against the MPLA. This policy of making life difficult for the Soviets boomeranged.[19] Washington's refusal to work with the MPLA and its decision to close the U.S. consulate, which had been guarded by the MPLA, narrowed the options available to that group. According to Klinghoffer:

> The MPLA itself recognized that an opening to the United States would give it greater freedom of action *vis-a-vis* the Soviets, and it sent a message to Kissinger which indicated that PRA welcomed talks with American representatives and did not insist on diplomatic recognition as a precondition.[20]

American policymakers' emphasis on a military solution together with the OAU's failure to provide peacekeeping forces and to present a unified position against external involvement created opportunities for the Soviets to escalate military supplies to the MPLA.

Available evidence suggests that the Soviet Union reluctantly became deeply involved in the Angolan conflict and that its decision to do so was strongly influenced by Cuba's commitment to Neto in particular and the MPLA in general. According to Bender, Moscow actually dropped all support for the MPLA one month before the April 1974 coup in Portugal and continued to withhold aid for approximately seven months.[21] Only in March 1975, following an attack by the US and Chinese-backed FNLA on an MPLA training camp at Caxito in which sixty MPLA activists were killed, did the Soviets begin significant arms shipments to the MPLA.[22] There is no evidence to support the view that Cuba and the Soviet Union suddenly escalated their military activities in Angola or that Cuba was a Soviet proxy.[23] Indeed, it is quite clear that Moscow responded to Havana's need for military assistance in order to protect the MPLA from South African forces.

As the FNLA escalated its attacks on the MPLA in March 1975, Neto turned to Castro for military aid, and about 250 Cuban military advisers were sent. When the MPLA later requested military specialists from Moscow, the Soviets advised that they call on Cuba again. While the Soviets were sympathetic, they were unwilling to become directly involved, and had hoped that a compromise could be reached between UNITA and the MPLA and the FNLA.[24] In the struggle for Luanda, UNITA and the FNLA were joined by Portuguese Angolans, Zairians, European, and American mercenaries, and approximately 6,000 South African troops. Cuba responded with Operation Carlotta, which involved a large scale infusion of Cuban troops.[25] This operation was a Cuban initiative, with Cuba providing ships and aircraft. It was only after the United States convinced Barbados and other Caribbean islands not to allow Cuban transfer flights that the Soviet Union supplied Cuba with longer-range IL-62 aircraft, and in January 1976 began a direct airlift of Cuban troops.[26]

It is estimated that 150,000 tons of military equipment were supplied by Moscow in the final stages of the Angolan conflict. Included were automatic weapons, ammunition, explosives, armored personnel carriers, anti-aircraft guns, mortars, rockets and ground-to-air missiles. This exceeded by far the scale of any previous Soviet assistance to an African liberation movement. Furthermore, there was the unprecedented Cuban military involvement. Eventually, approximately 25,000 Cuban troops were flown to Angola to fight with the MPLA and protect the new regime from the UNITA and FLNA.[27]

Several reasons can be advanced for this massive military involvement. First, the Soviets perceived the Chinese as serious competition for influence in southern Africa. Second, the Soviets were sensitive to charges of inaction or indifference to attacks on a progressive, Marxist National Liberation Movement.[28] Third, Moscow viewed Zaire, South Africa, and the United States as collaborators in an attempt to prevent decolonization of the region in order to protect capitalism and perpetuate minority rule in South Africa. South Africa's decision to use its helicopter gunships and armored units to take Luanda was seen as part of an American plan, especially after "high officials in Pretoria claimed that their intervention was based on an understanding with the United States."[29] Cuba and the Soviet Union had taken a greater number of factors into consideration. The United States was only one of them. Because of Kissinger's perception of the conflicts as communists versus anticommunists, he unwittingly involved the United States in what was primarily Sino-Soviet competition for leadership of Third World socialist regimes.

U.S. policy toward Angola was characterized by confusion, inconsistency and expediency. Initially, American policymakers supported Portuguese colonial rule. Later, in light of Soviet-Cuban backing of the MPLA, that policy shifted to support of the FNLA and UNITA, assuming that they would eventually defeat the much smaller MPLA. In addition to the possible Soviet-Cuban military escalation, the United States overlooked the obvious cooperation between the MPLA and Gulf Oil, a U.S. corporation which was paying huge royalties of approximately $125 million to protect its investments. It also underestimated the damage any perceived alliance would cost the FNLA, UNITA, and how much it would contribute to MPLA success by legitimizing Soviet-Cuban involvement and galvanizing African support against both South Africa and the United States. Rather than hurting the Soviets, South African troops in Angola resulted in a tremendous diplomatic and military victory for the Soviets. Soviet credibility as an ally of liberation movements was consolidated. While previously expressing opposition to Soviet interference in Angola, African states dramatically shifted because, in their view, Soviet involvement was preferable to the extension of white minority rule, symbolized by South Africa's entry into the conflict. The South African factor further reduced U.S. effectiveness in mobilizing world opinion and domestic support against Moscow. Kissinger's efforts to secure additional covert aid for UNITA and FNLA met with strong resistance from the Senate partly because of a certain degree of post-Vietnam paralysis and, more importantly, alliance with South Africa could only further strain relations with black African countries. Nigeria, for example, then the second largest supplier of oil to the U.S., was clearly vehemently opposed to U.S. participation in Angola.[30]

Having misread Soviet-Cuban commitment to the liberation movements, strong African feelings on the racism practiced by South Africa, and U.S. reluctance to actively oppose communism after the traumatic experiences of Vietnam and Watergate, Kissinger eventually decided to modify U.S. objectives in Angola and to apply diplomatic pressure on the Soviets to achieve their compliance in a compromise settlement. The leverage that would be instrumental in accomplishing this, namely $28 million to anti-MPLA forces, was denied by Congress in the Clark Amendment. As George suggests, Kissinger's belated effort to convert the competitive game, which he had lost, into a cooperative U.S.-Soviet solution came too late. As a result, the Ford administration needlessly suffered a humiliating setback in Angola.[31] Not only was U.S. credibility further shattered and its position as a global power seriously eroded, but its indecisiveness and awkward approach to Angola paved the way for increased Soviet-Cuban involvement in Ethiopia.

Perhaps the key lesson of Angola is that an anticommunist reaction which fails to take into consideration the interests and aspirations of countries in the immediate region and overlooks the nature of the conflict will inadvertently assist Soviet policy objectives at the expense of U.S. prestige and influence. By focusing on the problems instead of ideology, U.S. policy toward southern Africa could be less costly and increasingly effective. Although Angola is important, the major challenge for American policymakers is in relation to South Africa's occupation of Namibia and its pervasive apartheid laws. Escalating violence in South Africa and the white regime's militaristic policy toward black South Africans and neighboring states are conducive to Soviet involvement.

SOUTH AFRICA AGAINST ITSELF

What distinguishes South Africa from the vast majority of modern nation-states is its fervent commitment to the perpetuation of a racially segregated society dominated by a white oligarchy comprising approximately 14 percent of the total population. Rather than being imaginative in its search for accommodation and compromise that would safeguard the basic rights of all South Africans, the government continues essentially to redecorate the anachronistic system of apartheid at a time when the various race groups are obviously interdependent and in a world in which racism is rejected as an abhorrent abnormality. Rotberg accurately contends that no country in history has so recklessly risked its own survival for political premises that can only be perpetuated against enormous demographic, social, and economic odds.[32] As the external environment becomes increasingly inhospitable to apartheid, domestic conditions conspire to undermine racial domination. Due to skilled labor shortages in a growing economy, more blacks are being trained for skilled jobs previously monopolized by whites. As has always been the case, blacks supply labor for the mines, are domestic servants in white homes, work on white farms, and are employed in menial jobs throughout society.

In less than fifteen years, South Africa will have about 50 million people, 37 million of whom will be black, compared to only 6 million whites. Blacks currently outnumber whites two to one in cities which, theoretically, are white preserves. By the year 2000 blacks will be four times as numerous as whites.[33] Despite the military strength of the South African regime, developments in 1985 showed that there are highly visible structural cracks in the system of apartheid. All involved realized that 1985 marked a fundamental shift in power away from the military regime to the growing militant black population. South Africa's response to that reality, and not primarily Soviet designs, is determining the extent to which communism is consolidating its foothold there, a foothold gained because of the system of apartheid itself.

Although the system of apartheid was implemented by the National Party in 1948, its origins can be traced to the initial contacts between the Afrikaner people who settled Cape Colony in 1652 in the employ of the Dutch East Indian Company and the Bantu-speaking people, the San, and the Khoikhoi. While the company exercised jurisdiction over Afrikaners in Cape Town and maintained a semblance of law and order, even appointing ministers in the Dutch Reformed Church, most Afrikaners soon emigrated to areas beyond the Cape and became self-sufficient and a law unto themselves. They quickly established racial dominance over the Africans and used the Dutch Reformed Church and the Bible to buttress their claim to racial superiority. Their resentment of blacks intensified when, after being defeated by the British in the Boer War (1899–1902), they found themselves in direct competition with Africans for jobs in the cities and mines. British oppression of the Afrikaners only strengthened Afrikaner nationalism and determination to dominate non-Afrikaners.

The National Party's victory in the elections of 1948 provided the Afrikaners with the long-awaited opportunity to consolidate their power and implement apartheid as official government policy. They used legal and extralegal means to increase their own parliamentary majority and hinder the effectiveness of opposition groups both within and outside parliament to stress rigid conformity and to eliminate dissent within Afrikaner unity and adherence to the decisions made by the elites in the Afrikaner party hierarchy. Furthermore, they prevented the courts from reviewing parliamentary actions through the creation of parliamentary supremacy. Subsequently, legislation buttressing apartheid was enacted without fear of judicial review.

Nonwhites were denied the few political rights they had enjoyed, denied the right to participate in politics, their movement and job opportunities restricted by Pass Laws and job reservation legislation, and habeas corpus rescinded. When Africans, Coloureds, Asians, and a small number of whites challenged the erosion of civil rights and liberties, the government responded with even harsher measures, going so far as to equate dissent with communism, and communism with treason. Arbitrary arrest and detention became widespread and, despite its democratic veneer, South Africa became an authoritarian police state in order to control 80 percent of its population. The press, nominally free, was seriously restricted in what it could report. It is this system of apartheid, South Africa's claim to be a Western democracy (a claim most Western countries reject), strong international opinion against racism, and growing nationalism in Africa and within South Africa that combine to give the Soviets an opportunity to appear as the champions of freedom and decolonization. South Africa's refusal to grant independence to Namibia only serves to exacerbate this extremely dangerous situation.

Namibia, or South West Africa, has been one of the most unfortunate countries in southern Africa. Comprised primarily of the Namib desert, it was ruthlessly conquered by the Germans who massacred many of the inhabitants. At the end of World War I when the Germans lost their colonies, South Africa wanted to incorporate Namibia as its fifth province, but President Wilson objected. Instead, Namibia became a Class C Mandate under the League of Nations, to be administered by South Africa and to eventually emerge as an independent country. South Africa soon ignored its own documentation of German atrocities contained in the Blue Book and commenced implementing apartheid legislation in Namibia by an all-white legislative assembly. Blacks who make up 90 percent of the population were deprived of civil and political rights, their best land confiscated, and native reserves established on the remaining 40 percent of the land area.[34]

These actions, together with the South African contention that the mandate had elapsed with the demise of the League of Nations and was not continued under the United Nations, led to growing international concern for Namibians. In 1950 the International Court of Justice (ICJ) issued an Advisory Opinion on Namibia, which South Africa decided to ignore, stating that the mandate continued to exist despite the dissolution of the League, that the General Assembly of the United Nations had the authority to supervise South Africa's administration of Namibia, and that South Africa could not unilaterally change the mandate's status by annexing it without the approval of the General Assembly.[35]

In response to South Africa's disregard of the Advisory Opinion, Liberia and Ethiopia petitioned the court to force South Africa to comply. The Court took six years to conclude that since Liberia and Ethiopia were not directly affected by the Namibia, they had no standing and therefore refused to issue a ruling in the case. Directly reacting to the Court's inaction, the General Assembly overwhelmingly voted (114 to 2—South Africa and Portugal) in favor of Resolution 2145 revoking South Africa's mandate and bringing Namibia directly under the jurisdiction of the United Nations; South Africa was now in violation of international law by continuing to administer Namibia. In fact, as if to defy openly World opinion, South Africa proceeded to implement the Odendaal Plan which essentially made Namibia part of South Africa and created a system of homelands, similar to South Africa's.

It is out of these circumstances that the South West African Peoples Organization (SWAPO) emerged. Efforts to link independence for Namibia to the withdrawal of Cuban troops from Angola or view Moscow as the major source of instability overlook this central fact. Similar to the nationalist movements elsewhere in Africa Namibian nationalism found expression through students who attended various universities in South Africa. By 1956 the South West African Progressive Association (SWAPA) was formed by the students to secure greater access to university education. Meanwhile, laborers in mining and fishing industries went on strike and Namibians working in South Africa formed the Ovamboland People's Organization (OPO) in 1958 to terminate the system of contract labor. By 1960 the OPO transformed itself into SWAPO in order to highlight national, as opposed to regional, aspirations and to broaden the base for popular participation.[36] South Africa's determination to eliminate dissent and opposition to its control influenced SWAPO to integrate armed struggle with its political efforts to obtain independence and, consequently, to seek military training from African as well as communist countries. These actions have been sanctioned by the OAU and the United Nations. The "Contact Group" of five Western countries—the United States, Canada, West Germany, Britain, and France—collectively persuaded South Africa to abandon its Turnhalle constitutional provisions and move toward universal suffrage and a United Nations' role in the election process. However, linking Namibia with Cuban involvement in Angola effectively arrested progress on Namibia despite meetings of South African and SWAPO representatives in the Cape Verde Islands. Although little progress in these talks can be expected, the significant factor is that South Africa is coming to the realization that change is essential not only in its relations with SWAPO and its neighbors but also domestically.

WHY SOUTH AFRICA IS ATTEMPTING TO CHANGE

What was regarded as the impregnable fortress, or, perhaps more appropriately, *laager* (protective circle or fortress) of apartheid, is beginning to crack and fissures are visible even within the Afrikaner National Party. Although the strength of apartheid cannot be underestimated, there are several manifestations of a society which is undergoing change, albeit reluctantly. The split between the relatively more moderate Afrikaners (the *verligtes*), who wish to modify apartheid, and the extremely conservative (the *verkramptes*), who want to return to the pure system of apartheid as envisioned in 1948, is an indication of growing uncertainty about the future within the Afrikaner community. This schism also symbolizes the indecisiveness that characterizes most governmental action. For example, while granting limited political rights to Indians and Coloureds in two separate parliaments, South Africa is inexorably pressing ahead with its homelands policy for blacks who comprise 72 percent of the population. But this also demonstrates apartheid's dilemma. Despite vehement denial of the right of blacks to South African citizenship, blacks are becoming more permanent in urban areas, have more trade union rights, are increasing their economic power, and are increasingly militant and politicized. The government fluctuates between more repressive measures and a commitment to less repression. These developments are the hallmarks of a society in flux, a country which has come to the realization that change is inevitable but is unwilling or unable to alter the fundamental structure which preserves the privileges for the white oligarchy. Being so uncertain of itself, South Africa threatens its neighbors and itself by creating the climate conducive for violence and Soviet-Cuban involvement.

The impetus for change in South Africa resulted from the removal of the buffer provided by Portuguese control of Angola and Mozambique and growing domestic and international opposition to apartheid. Soviet-Cuban commitment to liberation movements in southern Africa was dramatically demonstrated by unprecedented military activity. Not only was South Africa exposed to a hostile, nationalistic black Africa, but for the first time South Africans were confronted by a superpower determined to assist the demise of apartheid. For the first time, South African troops were actually defeated. Zimbabwe's independence, in which South Africa played a role, exacerbated the situation in South Africa by creating greater expectations on the part of the nationalist movements in Namibia and South African blacks. It is generally agreed that any large scale Soviet involvement would be on behalf of black nationalists attempting to dismantle apartheid, or more immediately, on behalf of SWAPO if a peaceful settlement is not negotiated.[37] The Soviet Union continues to be the primary non-African supporter of both the African National Congress (ANC) and SWAPO.

Yet Soviet interest in southern Africa presents a paradoxical situation for the proponents of apartheid. On the one hand, government officials in Pretoria admonish the white minority to prepare against the "total onslaught" by supporting huge military budgets and training themselves to use firearms. They also argue that it is Western lack of resolve that allows the Soviets to operate and extend their influence in southern Africa. On the other hand, South Africa finds Soviet-Cuban activities beneficial. It can justify military action against neighboring states and count on Western acquiescence and domestic approval; and it can use the Cubans in Angola as the reason to refuse to relinquish control of Namibia; and it can dismiss ANC activities as externally induced, supplied, and directed, and thereby limit internal reform.[38] While both Moscow and Pretoria may share a common interest in postponing a settlement to the Namibian dispute and blaming the West—the United States in particular—for the stalemate, this strategy is far more beneficial to Soviet long-term objectives than it is to South Africa. This is equally applicable to Pretoria's refusal to deal creatively with domestic opposition.

Prior to the implementation of apartheid in 1948, several organizations demonstrated their opposition to racial discrimination. These included the ANC (founded in 1912), the South African Indian Congress (founded in 1920), and the African Political Organization comprised of members of the Coloured groups. All three groups aspired to political equality. They were essentially Western-oriented, middle-class South Africans who were represented by lawyers, clergy, and journalists. The leaders of the ANC, for example, interacted with white liberals and occasionally sponsored multiracial conferences.[39] Many of the early leaders of the ANC, like other African nationalists, were educated in Europe and the United States and found inspiration in American ideals. Not surprisingly, the ANC's Freedom Charter of 1955 contained the categorical declaration that South Africa belongs to all who live in it, black and white. This multiracial policy triggered a split in the ANC, with those opposing collaboration with whites, Coloureds, and Indians supporting the Pan-Africanist Congress in 1959.[40]

Apart from the fact that the ANC directly challenged apartheid and thus violated the broad Communism Act, ANC leaders formed an alliance with the outlawed South African Communist party in the mid-1920s in order to become a more effective agent of change. By the 1940s some of the African communists who had displaced many of the white communists assumed greater decision-making positions within the ANC but did not actually control it. In 1969 the ANC-communist alliance culminated in the establishment of a revolutionary council empowered to direct Unkhonto, the ANC's military wing, and the armed struggle against South African authorities. The Council's vice-chairman was Dr. Yusuf Dadoo, chairman of the Communist party. Furthermore, approximately 90 percent of the ANC's military support is provided by communist sources, particularly the Soviet bloc countries, with military training for ANC recruits occurring in Angola and elsewhere by ANC instructors who were trained in the Soviet Union and East Germany. On the other hand, financial assistance comes from a wide variety of sources, which includes Nigeria, Egypt, Sweden, Norway, Denmark, the Netherlands, Austria, Italy, and Finland.[41] Broad acceptance of the ANC is evidenced by its recognition by the OAU and the United Nations.

Beginning in 1961 antiapartheid groups, such as the white-led National Liberation Committee, the ANC and the Pan-Africanist Congress, resorted more frequently to urban violence, attacking power stations, government buildings, police stations, and railway lines. Since then guerrilla activity within South Africa has become more violent and widespread. In 1981–82, a coal-to-oil plant (Sasol) was attacked, an army recruiting office blown up, power stations attacked and rockets used against South Africa's main military base at Voortrekkerhoogte. This pattern continued in 1983–84. In Bloemfontein a bomb blew up under a parked car causing some damage, just six days after a car bomb which killed 18 people and wounded 217 in Pretoria. As neighboring black-ruled states signed nonaggression agreements with South Africa, violence within South Africa escalated. On May 15, 1984 there was a rocket attack on an oil refinery near Durban during which four guerrillas — three blacks and one Coloured — and three civilians were killed in the unprecedented five-hour gun battle with police.[42] In November 1985, land mines along the border with Zimbabwe injured four South African soldiers, and there was a rocket attack on Sasol. Given the growing discontent among younger, better educated, and more urbanized blacks, the widespread violence of 1985 was predictable.

Unable to control the violence with available local law enforcement officers, the South African government declared a state of emergency in July 1985, and stationed soldiers in armored cars in the black townships to restore order. By December 1985 more than 800 blacks had been killed by South African police and soldiers, and violence escalated. Hand grenade attacks increased in the Western Cape Province, schools became battlegrounds, violence spread to the previously unaffected white areas, and approximately 10,000 South African Moslems called for a holy war against apartheid after a Moslem student was killed by the police.

As violence continued in 1986 and 1987 the white minority government faced increasing opposition from extreme right-wing Afrikaners such as Terre Blanche and his Afrikaner Resistance Movement. Believing that the government should use more force against blacks, they prevented Foreign Minister Pik Botha from speaking in Pietersburg. Meanwhile attacks on soft targets increased. The Johannesburg Stock Exchange was bombed in July 1986 as were numerous hotels, restaurants, businesses, and police stations. Black South Africans were indiscriminately killed by white soldiers and policemen in full view of television cameras. Growing increasingly defiant and confident that apartheid forces would eventually be defeated, blacks buried their dead not in mourning but in protest. Unable to stop the violence under the existing state of emergency, the government banned television coverage and imposed martial law on June 12, 1986.[43] Arguing that renewed violence would erupt if martial law were lifted, Botha extended the severe restrictions on June 11, 1987.[44]

Peaceful attempts to change apartheid have also increased. It is not surprising that the large black labor force of more than 7 million workers is having a significant impact on apartheid. Unwittingly, South Africa created a system whose survival depends primarily on the cooperation of black labor throughout society. The white minority cannot maintain its high standard of living without it. Increasingly cognizant of their potential power, blacks have turned to labor unions as instruments of change. As early as 1974 the Trade Union Council of South Africa (TUCSA) invited African unions to join. By 1981 TUCSA, embracing the principle of multiracialism, had an estimated 300,000 members (45,000 Africans in ten affiliated unions, 188,000 Coloured, and 74,000 whites).[45] Shortages of skilled and semiskilled workers caused by the country's economic growth, estimated at 8 percent in 1980 and 5 percent in 1981, forced the government to reverse some of its industrial apartheid policies. Due to declining immigration, there were not enough whites available to maintain the high rate of growth deemed essential to South Africa's stability. Consequently, more blacks were permitted to participate in training programs once reserved by law for whites and enjoyed higher wages than previously allowed by law.

The vast majority of blacks did not share the benefits brought about by the shortage of white labor in 1981, and even those who did were constantly exposed to the multitude of apartheid restrictions which have a negative impact on the most fundamental human need—respect as a human being. As St. Jorre observed, those developments in industry must be set against the cold realities of the apartheid system, whose strength, durability, and ideology are manifest in hundreds of different laws and enforced in thousands of different ways.[46] Without movement toward political and social rights for blacks, peace and prosperity will be elusive.

The precipitous decline of the rand in 1985 to less than half its value in 1984, and the refusal of Western banks to refinance South Africa's foreign debt, estimated at $24 billion in 1985, reversed the economic gains enjoyed by South Africa in 1980 and 1981. Concerned about the government's inability to control the violence, many foreign investors reduced their investments, and about 3,000 white South Africans were leaving the country monthly by the end of 1987. Equally important, South African business leaders severely criticized the government, and Gavin Relly, chairman of Anglo-American mining corporation, led a group of businessmen to Zambia to discuss South Africa's future with the outlawed ANC. For Relly and others apartheid had become a threat to free enterprise.[47] Growing dissatisfaction with Pretoria's progress toward the abolition of apartheid and a greater awareness of the government's draconian measures were translated into actions against apartheid. So widespread were antiapartheid activities in the United States that despite Reagan's opposition to sanctions against the white minority regime, the Republican-controlled Senate voted 84 to 14 in favor of sanctions.[48] In the meantime, major corporations such as IBM, General Motors, and Barclays decided to leave South Africa as pressures for disinvestment escalated.

South Africa's formula for stability has clearly unraveled. The courts have issued rulings, connected with black labor, which have significant implications for apartheid, the most notable being the Rikhoto ruling which applies to migrant workers' rights to permanent residency in urban areas. Essentially, South Africa's highest court decided that the Black (Urban Areas) Consolidated Act, must be interpreted literally when it says a black can gain the right of residency in an urban area if he has worked there for fifteen continuous years, or for a single employer for ten years. The Rikhoto ruling, like many reforms in South Africa, only restores a situation which existed fifteen years before the decision. The government officials interpreted the law in such a way as to make it impossible for migrants to gain residency rights by requiring them to return to their homelands annually, thereby interrupting their employment. By so doing, the government could argue that their employment was not continuous. Many Afrikaners viewed the court's ruling as opening up urban areas to large numbers of blacks (estimated by some to be 1.5 million). But as Lelyveld noted, other apartheid laws and regulations clearly limited the ruling's impact in key industrial areas such as Durham, Pretoria, and East London where most urban blacks have been gerry-mandered out of South Africa and into black homelands.[49]

In addition to the courts, the press, various churches, Black Sash, and Afrikaner scholars and students have openly voiced discontent with some apartheid regulations. In 1982 more than a hundred theologicans signed a letter condemning apartheid on scriptural grounds, and the Reformed Churches of the Netherlands openly pledged support for opponents of apartheid, such as the ANC and trade unions. In Ottawa the World Alliance of Reformed Churches, composed of Reformed, Presbyterian, and other churches of Calvinist heritage, with a combined membership of over 700 million, declared that apartheid is a heresy. As to underscore their opposition to the white Afrikaner Dutch Reformed Church, the World Alliance elected Dr. Allan Boesak as its president. Boesak, a Coloured minister of a Dutch Reformed Church for Coloureds, had earlier rejected segregated churches and accused the white church of being guilty, on theological grounds, of heresy and idolatry in its support of apartheid.[50] In 1984 the World Lutheran Federation suspended two white South African churches because of their support for apartheid. Newspaper editors such as Ton Vosloo of the Beeld newspaper openly stated that the South African government will be forced to negotiate with the ANC as it is currently attempting to do with SWAPO. Another Afrikans editor, Dr. Willem DeKlerk, editor of the *Transvaler*, also advocated conciliation between the various groups, contending that only a political solution acceptable to all the population groups would guarantee whites' survival in South Africa. In 1985 Tony Heard, editor of *Cape Times*, published an interview with Oliver Tambo, President of the ANC, and faced criminal charges for violating the law against publishing the words of someone who is banned. Throughout 1986 and 1987 groups of Afrikaner students and faculty openly protested apartheid, and were beaten and tear-gassed by riot policemen.[51] Frederick van Zyl Slabbert, the former leader of the Progressive Federal party, met with ANC representatives in Lusaka, Zambia in November 1985 and in Dakar, Senegal in July 1987. South Africa's response to these developments is determining, to a large extent, the scope of future Soviet-Cuban involvement in southern Africa.

SOUTH AFRICA'S SOLUTION

South Africa exhibits the characteristics of a state facing a potential revolution. It realizes that past solutions are no longer suitable but, simultaneously, is unwilling or unable to implement imaginative strategies for change that would guarantee its own security and provide a peaceful transition to a democratic government for all South Africans. This uncertainty and lack of creativity is manifested by some important policy changes on the one hand and ruthless repression and strengthening of apartheid on the other. Despite the encouraging changes, however, South African authorities are attempting to modernize apartheid by redecorating it. As South Africa grows more dependent on black labor and the interests of the various groups become inextricably intertwined, the government stresses ethnic fragmentation and tribalism. This reality is camouflaged with arguments for a "confederal structure" based on tribal homelands for South Africa's 22 million blacks, 10 million of whom are essentially permanent urban residents in the so-called white areas of the country. The government's response to the reality of uncontrollable violence was not to let white South Africans and the outside world see it on television. Instead of focusing on the causes of violence, South African officials decided in 1985 to restrict press coverage of violent confrontations between blacks and white police.

As early as 1948, many Afrikaners expressed concern about the extent to which large numbers of blacks had penetrated white reserves as farm laborers and workers in an increasingly industrialized South Africa. It also pointed to the fundamental contradiction which defines South Africa: whites were becoming more dependent on black labor in order to maintain their standard of living and develop the country at a time when their obsession with racial purity was growing. The Homelands policy, designed to remove black South Africans from South Africa, is a continuation of this dilemma. Ten different homelands, consisting of approximately 97 separate pieces of land widely scattered around the periphery of the country, particularly in the north and southeast, comprise only 13 percent of the land area. Ten million blacks live there permanently and another 13 million will reside outside these areas in a "situation of dualism," meaning that they will live and work in white South Africa but be connected with their homelands. According to Frederick W. de Klerk, minister of the interior, the Homelands policy "makes provision for nationalism to come to fruition without destroying other nationalisms and for cooperation on matters of common concern."[52]

Basically, reform means rigid racial separation in homelands which will eventually be independent, thus depriving blacks of South African citizenship. Four of the homelands—Transkei (1976), Bophuthat-Swana (1977), Venda (1979), and Ciskei (1981)—have already been granted independence, although South Africa is the only country to recognize them as sovereign states. The reality is that these homelands are not economically viable or politically independent. In Ciskei, for example, malnutrition is evident among half of all two and three-year-olds, and only about 27,000 people out of a total population of 554,000 have land to cultivate for their existence. The overcrowded shacks, with their accompanying squalor, are surrounded by rolling acres of vacant land that the government has reserved for cattle grazing.[53] Unemployment is very high, despite government attempts to stimulate border industries and encourage economic growth on the homeland. In direct contradiction with the Homelands policy, most of the jobs are located in "white" South Africa. Therefore, rather than removing them from white urban areas, blacks reappear as migratory workers after securing a job through a labor bureau in their homeland. Furthermore, urban sections of homelands such as Kwa Zulu, Bophuthat-Swana, and Ciskei are located in close proximity to the industrial, urban centers of Durban, Newcastle, Pretoria, and East London. As Rotberg noted, areas within these homelands have become dormitories in much the same way as Soweto houses and supplies much of the labor force of Johannesburg.[54] Thus, while resettling blacks to deprive them of claims to South African citizenship, South Africa is even more dependent on black labor, a fact which directly contradicts the idea of separate development and "national independence." Yet the government continued to implement this "political dispensation" for blacks as it moved toward accommodation with Coloureds and Asians through limited ambiguous constitutional reform. Growing black unrest and external pressures forced South Africa to stop removing blacks from urban areas in 1985 and to restore South African citizenship to 10 million blacks who lived in "white" South Africa in 1986.[55]

Former Prime Minister John Vorster in early 1978 advocated an association of Coloureds, Asians, and Whites in a three-parliament executive presidential system and by July 1979, the new leader, P. W. Botha, appointed the Schlebush Commission to serve as an advisory group on new constitution arrangements. These efforts culminated in a referendum in November, 1983 on a new constitution which included Coloureds and Asians in a three-chamber parliament. Under the new arrangement each group addresses issues of concern to them, while matters of "mutual concern" are handled by all three parliaments. Disputes between the chambers are settled by the President's Council which is dominated by the numerically larger whites-only assembly controlled by the Afrikaner Nationalist Party. The president has the power to dissolve all three houses of parliament and proclaim martial law. The role of the small opposition Progressive Federal party remains ambiguous under the new constitutional arrangements. Pointing out that he was responding to political realities when he initiated constitutional reform, Botha viewed the majority vote in favor of his proposed three-chamber parliament as support for his attempt to "secure security, peace, stability and prosperity for South Africa."[56] Excluded from this reform are the 22 million blacks who comprise 72 percent of South Africa's population. Nor does it mean that apartheid will be dismantled for Coloureds and Asians.

Debate on the implications of Botha's reforms brought together groups which generally oppose each other and divided the relatively liberal Progressive Federal party which receives most of its support from the English-speaking whites. It also created a dilemma for Indians and Coloureds. Like the Homelands policy, the constitutional reforms are ambiguous and contradictory—a factor contributing to the strange alliances that emerged. Racial classification, the cornerstone of apartheid, remain unaltered and continue to affect political and civil rights. For example, the laws prohibiting integrated residential areas, schools, churches, and political parties remain. Coloureds and Indians who participate in the segregated parliament are denied equality in South Africa, and this is essentially why the reforms were resisted by large numbers of Indians and Coloureds, especially professional and student groups. While some Indians and Coloureds endorsed the change, others viewed it as an attempt to use these groups as a buffer between the white minority and the black majority, especially in light of their conscription into the army whose major role is to combat black nationalism.[57]

For the first time since the Boer War Afrikaners found themselves divided on apartheid, despite reassurances from Botha that this did not represent a departure from the basic principles of the National party nor would lead to a fourth parliament for blacks in his children's lifetime. While most Afrikaners reluctantly agreed that change is essential for the conservation of Afrikaner power and control, others led by Dr. Andries Treurnicht saw the move as a dilution of apartheid and white supremacy. Nevertheless, the underlying assumption among the rival Afrikaner factions is basically the same: whites must continue to dominate, not just for the immediate future but for the decades to come.[58] The difference between them is the strategy for achieving this. Botha viewed the inclusion of Indians and Coloureds as easing the threat of racial confrontation, thereby maintaining white control. Treurnicht, on the other hand, saw it as eventually leading to black domination. For groups which have long advocated fundamental changes, such as Black Sash and the Institute of Race Relations, Botha's proposal was seen as further alienating the black majority, decreasing the probability of peaceful change, and increasing the likelihood of Soviet-Cuban involvement. The whites-only election of May 6, 1986, while strengthening Botha's position in the National party, did not change this reality.[59]

Constitutional reform simultaneously weakens apartheid by demonstrating in a concrete way Afrikaner vulnerability and their realization that change is necessary to preserve most of their power. This unusual indirect admission of weakness by a government whose control rests on force rather than the consent of the governed can only contribute to demands for the total dismantling of apartheid by the Asians and Coloureds on whom the government is relying for manpower to help defend the country in the face of a relatively small white manpower source. Asian and coloured soldiers will expect equality. Furthermore, despite the fact that 66 percent of the voters approved the proposal, the Afrikaners have been badly fragmented. The majority included many English-speaking whites, and the opposition was composed primarily of more conservative Afrikaners who have vowed to fight to undo the new constitution. Subsequent by-elections in the Johannesburg suburb of Rosettenville and in the town of Potgietersrus in the Transvaal seemed to indicate that whites are reconsidering their vote on the referendum, and that previously contending groups are uniting around opposition to the proposed changes. One consequence of this development is that Botha's Afrikaner supporters will have to collaborate with an English-speaking constituency that has traditionally been more liberal. Thus, by embarking on piecemeal reform designed to perpetuate apartheid, Botha may have added another more "explosive element."[60] The contradictions of South African society make confrontation more likely, particularly because a "yes" vote on the referendum could have meant different things to the Afrikaners and English-speaking whites, the former seeing it as buttressing the status quo and the latter as the beginning of serious social and political reform. In either case, more change appears inevitable as Afrikaner cohesiveness weakens. In addition to these concerns, South Africa must deal with its neighbors to solve some of its problems.

South Africa's relationship with the neighboring states of Mozambique, Swaziland, and Angola is characterized by economic cooperation and military conflict, by reconciliation and destabilization – all designed to safeguard its system of apartheid. In Angola, South Africa is primarily concerned about the activities of SWAPO, and in Mozambique, potentially the more dangerous, South Africa's objective is to reduce ANC operations against its territory. Similar to the Homelands policy and the constitutional reforms, South Africa's ties with its neighbors are characterized by contradictions and paradox – both stemming from regional interdependence. The British and Portuguese who controlled the region created economic and transportation links between the various countries that differing ideologies cannot easily dismiss. Yet these countries' significant disagreements with apartheid, and Angola's and Mozambique's successful revolt against the Portuguese who had cooperated with Pretoria to perpetuate minority rule in all three countries, present severe impediments to full peaceful cooperation. While South Africa would like Mozambique to continue being dependent on it because of the resulting leverage, Mozambique strives for greater independence.

Mozambique is clearly vulnerable to South Africa's economic and military pressure. In 1980 approximately 56,000 workers from Mozambique were employed in South African mines and industry, providing precious foreign exchange for Mozambique. However, following the imposition of sanctions, South Africa threatened to send them home. The sale of electricity from the Cabora Bassa dam to South Africa and fees charged for the use of Maputo-Matola port complex and rail lines also provide important income for Mozambique. Despite serious efforts to reduce its dependence on Mozambique's ports and railways, much of South Africa's chrome and citrus crop going to Europe is exported through Maputo. South Africans have been instrumental in keeping rail and port facilities functioning properly even as Mozambique provided sanctuary and training bases for the ANC and as South Africa gave military support to the Mozambique Resistance Movement and bombed suspected ANC targets in Mozambique.

As Mozambique tried to decrease its dependence on South Africa and frustrate its attempt to create a constellation of states by joining the Southern African Development Coordination Council (SADCC), South Africa's policy became more confrontational. SADCC's formation is a direct response to South Africa's use of economic interdependence as leverage against states opposing apartheid. SADCC's primary objectives are to reduce dependence on South Africa by finding alternatives to South African rail services and to promote economic growth through coordination of economic development policies.[61] Many countries still remain vulnerable to South African pressure because little progress has been made in achieving SADCC objectives. Not surprisingly, despite the political antipathy between Mozambique and South Africa, the two countries signed a nonaggressive pact in 1984. This was accomplished partly because of this historic interdependence between them and the relatively low level of Soviet and Cuban involvement in Mozambique. However, South Africa's continued support of the Mozambique Resistance Movement influenced the government of Mozambique to increase the number of Cuban and Soviet troops there in 1986.[62]

Angola represents a different challenge for South Africa, given the large number of Cubans in Angola, estimated to be 35,000, and the Soviet and Cuban commitment to SWAPO. Although Mozambique's border with South Africa provides many opportunities for the ANC to penetrate South African defense lines and sabotage various government facilities, Mozambique is not as dependent on communist assistance and is extremely susceptible to South African pressure. Thus, a sharp paradox in South Africa's policy of destabilizing Angola to retaliate for its support to SWAPO and force Angola to send the Cubans home is that by so doing Angola has few alternatives to becoming more dependent on Soviet-Cuban support.[63]

South Africa's determination to eliminate Soviet-Cuban activities in Angola through military attacks can only culminate in the MPLA reluctantly becoming closer to Moscow. Because Moscow has invested heavily in Angola's independence, it can be expected to provide even more sophisticated weapons so that Angola can discourage South African invasions. Ironically, the Soviets appear to be the only beneficiary of Pretoria's policy. So obsessed is South Africa with communism that it ignores the lessons of Angola in 1975 when it aided UNITA. By intervening in that conflict, South Africa inadvertently contributed significantly to the MPLA's victory by legitimizing the Soviet-Cuban massive military assistance. Its decision to support UNITA in its continuing conflict with the MPLA-controlled government in Luanda is actually detrimental to U.S. interests as well as its own. Washington's decision to fund UNITA in 1986 and 1987 and to supply Stinger anti-aircraft missiles overlooked long-term implications.[64]

Short-term benefits accrue to both UNITA and South Africa from their collaboration to destabilize Angola. South Africa assists UNITA in several ways. It provides supplies and logistical support from Mabia. This includes weapons, ammunition, trucks, fuel, radios, food, medicine, and even uniforms. Furthermore, South Africa allegedly buys ivory and diamonds from UNITA thereby allowing it to purchase more arms and supplies on the international market.[85] UNITA also benefits from access to bases, training, medical treatment, intelligence, and air cover from South Africa for its military attacks on Angola. By fighting the Angolans, South Africa helps to advance UNITA's military objectives. Similarly, UNITA's activities divert the MPLA's resources away from much needed projects and services. Constant military threats impede economic growth and political development. UNITA has managed to hamper agricultural productivity in important food growing regions at a time when Africa is experiencing the most severe famine in recent history. Faced with starvation, the only option available to over half a million Angolans in 1987 was to become internal refugees. Another 55,000 Angolans have fled to Zaire.[66] Harsh consequences also result from UNITA's sabotage of the Benuela railroad in Angola, a crucial transportation link for both Zaire and Zambia whose dependence on copper and cobalt exports has increased. South Africa gains from this because continued reliance on South African railroads frustrates SADCC's objectives and reminds southern African countries of their vulnerability. And, somewhat paradoxically, UNITA helps to keep the Cubans in Angola (at considerable cost to the Angolan government), thereby providing partial justification for its attacks against SWAPO and support for its view of Soviet-Cuban imperialism in southern Africa.[67] Fear of communism serves to unify South Africans and build domestic consensus for government policies which are ultimately detrimental to South African and Western interests, and beneficial to the Soviet Union.

The danger of this policy, apart from the fact that it does not address apartheid which is the real cause of South Africa's insecurity, is that it will become a self-fulfilling prophecy. Trapped by its ideology of racial superiority, South Africa seems to believe that Angolan forces should not retaliate. For example, in 1983 the South African General Viljoen announced that, "We are deploying the necessary troops because we intend to meet SWAPO as far north as possible so that we can prevent, if possible their operation into Ovambo and farther south."[68] Pointing out that the guerrilla forces were being supplied with Soviet arms landed at Angolan ports by Soviet ships, Viljoen blamed Angola for the deaths of five South African soldiers and warned Angola "not to become involved in the operation!"[69] Not only were the Angolans forced to defend their country, the Soviets were placed in the position of having to proclaim its commitment to Angola in the United Nations and elsewhere. More significantly, Moscow indicated to Pretoria that future military ventures would be more dangerous by agreeing to increase military aid to the Angolan government and Cuban troops. Reports in TASS linked new supplies of weapons to South Africa aggressive actions and accused the South Africans of acting with U.S. support to create a "cordon sanitaire" in southern Angola.[70]

By 1987 the Soviets and Cubans had clearly strengthened their position in southern Africa. South Africa's raids on Zimbabwe influenced Mugabe to turn to the Soviet Union for MiG-29s to intercept South African planes and to ask Cuba for over 100 military advisers.[71] The situation in Angola had grown very serious, with Moscow making round-the-clock deliveries of heavy equipment and military supplies, and transporting Cuban and Angolan troops to bases near the territory controlled by Savimbi.[72] There was also an increase in the number of Soviet pilots, officers, and military commandos who guard airports where sophisticated equipment is used.[73] Instead of driving the Cubans and Soviets out of Angola, South African and U.S. policies have inadvertently given the Soviet Union and Cuba an opportunity not only to consolidate their position in Angola but also to develop stronger ties with Zimbabwe.

These developments clearly demonstrate that a conventional anti-communist approach to southern Africa is a formula for disaster. The challenge for American policymakers is to develop a more creative and imaginative policy that will remove the conditions conducive to Soviet involvement and thereby remove the Soviets from southern Africa — or at least significantly reduce their influence in the region.

UNITED STATES' POLICY TOWARD SOUTH AFRICA

Despite the rhetoric of opposition to apartheid and support for majority rule, U.S. policy toward South Africa has been essentially one that favors the status quo in order to contain communist expansionism in southern Africa. South Africans have been very adroit in taking advantage of U.S. anticommunist ideology. Even President Carter, who initially admonished Americans against an "inordinate fear" of communism, eventually came to the conclusion that anticommunism was the best policy in southern Africa and for the 1980 elections. Following Carter's strong condemnation of external intervention in Africa in 1978, former prime minister Vorster said: "They said we saw ghosts behind every bush. It took Angola, the Horn of Africa, and Shaba (in Zaire) to wake them up."[74] Thus, U.S. obsession with anticommunism allowed Pretoria to argue convincingly that the best way to stop communist encroachment is in alliance with South Africa. Because South Africa's definition of communism includes any protest against apartheid, Western alliance with South Africa against communism will be construed as support for apartheid and actually dignify the Soviet Union in the eyes of all antiapartheid Africans.[75] Despite the fact that both South Africa and the West will ultimately assist the Soviets in gaining greater influence in southern Africa by focusing on the symptom rather than the cause (apartheid), U.S. policymakers continue to pursue a policy of self-victimization.

President Reagan's view of the world in terms of East versus West and Moscow as the evil expansionist empire pleased Pretoria. Not only were South Africans pleasantly surprised to hear Reagan say how valiantly they fought for freedom in World War II, especially since many Afrikaners were Nazi sympathizers, but they also understood his strong anticommunist position. As J. E. Spence observed, the right-wing elements in South Africa saw Reagan's success as indicating that there would be little U.S. pressure for internal reforms; indeed, the communist threat could now be used as an argument against radical internal change.[76]

But even before Reagan was elected, a member of his foreign policy advisory panel reportedly told a South African television audience that they could "well assume that the new government in Washington would be better disposed to the white regime in Pretoria"[77] and therefore there was no need to implement significant changes regarding blacks. This was the policy of "constructive engagement."

Constructive engagement was based on the assumption that interacting with South African officials and pursuing a policy of quiet diplomacy will be more effective than a policy which is clearly antiapartheid and puts pressure on Pretoria to implement meaningful reform. The obvious danger of constructive engagement was that it drew Washington closer to South Africa and implicated it with apartheid. Constructive engagement was based on the assumption that whites, not blacks, will transform the South African society, and those blacks who tried to dismantle apartheid were viewed as communists. What was overlooked was that only substantial economic and diplomatic pressure would influence South Africa to change, and that greater communication with the black majority was essential to efforts to bring about change. South Africa became increasingly repressive during a time when international and domestic pressures were not strong. The homelands policy was expanded and strengthened, and the Sharpeville massacre occurred while the Portuguese in Angola and Mozambique provided a buffer zone and Western powers appeared indifferent to majority rule. The economy was also growing, and black resistance was minimal. Indeed, the history of South Africa has been characterized by movement into a defensive *laager* founded on the unencumbered consolidation of white power through the legal separation and subjugation of blacks.[78] Developments between 1985–88 clearly show that Washington must work with the black majority to protect its interests in South Africa.

One of the first major departures by the Reagan administration from Carter's policy toward South Africa came with the reception of high-ranking South African intelligence officers by UN Ambassador Kirkpatrick and condemnation of SWAPO as a pro-communist terrorist organization. Reagan's South African policy was further articulated by Chester Crocker, undersecretary of state for African affairs. While indicating that the United States would not align itself with apartheid, Crocker made it clear that the "Reagan administration had no intention of destabilizing South Africa in order to curry favor elsewhere."[79] The appointment of Donald E. de Keiffer, a former lobbyist for the South African government, as general counsel in the White House trade representative's office, and his official trip to South Africa demonstrated a shift toward the apartheid regime of South Africa. Relaxing restrictions on trade with South Africa and approving the sale of so-called nonmilitary goods to its military and police forces represented a reversal of Carter's policy of prohibiting sales of even nonmilitary goods to South Africa.[80] This action was clearly inconsistent with the claim made by Lawrence Eagleburger, Reagan's former undersecretary of state for political affairs, that constructive engagement supports those inside and outside of government in South Africa who are committed to peaceful change away from apartheid.[81]

Reagan's general insensitivity to growing demands in South Africa and the United States for the adoption of policies aimed at dismantling apartheid contributed to the demise of constructive engagement and the imposition of sanctions against Pretoria. Opponents of constructive engagement believed under Reagan the U.S. had moved too close to the white minority regime.[82] Despite some obvious changes in U.S. policy that indicate a shift away from the minority government, Reagan's decision to provide UNITA with an additional $15 million in military assistance is perceived as supportive of South Africa's efforts to destabilize neighboring states and perpetuate the status quo.

However, as long as change remains a secondary objective to containing communism, while South Africans will continue only to modernize apartheid rather than develop mechanisms for genuine power sharing or granting independence to Namibia.

As indicated earlier, the international community has opposed South African control of Namibia and consistently insisted on independence for that country. Significant, albeit slow, progress was being made by the Western Contact Group (composed of Canada, the United States, France, Britain, and West Germany) to get South Africa to relinquish its rule. So troubled was Reagan by Cuban troops in Angola and determined to get them out that he decided to link the unrelated issues of Namibian independence and Cuban withdrawal. Not even the South Africans thought of devising such a plan. The idea was suggested by Chester Crocker and former Deputy Secretary of State William Clark in Cape Town in June 1981. Now the South Africans routinely demand the withdrawal of the Cuban troops as a condition for Namibian independence. The irony is that the Angolans refuse to budge on the linkage and continue to rely on Cubans to protect their territory against South African invasions; the South Africans "can put their hands on their hearts and say it was not their fault; they were ready to pull out but the Angolans refused to move the Cubans."[83] Apparently, South Africans now have a vested interest in keeping the Cubans in Angola. Unfortunately, this has only escalated tensions in the region, imposed greater security burdens on South Africans, alienated moderate African leaders, and provided justification for increased Soviet-Cuban involvement. The irony is that the U.S. policy of constructive engagement designed to bring about peaceful change was actually an invitation to conflict, a development from which the Soviets will benefit.

Toward a Pragmatic U.S. Policy

It is in the interest of the United States and South Africa for South Africa to move toward a peaceful resolution of its racial problems. American foreign policy should take into consideration that the Cubans and Soviets, rather than being a major threat to U.S. national security interests can, paradoxically, be instrumental in effecting change in South Africa. They can assist the United States in the achievement of its foreign policy objectives, while simultaneously undermining their own influence through the elimination of conditions conducive to their involvement. The argument that the Soviets can be utilized to the benefit of the United States may be easily dismissed if one takes a simple East-West approach to global problems. Southern African politics are far too complex to rely on the conventional strategy of being on the opposite side of every issue supported by the Soviets. In southern Africa, the Soviets are safely on the right side of the issue, going with the prevailing winds of African politics. Both President Carter and Prime Minister Thatcher were cognizant of this in their negotiation of a peaceful settlement in Zimbabwe. Rather than focusing on Soviet-Cuban support of the liberation movements as evidence of communist expansion, they applied the pressure on the source of the problem — Ian Smith's minority regime. Indeed, British and American negotiators were strongly influenced to participate actively in efforts to obtain majority rule precisely because of increasingly successful Soviet-Cuban support of the liberation movements and because they realized that African and world public opinion was overwhelmingly in favor of majority rule. Furthermore, it was apparent that Ian Smith would not have negotiated a settlement to terminate a system he erroneously predicted would last a thousand years, without perceiving a credible and powerful threat from the liberation movements. The ability of the Carter administration to focus on the objective and identify the problem, rather than engaging in counterproductive anticommunist rhetoric, resulted in one of the major, though largely unsung, foreign policy victories in recent American diplomatic history — and without any military investments.

Rather than repeat foreign policy blunders which result when the United States, regardless of the circumstances, blindly supports the side opposing the Soviet Union, the United States must become more creative and less ideologically rigid in dealing with the Soviet threat in southern Africa. Although policymakers deridingly term Soviet policy "opportunistic," apart from the fact that all foreign policy is opportunistic, the pragmatism of Soviet policy is illustrated by the fact that in recent southern African conflicts they have been on the side of the issue favored by the vast majority of African states and the rest of the world, including our European allies. This is particularly valid in the case of South Africa. Although a peaceful resolution of South Africa's race problem is the desired objective, it is very unlikely that significant changes will occur without a clear credible threat. For the whites in South Africa apartheid has created such intense attitudes and beliefs about racial superiority that it is unrealistic to expect voluntary minority acceptance of meaningful majority participation in the political and economic life of the country. Despite the fact that many Afrikaners recognize the need for change, it remains an almost insurmountable undertaking to impress upon them that majority rule is, in reality, inescapable. While it is accepted wisdom to focus on the negative aspect of Soviet behavior, given the limited sources of leverage available to Washington and South Africa's military might, a pragmatic U.S. policy toward South Africa must seize the opportunity provided by Soviet activities. It must utilize the Soviet-Cuban threat as a catalyst for change in South Africa. South Africa represents an extremely good case where the U.S. can use the Soviets' strength against them, and to its advantage.

Work with the Soviets. The Soviet Union and the United States have different interests in southern Africa and different strategies for achieving their objectives. The Soviets will clearly benefit from violent change, whereas the United States is better served by a peaceful solution. Paradoxically, it is because of the plausible threat of violent change — that would favor Soviet expansionism — that America can support a less violent transition to majority rule in South Africa. Not even the South Africans doubt that change must come. The critical question, therefore, is under what circumstances will change come and what kinds of changes are expected.

As we have seen, while the South African government redecorates apartheid and advocates ethnic homelands, regarding this as change, black South Africans obviously do not. Their growing commitment to violence as an instrument of change kept South Africa in a state of constant unrest in 1987. The reality is that change is coming, and the United States gains nothing from supporting South Africa's solutions for stability. As Bull suggested, where a political regime is clearly doomed, the best prospects for stability in the long run lie not in helping to prop it up, but in allowing the inevitable to take place and preparing to do business with the successors.[84] The Soviets are supportive of the Africans on a very emotional issue. Assisting the white minority on the basis of an anti-communist approach to foreign policy would be extremely costly. It is through pursuing diplomatic and political initiatives which run parallel to Soviet military aid to the liberation groups that the United States can most effectively counter the Soviets.[85]

Such a strategy requires talking with the Soviets and deemphasizing the communist threat as the problem. Washington and Moscow could explore options for mutual gain. Both sides could benefit from South Africa's transition to majority rule. While continued conflict might be in the Soviets' interest, a significant change in apartheid regulations could be viewed by Moscow as a direct consequence of its policies. This means that Moscow could claim victory without committing additional military resources. But so could the United States. Both could win if the United States agreed to exercise leverage on the South African regime in exchange for Soviet willingness to restrain guerrilla movements struggling against it.[86] However, because both sides actually possess limited bargaining power to ensure compliance with such a strategy, the most workable solution is to take advantage of the Soviet threat by using it in combination with other pressures on South Africa to give the white regime an incentive to change apartheid. Since South Africa is now utilizing the communist threat to maintain apartheid, U.S. policymakers must clearly communicate to white South Africans that apartheid breeds communism.

Put Pressure on South Africa. The present apartheid regime is not a bulwark against communism. On the contrary, it is actually detrimental to Western security interests. Endorsing Pretoria's view of itself as the pro-Western, anticommunist, strategically important country is self-defeating. The United States must inform South Africa in unambiguous language and action that it will not come to its rescue in the event of Soviet-Cuban military attack in order to create a greater sense of urgency to take action. It must be clearly communicated that apartheid is a barrier to close Western association with South Africa and an invitation to growing Soviet-Cuban involvement, and that the United States will support change in order to guarantee continued U.S. access to the strategic minerals in a black-ruled South Africa. This approach would have a tremendous impact on South Africans because of their identification with a selected part of U.S. history and America, as they perceive it. South African whites really believe that because of historical similarities between the two countries, the United States will protect them in the event of conflict. Ironically, evidence indicates that Afrikaners are increasingly realizing the need for change. The vote on the constitutional referendum in 1983, the abolition of the Immorality Act in 1985 and the pass laws and influx control in 1986 signified ambiguity as well as recognition that change is inevitable. However, they are expecting the United States to confirm what they know is no longer possible. Emphasizing the realities involved, instead of helping to perpetuate their denial psychosis, would refocus Afrikaners' attention on what they know is the real threat. They really want to be considered part of the community of Western democracies. America must withhold this recognition until South Africa earns it.

An unequivocal condemnation of South Africa in international forums whenever it invades neighboring states would send Afrikaners a message inconsistent with their expectations and contribute to changing their perceptions. Rather than treating white South Africans as a mono-lithic group, Washington must continually explore openings to en-courage diversity of opinions and approaches to eliminating apartheid while simultaneously emphasizing the positives of changing apartheid for South Africa. At the same time, the United States must not demonstrate excessive optimism or praise when the Afrikaners appear to change apartheid by redecorating it. Unrelenting pressure on, and distance from, Pretoria are essential to impress upon that government the U.S. commit-ment to human rights. By so doing, Washington will protect its interests in a reformed South Africa and improve its image in Africa and elsewhere. Finally, because of Afrikaner perceptions of the United States, recently imposed sanctions have a real impact for they have a symbolic as well as practical meaning.[87] Since broad sanctions are generally ineffective, specific sanctions, such as curtailing new invest-ment or loans, have sent a powerful message. Specific sanctions should be tied to specific developments that perpetuate apartheid. In the process of distancing itself from the apartheid regime, Washington must work with the opposition.

Work with the Opposition. With frequent changes of administration in Washington, it is understandable that South African problems would be perceived as recent developments. However, the danger of this disregard for the history of protest against apartheid is that it leads to excessive op-timism about a peaceful transition to majority rule. Rather than being a progressive society, South Africa under Afrikaner domination has been extremely retrogressive. What passes for change in many cases is simply a return to a period prior to the full implementation of apartheid. Given the extremely long, arduous, and dangerous struggle against apartheid, it is unrealistic to expect change without violence. By working with the op-position, the United States would be in a better position to influence the dismantling of apartheid through a process involving less violence. U.S. disapproval of apartheid also provides hope for those advocating peaceful change, and that hope constitutes a form of moral pressure that Pretoria will find difficult to ignore.[88]

This requires a clear shift away from "constructive engagement" to a focus on the nonwhite majority in order to build a constructive relation-ship with potential leaders and make a democratic South Africa a greater reality. Greater interaction should be developed between the United States and Black Sash, a white women's organization that began as a pro-test movement in the early 1950s and later set up counseling offices in cities to help blacks who became entangled in apartheid's legal complexi-ties. Other groups would include the Institute of Race Relations, labor unions, black civic organizations and their leaders, churches, and the opposition Progressive Federal party. The United States' decision to allocate $4 million for an annual program of scholarships for black South Africans in the U.S. and South Africa, as well as AFL-CIO support for the training of labor leaders are very important steps in the direction of peaceful change.[89] But the United States must also work with groups which are engaged in violent conflict with apartheid, such as the ANC and SWAPO, to influence the nature of change and reduce their reliance on the Soviets. Working with these primary actors, who enjoy widespread popular support in South Africa and Namibia, respectively, is a pragmatic and essential policy. It is only through the inclusion of them that Washington's hopes for peaceful change can be realized. Schultz's decision in 1987 to meet with Oliver Tambo, leader of the ANC, is a step in the right direction. Constant contact should be maintained, despite the ANC's anti-American rhetoric and praise for Moscow.[90] The long-term benefits of this approach could include U.S. access to South African resources, an enhanced world image, and a diminished Soviet role in a future South Africa.

Listen to the Africans. Failure to listen to countries and groups directly affected by or closest to a situation continues to be a very costly mistake for the United States. Angola demonstrated that closer consultation with African leaders and collaboration with the OAU could have resulted in a peaceful resolution of the conflict. Greater U.S. efforts should be made to strengthen the OAU as a peacekeeping organization and its reponsibility for bringing about peaceful change emphasized. Involving the OAU would enhance U.S. prestige among Africans, give that organization greater power for resolving future disputes, and diminish Soviet-Cuban involvement by reducing African dependence on Moscow and Havana.

Recognize Angola: Labeling is Folly in Africa. The ideology of anticommunism blinds policymakers to African realities. The irony is that while Washington branded Angola as being Sovietized and Cubanized, Gulf Oil, an American Corporation, continued operations with Cuban troops guarding its facilities. Behind the propaganda is an Angola very much tied to the West. Approximately 60 percent of Angola's imports come from the West, and Angola is supported by a large segment of the American business community. Firms operating there include many European companies as well as Texaco, Mobil Corporation, Chase Manhattan, Citibank, First Boston Bankers Trust Company, Boeing Company, Lockheed Corporation, and General Electric.[91]

From the incipient stages of Angolan conflict and prior to massive Soviet-Cuban military involvement, the MPLA attempted to establish ties with Washington. Obsessed with meaningless labels, Washington ignored the MPLA and all attempts at a peaceful solution until after the Soviets and Cubans had invested significant military resources. Linking Angola and Namibia only complicated problems for U.S. policy. In addition to delinking Namibia and Angola, recognizing Angola would be a pragmatic step toward reducing Soviet-Cuban involvement. At an estimated cost of $600 a month per soldier, the Angolan government has a strong incentive to send the Cubans home.[92] However, it is unrealistic to expect them to do so as long as UNITA, supported by South Africa and the United States, and South African troops continue to threaten the Angolan regime. A strong independent Angola is in America's interest. Relations with Angola would make it more likely that the United States would be in a position to bring the MPLA and UNITA to the negotiating table. In order to move in this direction Washington must stop funding UNITA.

Focus on Regional Economic Development. One of South Africa's strategies in its effort to modernize apartheid is to demonstrate to its neighboring states their vulnerability to economic pressure from Pretoria. Given their historical interdependence, it is extremely difficult for them to become less dependent on South Africa without substantial Western assistance. Washington should not be persuaded by South Africa's anticommunist rhetoric to focus primarily on military solutions. What is often overlooked is that the Soviet Union is unable and increasingly unwilling to go beyond military assistance to liberation groups. This support can be used to the benefit of the United States. It is the next stage, economic reconstruction and development, which is generally the most crucial, and it is here where Moscow is weak and the United States is strong. By providing more economic assistance, particularly agricultural, to southern African countries and contributing to the achievement of SADCC's objectives, Washington will reduce Pretoria's leverage and force it to deal seriously with reforming apartheid instead of buying time. Furthermore, providing resources for the peaceful stage of nation-building, after the Soviets have rendered military assistance, can undermine the close ties betwen Angola, Mozambique, and the Soviet Union created by and based on military dependence.[93] European cooperation should be enlisted in this endeavor.

Use the Pressure of Business. Because economic growth is essential for political stability, especially in South Africa, American firms are in a position to put pressure on the South African government to abolish apartheid and simultaneously create a safer investment climate in South Africa—as well as in other African countries—now and in the future.

Total U.S. investment in South Africa is estimated to be $15 billion: $3.7 billion in bank loans, $3 billion in direct investment, and $8 or $10 billion in securities, primarily gold stocks. Trade between South Africa and the United States totals $4.4 billion. The conclusion generally reached after examining these figures is that U.S. investment should be withdrawn to force South Africa to change. Economic considerations and political pressures forced many companies to withdraw from South Africa in 1986 and 1987. Now that sanctions have been enacted, there is increasing evidence that business can play a role in ending apartheid. The objective must be to utilize the business leverage of U.S. firms to bring about the social and political transformation of society.

The importance of stability for business was evidenced by major corporate actions following the Soweto demonstration, and the decision by Gavin Relly of the Anglo American Corporation of South Africa to visit ANC representatives in Zambia in 1985 to discuss change in South Africa. Based on efforts of two of South Africa's wealthiest industrialists, Harry Oppenheimer and Anton Rupert, a conference of blacks and businessmen was called to discuss the quality of life in urban communities. Out of this came the Urban Foundation, an organization supported by business to provide better communication between different interests and racial groups. It also gives financial assistance for self-help community development, housing and education projects for urban blacks. Another corporate action is the implementation of the Sullivan Principles which grew out of the disinvestment debate in the United States and the charge that U.S. firms are legitimizing apartheid. It was felt that although U.S. firms employ less than 1 percent of the black workforce, they are involved in crucial industries upon which South Africa depends. Because British companies account for half of South Africa's total foreign investments, efforts had to be made to include them in any attempt to change apartheid. Fair employment codes were subsequently developed by Canada and the European Economic Community.

Overall, the Sullivan Principles have contributed to the growth of black labor unions and the removal of physical barriers which segregated the different races in the workplace. There are now desegregated lockers, rest rooms, and eating areas. Many companies—Ford, Goodyear, Union Carbide, IBM, Caterpillar Tractor, General Motors, the Kellogg Company, Borg-Warner Corporation, and Johnson and Johnson—have made significant changes not only in the workplace but have assisted in housing and education. These actions by U.S. companies have a positive effect on South African companies. Despite the fact that in 1987 Sullivan himself called on companies to withdraw and for the U.S. to enact an economic embargo on South Africa, many companies will continue to follow the Sullivan Principles.[94] Nevertheless, even the companies agree that more must be done.

Washington should encourage the establishment of a permanent business lobbying organization in South Africa to work against apartheid — based on reciprocity. If South Africa refuses to allow this, we should curtail their lobbying efforts in the U.S. for apartheid. U.S. companies must become more vocal. Because South Africa needs the companies for stability, they have significant leverage and must use it to challenge apartheid beyond the factory. Supporting change is in their own interest. While South Africa is willing to improve the skills of black workers, it is adamant about not having blacks supervise whites. Kellogg Company's approach challenged this. Kellogg has introduced modification courses designed to help white workers deal with skilled blacks. The courses also include role reversals in which blacks act the part of supervisors.[95] Now that the relatively easy problems have been solved, companies realize that the more difficult issue of education, community development, and black entrepreneurship must be tackled, which essentially means greater confrontation with apartheid. Washington should endorse laws passed in more than 10 states and 30 U.S. cities providing that the state employees' pension funds cannot be invested in companies which are not actively involved in implementing the Sullivan Principles or which sell strategic products to South Africa.

South Africans will not relinquish their power unless they are pressured to do so. It is in South Africa's interests as well as Washington's to have fundamental changes in apartheid. America must communicate its profound disagreement with apartheid not only rhetorically but also through tangible actions. As long as South Africa thinks that the West will rescue it in the event of further Soviet penetration, it will simply continue to modernize apartheid and, inadvertently, increase the probability of Soviet involvement against racial domination. It would be an extremely costly mistake for Washington to continue its support of a minority regime. The best way to reduce Soviet-Cuban activities is to use their strength as a catalyst for change together with unrelenting pressure on South Africa and greater cooperation with African states.

7

Conclusion

Discussions between President Reagan and Soviet leader Mikhail S. Gorbachev at the 1985 Geneva Summit and at Reykjavik in 1986 marked a movement away from counterproductive rhetoric on both sides to a more constructive superpower relationship. Although regional crises were not addressed, the climate between Washington and Moscow had improved sufficiently to allow follow-up summits during which issues such as Afghanistan, Angola, Nicaragua, and the Horn of Africa might be discussed. After six years of emphasizing military solutions to regional problems and refusing to meet each other, Soviet and American leaders decided that they would attempt to achieve foreign policy objectives through negotiation.

Both countries, and their allies, recognize the high costs and dangers of relying primarily on military force as an instrument of foreign policy. Afghanistan clearly demonstrated to the Soviet Union that there are limits to military power. Supporting the Contras in Nicaragua only increased problems for the United States in the region, at home, and internationally. South Africa's state of emergency vividly showed that apartheid, not communism, was the problem that the U.S. should address. Economic difficulties in Cuba and the Soviet Union also had a moderating influence of Soviet-Cuban expansionism. Furthermore, Gorbachev's desire to improve the Soviet Union's image by taking the moral high ground opened up opportunities for superpower cooperation and dialogue.

Of the various regional conflicts examined, the Commonwealth Caribbean is the least problematic for the United States. The most appropriate strategy for safeguarding both U.S. and Caribbean security interests is to address the region's deeply-rooted economic problems and to demilitarize the area. Soviet-Cuban penetration of Jamaica and Grenada was largely due to the islands' frustrations with finding an economic system most apropriate for mobilizing their human and material resources.

Small steps taken by the U.S. to improve economic well-being of Caribbean countries can make a difference. For example, Peace Corps Volunteers can be extremely effective because of the small size of the islands, their close cultural, economic, political, geographic, and demographic ties with the United States. American students should be encouraged to participate in winter work-study programs in the Caribbean, and summer programs in the United States should be implemented for Caribbean students interested in studying agriculture, forestry, solar energy, family planning, and general health care. Another way to reduce poverty is to promote economic integration. Rather than excluding some islands because of their ideology and attempting to divide the region, efforts should be made to construct economic and political bridges among all the islands. Countries that are interdependent obviously find it more problematic to ignore the view of those with whom they interact.

American policymakers must avoid confusing the Commonwealth Caribbean with Central America and deemphasize the East-West rivalry in the Caribbean. Rather than stressing the communist threat, the strong, deeply-rooted democratic institutions in the Commonwealth Caribbean should be highlighted. The United States must be more confident that its military presence in the region is sufficient to defend both Caribbean and U.S. interests against external threats. Grenada demonstrated that neither Cuba nor the Soviet Union will engage in direct confrontations with the U.S. in the Caribbean. Consequently, a general demilitarization of the region is a low-cost strategy for protecting U.S. interests.

The implications of U.S. policy toward Nicaragua are obvious. By early 1988, economic and political conditions had deteriorated within Nicaragua, Honduras, El Salvador, and Costa Rica. Congress was increasingly reluctant to continue supplying "humanitarian" assistance to the Contras because of their blatant violations of human rights, divisions among them, problems created for Honduras and Costa Rica due to their presence, the Iran-Contra scandal, and widespread support for the Central American peace plan, for which Arias was awarded the Nobel Peace Prize. U.S. preoccupation with controlling events in Central America in an effort to eliminate the communist threat actually contributed to the reduction of freedom for Central Americans.

A pragmatic U.S. policy must begin with a clear definition of U.S. interests in the region, an assessment of the costs involved in achieving them, a recognition of the limits of our power to transform societies according to our wishes, and greater appreciation for Central America's economic, social, and political development needs and the changes necessary to meet them. The most effective way to diminish Soviet-

Cuban involvement in Nicaragua is to support the revolution which we could not prevent because of indigenous social, political, and economic realities. Rather than seeing the revolution as a threat to U.S. interests, Washington should regard it as an opportunity to influence the Sandinistas by acting inconsistently with our past behavior in Latin America. By supporting the revolution, we improve the possibility of moderating it. U.S. opposition to the Sandinistas clearly did not persuade them to move closer to a democratic political system.

As in Afghanistan and Grenada, Nicaragua demonstrated that utilizing military force as a substitute for diplomacy is extremely costly to all parties involved. Ordinary Nicaraguans suffer most from Contra violence and Sandinista restrictions. There were deaths among farmers along the Nicaraguan-Honduras border in 1987, and many were ruined financially because of violence. Reductions in regional military forces will eventually help to alleviate economic and political hardships for Central Americans.

Instead of imposing economic hardships on Nicaraguans, the United States should encourage regional economic integration. That is more likely to moderate the Sandinista regime because it would create webs of interdependent Central American states. Focusing on economic development would shift the emphasis from military confrontations, which is beneficial to Havana and Moscow, to economic prosperity, which is a U.S. strength and Central America's desire.

Finally, American policymakers must shift their focus from Havana to Costa Rica and Mexico City. Focusing on communism and Cuba made the United States appear insensitive to much needed reforms, and put it in opposition to the Contadora group and its efforts to peacefully resolve the problems. Mexico's interests preclude a major role for Cuba in Central America. Its fear of instability is no less than that of the United States. Mexico, however, realized that change is an inevitable component of Nicaragua's political and social development. Washington must give Mexico a greater role in finding solutions to the turmoil in the region. Serious efforts must be made to negotiate with the Sandinistas and to support the Contadora process as well as the 1987 Central American peace plan.

Afghanistan, unlike the Commonwealth Caribbean and Nicaragua, is an area where U.S. power is seriously limited. Failure to clearly define U.S. interests there and to recognize the limits of U.S. influence on Soviet behavior contributed to the deterioration of overall U.S.-Soviet relations during 1979–87, highlighted U.S. foreign policy failures, and diminished the negative consequences of brutal aggression for the Soviet Union. Despite Reagan's attempt to include Afghanistan in the 1985 Geneva Summit and the 1986 Reykjavik talks with Gorbachev, little progress was made toward resolving the conflict. Moscow remained bogged down in the quagmire it created by resorting to force as an instrument of foreign policy. The Soviet Union's ruthless policy demonstrated its determination to pay a heavy price for subjugating the Afghans. More than 10,000 Soviet soldiers were killed and another 20,000 wounded in Afghanistan by the end of 1987, and it was increasingly obvious to all parties that the struggle in Afghanistan could be terminated by a political solution, not continued military force. Such a solution will have to take into consideration the Soviets' perception of their security, Indo-Pakistani rivalry, and the complex relationships among India, China, Afghanistan, the Soviet Union, and Pakistan.

American policymakers must realize that leverage *vis-a-vis* the Soviet Union in Afghanistan is significantly reduced when Washington emphasizes the military option in Nicaragua. By strongly endorsing international law as the basic framework for world order and by refraining from military intervention and activities contrary to the law, the United States will strengthen domestic support for its foreign policy objectives and improve its credibility with allies and adversaries alike. Gaining the moral high ground, recognized even by Gorbachev as a critical element of a successful foreign policy in a nuclear age, creates more leverage to counteract those Soviet activities which are widely regarded as obviously contrary to accepted principles of international behavior. Within this context, nonalignment and national autonomy should be stressed.

The United States can utilize Soviet involvement in Afghanistan to reconcile India and Pakistan. India's Prime Minister Rajiv Gandhi met with Pakistan's leader Zia Ul-Haq at the United Nations' 40th anniversary celebration in October 1985 partly to reduce tensions between their countries. It is in India's interest to have a strong, nonthreatening Pakistan on its border to prevent further Soviet expansion. The United States should move aggressively to build strong ties with India to limit Soviet influence in South Asia. Focusing solely on Pakistan as a bulwark against Soviet expansion can only exacerbate difficulties between India and Pakistan, and thereby contribute to the advancement of Soviet objectives in the region.

Escalating violence in South Africa at the end of 1985 and continued government repression in 1988 clearly showed that an anticommunist U.S. policy in southern Africa is self-defeating and, inadvertently, beneficial to the Soviet Union. The problem in South Africa is the system of apartheid by which approximately 86 percent of the population is subjugated to the will of the white minority. Neither white South Africans nor the Reagan administration could ignore the fundamental shift which occurred in South Africa in 1985. The imposition of a state of emergency in July 1985 only helped to escalate violence and made blacks more confident of ending apartheid. The deaths of over 700 black South Africans in 1985 focused international attention on apartheid and forced the Reagan administration to abandon "constructive engagement" and enforce sanctions against the minority government. Business leaders openly advocated dismantling apartheid and met with the outlawed African National Congress.

American policymakers must continue to apply economic and diplomatic pressure on South Africa in order to influence the government to make fundamental reforms that would provide blacks with equal citizenship rights. And they must utilize the Soviet threat as leverage against apartheid. Opposing the Soviet Union on the issue of apartheid can only be detrimental to long-term U.S. interests in southern Africa in particular and in Africa in general. The United States must continue its focus from the white minority to the black majority to moderate change and deprive the Soviets of an opportunity to be regarded as the champions of human rights. Rather than regarding the African National Congress as a communist organization and refusing to talk with its leaders, Washington must pursue a policy that is essentially similar to Soviet policy in southern Africa. This requires talking with Moscow, supporting change, deemphasizing the communist threat as the problem, and working with various opposition groups within South Africa to end apartheid.

Similarly, the United States should recognize the Angolan government and discontinue assistance to UNITA. This would be a pragmatic step toward reducing Soviet-Cuban involvement in Angola. It is unrealistic to expect the Angolan government to send Cuban soldiers home as long as UNITA, supported by South Africa, and South African troops continue to threaten the Angolan regime. A strong, independent Angola is in America's best interest. Establishing diplomatic relations with Angola would place the United States in a better position to bring the MPLA and UNITA to the negotiating table. Linking the withdrawal of Cuban troops from Angola to independence for Namibia is self-defeating and detrimental to U.S. interests in southern Africa.

Development on the Horn of Africa between 1974 and 1988 demonstrated the pragmatism of U.S. policy in the region. The United States, despite pressure for a belligerent reaction to Soviet-Cuban intervention on behalf of Ethiopia, carefully assessed its influence on the Horn, its ability to influence local events, indigenous factors and their impact on Soviet-Cuban influence, and the broader implications for its interests in Africa. Ethiopia's problems remain unresolved and increasingly burdensome for the Soviet Union. Western food aid is a vivid reminder to Ethiopians that their interests are best advanced through improved relations with the United States, Canada, and Western Europe. Even government officials in Ethiopia are obviously disillusioned with the Soviets because of their inability to provide substantial economic assistance. The Horn represents a case where neither Moscow nor Washington stands to benefit significantly from military conflict. Both superpowers can cooperate to solve the crisis of Eritrea and restrain Somalia and Ethiopia, thereby reducing their liabilities in the region and setting the stage for future superpower collaboration in the interest of regional stability.

By maintaining a relatively neutral position on the Horn and not strongly supporting Somalia militarily, the United States can avoid antagonizing Ethiopia and the OAU, and be in a position to capitalize on future developments in Ethiopia. U.S. allies, the Italians in particular, are better suited to play the leading role on the Horn. However, given our close relationship with Kenya, we could encourage improved relations between Kenya and Somalia. Somalia has already agreed to relinquish its claims to Kenyan territory settled by Somalis.

American policymakers must continue to search for opportunities created by Soviet Union activities, and find innovative approaches for facing up to the dangers inherent in Soviet-Cuban expansionism. By clearly defining our interests and deemphasizing ideology as the basis of foreign policy actions, we may avoid costly blunders which provide opportunities for Moscow and Havana in areas we consider vital to our security interests.

The importance of having accurate information about developments in societies characterized by instability and volatility should not be underestimated. U.S. difficulties in Iran, the Senate's confusion over our involvement in the mining of Nicaraguan harbors, and the Beirut tragedy in which 241 marines died demonstrate the cost of inadequate information, due partly to half-hearted efforts to obtain information and not listening to those intimately involved in the situation. Access to information might give the United States a better opportunity to influence the course and direction of revolutionary change or otherwise moderate the impact of the internal political transformation. In order to have accurate information, in addition to traditional diplomatic information gathering, greater emphasis should be given to grassroots diplomacy. Too often diplomats find it difficult to get beyond the capital city or outside diplomatic circles. The establishment of informal contact groups composed of U.S. citizens, as well as citizens of the host countries, to keep diplomats and others aware of developments at all levels of society would contribute valuable input in the foreign policy-making process. Such nonofficial sources of information would also increase awareness among a broader cross-section of American society of the causes of Third World instability and redirect the focus away from military to diplomatic and economic solutions. It is imperative that the United States address the causes of conflicts and the conditions which are conducive to Soviet-Cuban involvement.

Although a preventive policy should include a military component, overreliance on military capability in Third World countries inevitably leads to military rather than political solutions; for as long as factions know that Washington will supply military weapons, they have no real incentive to search for alternative solutions. Stressing military solutions is an inappropriate strategy for the overwhelming majority of Third World conflicts. Not only does it give the Soviets a definite advantage because of their military strength and a domestic American consensus against our military involvement abroad, but in many cases, because we are reacting to the Soviets, it means supporting the side that is eventually defeated. This makes reconciliation and reconstruction more formidable than prior to the escalation of fighting. It also means continued conflict over which neither Moscow nor Washington has meaningful control, creating a vicious circle of widespread destruction of human and material resources and superpower confrontation. An ideological approach to foreign policy obscures this reality.

LABELING IS CONVENIENT BUT DANGEROUS

A foreign policy based on the ideology of communism is by its very nature designed for failure. Because it is based on an "inordinate fear of communism," there is a real danger that such fear will determine reality. As Fisher observes, people tend to assume that whatever they fear, the other side intends to do.[1] Eventually this becomes a self-fulfilling reality because the most negative interpretation is given to the actions or rhetoric of the other side. By simplifying problems in terms of East versus West, the evil empire versus the good empire, the Russians versus the Americans, it is extremely tempting to blame the other side for any unpleasant developments. But blaming is not an effective strategy; it is generally counterproductive. Furthermore, it can lead to self-victimization, as demonstrated by Carter's awkward attempt to enhance his reelection chances by drawing attention to the Soviet brigade in Cuba. Rather than getting the Soviets to leave, he only drew attention to his impotence and greatly diminished his credibility and perhaps reelection chances.

Labeling is dangerous because it stifles imagination, leads to hypocrisy, exaggeration, and oversimplification of complex realities. It often influences us to define our adversaries by their ideological orientation and to automatically view ourselves in a more positive light. At the heart of this suggestion is the realization that it is far easier and less costly to work with potential Soviet-Cuban targets than to influence Soviet behavior through inducements and punishments. As Brown put it, a more efficient and effective strategy of containing Soviet expansion is to help other people to attain what they value through means that enlarge their pride in themselves as capable of determining their own way of life.[2]

Recognizing the diversity which exists and actively encouraging it would remove the temptation for developing countries to play one superpower against the other, often to the detriment of their own society. In a less polarized environment there may also be opportunities for Washington to develop dialogue and cooperation with socialist-oriented states, thereby creating uncertainties for Moscow about the dependability of its supposed allies.[3] This policy would not only be consistent with Third World nationalism and quest for genuine political independence, to the extent that that is possible in an interdependent world, but would also reaffirm a U.S. commitment to the right of each nation to determine its own form of government, as long as basic internationally recognized human rights are protected. By accepting the reality of a diverse, pluralistic world, the United States would actually be adopting a very low-cost effective foreign policy in relation to frustrating Soviet-Cuban activities. Countries are not objects to be won or lost. Meaningful nonalignment is beneficial to U.S. and Third World interests.

UNDERSTAND THE SOVIET REALITY

Perhaps the best way to change Soviet perceptions of the United States as a hostile power is to send them a message different from what they anticipate. We must look for opportunities to act inconsistently with their perceptions. In order to do so, a greater effort should be made to understand their reality. Given the obvious fact that the future of mankind depends on the relationship between the nuclear superpowers, it is imperative that the U.S. put itself in Soviet shoes and vice versa. How each nation views the world depends on where it has been and where it is. Since an integral part of foreign policy is attempting to influence the external environment to achieve essentially domestic objectives and secure the nation's welfare, it is necessary to listen to those we want to influence and demonstrate that we understand them. They in turn are more likely to listen to us. As Fisher and Ury put it, if you want the other side to appreciate your interests, begin by demonstrating that you appreciate theirs.[4] Perhaps the greatest danger of ideology is that it dehumanizes those opposing it. It obscures the obvious fact that in foreign policy, as in domestic policy, we are dealing with human beings with emotions, with values they regard as sacrosanct, and with basic needs such as security, economic well-being, recognition, and a sense of belonging. They are unpredictable; we are unpredictable. Although we may never be able to make the Soviets feel secure, we have to weigh the costs of threatening them versus communicating with them and engaging in constructive diplomatic exchanges. We must also weigh the cost and effectiveness of confidence-building strategies — such as exchange programs, on-going regular, informal meetings between Moscow and Washington, financial support for Russian language programs at colleges and universities — versus the cost and effectiveness of the military aspect of defense.

Given the historical experience of the Russian people and the devastating effects of WWII on their country, military threats will only confirm the reality they have constructed. However, because their positions, interests, and experiences are changeable, it is likely that their construction of reality is also changeable in a way that is beneficial to U.S. interests. The USSR's leadership is not monolithic nor are all its leaders diametrically opposed to seeking a workable relationship with the West. We should make it easier for those in the Kremlin with interests similar to our own. There is no better way to undercut Soviet officials who might favor some accommodation with Washington than to follow policies that seem to postulate eventual war or improve China's military capabilities.[5] Understanding their fear will hardly mean an automatic swing of essentially nationalistic Third World regimes toward Moscow. On the contrary, if we treat Moscow like an international outlaw, rather than giving them a stake in the preservation of international order and promotion of global welfare, we will help promote a self-fulfilling prophecy.[6]

FOCUS ON THE FUTURE

Blaming each other for violations of international law and engaging in hateful rhetoric is counterproductive. Focus on the future. What kind of future do we want, and how can we get there? What kinds of international political and economic systems do we want to create? Rather than emphasizing what we are against, we should stress what we are for. The United States should use the positive aspects of Soviet-U.S. relations to improve ties between the two countries. In light of the Soviets' strong emotions about World War II, emphasizing Soviet-U.S. collaboration should strike a responsive chord. Why not invite the Soviets to Normandy and give them credit for their role in ending the war? This was an opportunity to act inconsistently with their perceptions and modify them.

Former President Richard Nixon demonstrated the effectiveness of focusing on the future and acting inconsistently with Soviet expectations. At a dinner in San Clemente he said to Brezhnev:

I only hope that Russians and Americans in future generations may meet as we are meeting, in our homes as friends because of our personal affection for each other, and not just as officials meeting because of the necessity of settling differences that may exist between our two countries.[7]

As Nixon's toast was translated, Brezhnev's eyes filled with tears. He got out of his chair and walked toward Nixon; Nixon walked toward Brezhnev, and they hugged each other.

THE OTHER SIDE OF DANGER IS OPPORTUNITY

Crisis situations are generally neither as good nor as bad as they initially appear. We must move from a negative policy to an affirmative policy. Possible benefits and opportunities resulting from Soviet-Cuban involvement in Third World conflicts should be explored. Each crisis is different and requires different solutions. Indeed, each problem is really a combination of many smaller problems, each calling for different solutions. The U.S. approach to Soviet-Cuban activities in southern Africa, for example, may be quite distinctive from its policy toward Afghanistan. Nevertheless, each situation presents dangers to and opportunities for U.S. foreign policy. The challenge of foreign policy is to find ways to take advantage of Soviet-Cuban activities.

Notes

CHAPTER 1

1. Stephen T. Hosmer and Thomas W. Wolfe, *Soviet Policy and Practice Toward Third World Conflicts*. (Lexington, Massachusetts: Lexington Books, 1983), p. 175.

2. Alan Tonelson, "The Real National Interest," *Foreign Policy*, No. 61 (Winter 1985–86), p. 49.

3. Donald E. Nuechterlein, *America Overcommitted: U.S. National Interests in the 1980s*. (Lexington, Kentucky: University of Kentucky Press, 1985), p. 10.

4. Ibid.

5. Thomas Perry Thornton, *The Challenge to U.S. Policy in the Third World: Global Responsibilities and Regional Revolution*. (Boulder, Colorado: Westview Press, 1986), p. 56.

6. Michael Mandelbaum and Strobe Talbott, "Reykjavik and Beyond," *Foreign Affairs*, Vol. 65, No. 2 (Winter 1986–87), p. 215.

7. Dimitri Simes, "The New Soviet Challenge," *Foreign Policy*, No. 55 (Summer 1984), p. 119; and Bill Keller, "Kremlin Economic Dreamers Outdoing Gorbachev's Vision," *The New York Times*, June 4, 1987, p. 1.

8. John M. Joyce, "The Old Russian Legacy," *Foreign Policy*, No. 55 (Summer 1984), p. 152.

9. Ibid., p. 137.

10. David K. Shipler, "Russia: A People Without Heroes," *The New York Times Magazine*, October 16, 1983, p. 94.

11. Rebecca V. Stroder and Colin S. Gray, "Empire and Soviet Power," *Problems of Communism*, Vol. 30, No. 6 (Nov.–Dec. 1981), pp. 9–15.

12. These views and suggested strategies for dealing with each are discussed by Seyom Brown, *On the Front Burner: Issues in U.S. Foreign Policy*. (Boston: Little, Brown, and Co., 1983), pp. 48–50. For grand strategy, see Richard Pipes, "Soviet Global Strategy," *Commentary*, Vol. 69, No. 4 (April 1980), p. 39.

13. Jonathan Steele, *Soviet Power: The Kremlin's Foreign Policy*. (New York: Simon and Schuster, 1983), p. 27.

14. John Lewis Gaddis, "Containment," in *Neither Cold War Nor Detente*, edited by Richard Melanson (Charlottesville: University Press of Virginia, 1982), p. 14. Giving political support to decolonization movements was relatively inexpensive for the Soviet Union compared to providing the massive amounts of economic aid needed today to improve Third World economies.

15. See Seweryn Bialer and Joan Afferica, "Reagan and Russia," *Foreign Affairs*, Vol. 61, no. 2 (Winter 1982–83), p. 257; Roger E. Kanet, *Soviet Foreign Policy in the 1980s*. (New York: Praeger, 1982), p. 12; Steele, *Soviet Power*, op. cit., p. 20; and Dimitri Simes, "The New Soviet Challenge," *Foreign Policy*, No. 55 (Summer 1984), p. 126.

16. Zhores A. Medvedev, *Gorbachev*. (New York: W.W. Norton, 1986), p. 227. Several Soviet leaders resented the growing burden of assisting radical regimes, especially in light of relatively minor returns on their investments.

17. See Francis Fukuyama, "Gorbachev and the Third World." *Foreign Affairs*, Vol. 64, No. 4, (Spring 1986), p. 715; and Daniel S. Rapp, *Soviet Perceptions of the Developing World in the 1980s*. (Lexington, Massachusetts: Lexington Books, 1985), p. 25.

18. Bill Keller, "Soviet, in a Shift, Expands Contact with Third World," *The New York Times*, May 25, 1987, p. 1.

19. Ibid.

20. Thompson, R. Buchanan, "The Real Russia," *Foreign Policy*, No. 47 (Summer 1982), p. 44.

21. Bruce McColm, "Castro's Ambitions Amid New Winds from Moscow," *Strategic Review*, Vol. 14, No. 3 (Summer 1986), p. 52.

22. See George Volsky, "The Soviet-Cuban Connection," *Current History*, Vol. 80, No. 468 (October 1981), p. 346; and George I. Dominguez, "The United States and its Regional Security Interests: The Caribbean, Central America, and South America," *Daedalus*, Vol. 109, No. 4 (Fall 1980), p. 42.

23. Carla Anne Robins, *The Cuban Threat*. (New York: McGraw-Hill Book Company, 1983), p. 17.

24. Ibid. p. 18; and Robert S. Leiken, *Soviet Strategy in Latin America*. (New York: Praeger, 1982), p. 45.

25. Leiken, *Soviet Strategy*, p. 24.

26. Mark Falcoff, "Cuba: First Among Equals," in *The Red Orchestra: Instruments of Soviet Policy in Latin America and the Caribbean*. Dennis L. Bark, editor, (Standford: Hoover Institution Press, 1986), p. 71.

27. Kenneth L. Adelman, *African Realities*. (New York: Crane, Russak, and Co., 1980), p. 42; and Jorge U. Dominguez, "Cuban Foreign Policy," *Foreign Affairs*, Vol. 57, No. 1 (Fall 1978), pp. 83-108.

28. W. Raymond Duncan, *The Soviet Union and Cuba: Interests and Influence*. (New York: Praeger, 1985), p. 127.

29. Volsky, "Soviet-Cuban Connection," p. 327.

30. Leiken, *Soviet Strategy*, p. 48.

31. Duncan, *The Soviet Union and Cuba*, p. 157.

32. Dominguez, "The United States and Its Regional Security Interests," p. 124.

33. Bialer and Afferica, "Reagan and Russia," p. 261; Leiken, *Soviet Strategy*, p. 43; John B. Martin, *U.S. Policy in the Caribbean*. (Boulder, Colorado: Westview Press, 1978), p. 138; and W. Raymond Duncan "Soviet and Cuban Interest in the Caribbean," in *The Restless Caribbean: Changing Patterns of International Relations*, edited by Richard Millett and W. Marvin Will (New York: Praeger, 1979), p. 138.

34. James D. Theberge, "Soviet Policy in the Caribbean," in *Soviet Seapower in the Caribbean: Political and Strategic Implications*, edited by James D. Theberge (New York: Praeger, 1972), pp. 3-5.

35. William M. LeoGrande, "Cuba Policy Recycled," *Foreign Policy*, No. 46 (Spring 1982), p. 114.

36. Falcoff, "Cuba: First Among Equals," p. 71.

37. Duncan, *The Soviet Union and Cuba*, p. 157.

38. Ibid., p. 159.

39. Ibid., p. 120.

40. Marshall D. Shulman, "Moscow Opportunities" *The New York Times*, July 10, 1983, p. E21.

41. Hosmer and Wolfe, *Soviet Policy and Practice*, pp. 166-167.

42. See Frederick H. Hartman, *The New Age of American Foreign Policy*. (New York: The Macmillan Co., 1970), p. 10; and Roger Fisher, *Dear Israelis, Dear Arabs: A Working Approach to Peace*. (New York: Harper and Row, 1972), p. 19.

43. John Lewis Gaddis, "Containment: Its Past and Future," in *Neither Cold War Nor Detente? Soviet-American Relations in the 1980s*, edited by Richard A. Melanson (Charlottesville: University Press of Virginia, 1982), p. 23.

44. Roger Fisher, *Points of Choice*. (New York: Oxford University Press, 1978), p. 23.

45. Selig S. Harrison, "Fanning Flames in South Asia," *Foreign Policy*, No. 45/Winter, 1981-82), p. 84.

46. Alexander George, "Detente: The Search for a Constructive Relationship," in *Managing U.S.-Soviet Rivalry: Problems in Crisis Prevention*, edited by Alexander George (Boulder: Westview Press, 1983), p. 26.

47. See Alexis De Tocqueville, *Democracy in America*, edited by J.P. Mayer (New York: Doubleday and Company, 1969), pp. 226-230; Gabriel A. Almond, *The American People and Foreign Policy*. (New York: Praeger, 1960), pp. 29, 53, 55, 56; George W. Ball, *Diplomacy for a Crowded World: An American Foreign Policy*. (Boston: Little, Brown and Co., 1976), pp. 199, 309, and 325; and George F. Kennan, *The Cloud of Danger: Current Realities of American Foreign Policy*. (Boston: Little, Brown and Company, 1977), pp. 4-14.

48. Henry A. Kissinger, *American Foreign Policy*. 3rd Edition (New York: W.W. Norton and Co. 1977), p. 31.

49. Ball, *Diplomacy for a Crowded World*, p. 328.

50. James L. Payne, "Foreign Policy for an Impulsive People," in *Beyond Containment: Alternative American Policies Toward the Soviet Union*, edited by Aaron Wildavsky. (San Francisco: Institute for Contemporary Studies Press, 1983), p. 216.

51. Joseph S. Nye, "Can America Manage Its Soviet Policy?" *Foreign Affairs*, Vol. 62, No. 4, (Spring 1984), p. 865.

52. Arthur Schlesinger, Jr., "Foreign Policy and the American Character," *Foreign Affairs*, Vol. 62, No. 2 (Fall 1983), p. 6.

53. Michael Parenti, *The Anti-Communist Impulse* (New York: Random House, 1969), p. 6.

54. Joseph de Rivera, *The Psychological Dimension of Foreign Policy*. (Columbia, Ohio: Charles E. Merrill, 1968), p. 22.

55. Stephen A. Garrett, "Illusion and Reality in Soviet-American Relations," *International Journal on World Peace*, Vol. 3, No. 2 (April-June, 1986), p. 28. Ole Holsti maintains that in situations of high stress, tolerance for ambiguity is reduced, information that is unpleasant tends to be suppressed, and responses are made in terms of personal predispositions. See "Theories of Crisis Decision Making," in Paul G. Lauren, editor, *Diplomacy*. (New York: Free Press, 1979), p. 110.

56. Richard Cottam, *Foreign Policy Motivations* (Pittsburgh: University of Pittsburgh Press, 1977), p. 15.

57. George, "Detente," p. 9.

58. Michael M. Harrison, "Reagan's World," *Foreign Policy*, No. 43 (Summer 1981), p. 8.

59. The growing war in Central America is forcing Nicaragua to use more of its scarce resources and to increase its dependence on the Soviet Union. It is estimated that Soviet and East bloc aid to Nicaragua reached $1 billion in 1986. See James Le Moyne, "Nicaragua Cuts back on Fuel because of War, *The New York Times*, June 7, 1987, p. 11.

60. Anthony Lake, *Third World Radical Regimes: U.S. Policy Under Carter and Reagan*. (New York: Foreign Policy Association, 1985), p. 50.

61. Thornton, *Challenge to U.S. Policy in the Third World*, p. 136.

62. Walter C. Clemens, "National Security and U.S.-Soviet Relations," in *Toward Nuclear Disarmament and Global Security*, edited by Burns H. Weston (Boulder: Westview Press, 1984), p. 351.

63. Jerry F. Hough, *The Struggle for the Third World*. (Washington, D.C.: The Brookings Institution, 1986), p. 272.

64. Carol R. Saivetz and Sylvia Woodby, *Soviet-Third World Relations*. (Boulder: Westview Press, 1985), p. 117.

CHAPTER 2

1. Mariana Ottaway, "Superpower Competition and Regional Conflicts in the Horn of Africa," in *The Soviet Impact in Africa*, edited by R. Craig Nation and Mark V. Kauppi (Lexington, Massachusetts: Lexington Books, 1984), p. 185.

2. Harry Brind, "Soviet Policy in the Horn of Africa," *International Affairs*, (London) Vol. 60, no. 1 (1983-84), p. 92.

3. David E. Albright, *The U.S.S.R. and Sub-Saharan Africa in the 1980s*. (New York: Praeger Publishers, 1983), p. 63.

4. Joanne Gowa and Nils H. Wessell, *Ground Rules: Soviet and American Involvement in Regional Conflict*. (Philadelphia: Foreign Policy Research Institute, 1982), p. 36.

5. Fred Halliday and Maxine Molyneux, *The Ethiopian Revolution*. (London: N. B. 1981), p. 218.

6. Tom Farer, *War Clouds on the Horn of Africa*. (New York: Carnegie Endowment for International Peace, 1976), p. 11.

7. Paul B. Henze, "Ethiopia," *The Wilson Quarterly*, Vol. 8 no. 5 (Winter 1984), p. 119.

8. Mariana and David Ottaway, *Ethiopia: Empire in Revolution*. (New York: Africana Publishing Company, 1978), pp. 3-4.

9. No compensation was given for expropriated land, but home owners were paid for the 409,000 houses seized by the government.

10. Robert F. Gorman, *Political Conflict on the Horn of Africa*. (New York: Praeger Publishers, 1981), p. 53.

11. Department of Defense, *Soviet Military Power* (Washington, D.C.: USGPO, 1985), p. 115.

12. Richard B. Remmek, "Soviet Policy in the Horn of Africa: The Decision to Intervene," in *The Soviet Union in the Third World: Successes and Failures*, edited by Robert H. Donaldson, (Boulder, Colorado: Westview Press, 1982), p. 129.

13. Harry Brind, "Soviet Policy in the Horn of Africa," p. 92.

14. Ibid.

15. Morris Rothenberg, *The U.S.S.R. and Africa: New Dimensions of Soviet Global Power*. (Miami: Advanced International Studies Institute, 1980), p. 138.

16. James E. Dougherty, *The Horn of Africa: A Map of Political-Strategic Conflict*. (Cambridge, Massachusetts: Institute for Foreign Policy Analysis, 1982), p. 25.

17. Gowa and Wessell, *Ground Rules*, p. 35.

18. Mariana Ottaway "Superpower Competition," p. 175.

19. Brind, "Soviet Policy in the Horn of Africa," p. 89.

20. Gorman, *Political Conflict on the Horn of Africa*, p. 55.

21. William M. LeoGrande "Cuban-Soviet Relations and Cuban Policy in Africa," in *Cuba in Africa*, edited by Carmelo Mesa-Lago and June S. Belkin, (Pittsburgh: University of Pittsburgh Press, 1982), p. 38.

22. Albright, *The U.S.S.R. and Sub-Saharan Africa*, p. 20.

23. LeoGrande, "Cuban-Soviet Relations," p. 41; and Mariana Ottaway, op. cit. p. 182.

24. Department of Defense, *Soviet Military Power*, p. 123.

25. Dougherty, *The Horn of Africa*, op. cit., p. 66; and James Brooke, "Ethiopians Officially Joining Ranks of Communist Nations," *The New York Times*, February 23, 1987, p. 4.

26. Mariana and David Ottaway, *Ethiopia: Empire in Revolution*, p. 166.

27. LeoGrande, "Cuban-Soviet Relations," p. 45.

28. David E. Albright, "The U.S.S.R. and Africa in 1982: Quest for Global Power Status," in *Africa Contemporary Record, 1982–83*, edited by Colin Legum, (New York: Africana Publishing Company, 1984), p. A160.

29. Ed Brown, "The U.S. and Africa in 1983," *Africa Contemporary Record 1983–84*, edited by Colin Legum, (New York: African Publishing Company, 1985), p. A279.

30. Henze, "Ethiopia," p. 124. About 85 percent of Ethiopia's exports are agriculture-based.

31. *Africa South of the Sahara 1984–1985* (London: Europa Publications, Ltd., 1984), p. 365.

32. Clifford D. May, "Ethiopia's Middle Class Increasingly Feels Pinch," *The New York Times*, July 4, 1985, p. 9.

33. This committee, better known as the Commission for Organizing the Party of Working People of Ethiopia, was formed partly in response to Soviet pressure on Mengistu to institutionalize the Ethiopian revolution. See Judith Miller, "New Ethiopian Party Established in Move to Entrench Communism," *The New York Times*, September 7, 1984, p. 6; and Colin Legum, "Document Spells out Alleged Soviet Role in Ethiopia," *The Christian Science Monitor*, June 3, 1985, p. 1.

34. "Ethiopia-Somalia: Confrontation turns to Consultation," *Beijing Review*, Vol. 29, No. 21, (May 26, 1986), p. 11. Barre and Mengistu had three meetings in January and in May 1986, Somali Foreign Minister Abdurahman Jama Barre and a 17-member delegation went to Addis Ababa for the first meeting of the newly created Somali-Ethiopian Joint Committee.

35. Donald Petterson, "Ethiopia Abandoned? An American Perspective," *International Affairs,* Vol. 62, No. 4 (Autumn, 1984), p. 645.

CHAPTER 3

1. *Granma Weekly Review*, January 27, 1980, p. 12. The full text of the speech of Ambassador Raul Roa is reprinted.

2. Carla Ann Robins, *The Cuban Threat.* (New York: McGraw-Hill Book Co., 1983), p. 253; and Jiri Valenta, "The Soviet-Cuban Alliance in Africa and the Caribbean," *The World Today*, Feb. 1981, p. 49.

3. H. Michael Erisman, *Cuba's International Relations.* (Boulder: Westview Press, 1985), p. 127.

4. Ibid., p. 129.

5. Edward Girardet, "Afghanistan: Bleak Scene for Muyahideen," *The Christian Science Monitor*, Dec. 22, 1986, p. 10.

6. Alvin Z. Rubinstein, "Afghanistan and the U.S.S.R.: Speculations on a National Tragedy," *Orbis*, Vol. 30, No. 4 (Winter 1987), pp. 592–594. Rubinstein contends that the international costs have long since been paid by

Moscow and military costs alone will not consider the wisdom of its policy, despite Gorbachev's allusion to Afghanistan at the 27th Congress of the CPSU as a bleeding wound.

7. Anthony Arnold, *Afghanistan: The Soviet Invasion in Perspective.* (Stanford: Hoover Institution Press, 1981), p. 2.

8. Henry S. Bradsher, *Afghanistan and the Soviet Union.* (Durham, North Carolina: Duke University Press, 1983), p. 4.

9. Shaheen F. Dil, "The Cabal in Kabul: Great Power Interaction in Afghanistan," *American Political Science Review*, Vol. 71, no. 2 (June 1977), p. 468.

10. Arnold, *Afghanistan*, p. 34.

11. Ibid., pp. 41–42.

12. G. S. Bhargava, *South Asian Security After Afghanistan.* (Lexington: D. C. Heath and Company, 1983), p. 51.

13. John C. Griffiths, *Afghanistan: Key to a Continent.* (Boulder, Colorado: Westview Press, 1981), p. 181.

14. Shirin Tahir Kheli, "The Soviet Union in Afghanistan: Benefits and Costs," in *The Soviet Union and the Third World: Successes and Failures*, edited by Robert H. Donaldson (Boulder, Colorado: Westview Press, 1981), p. 225.

15. Alvin Z. Rubinstein, "Afghanistan: Embraced by the Bear," in *At Issue: Politics in the World Arena*, edited by Stephen L. Speigel (New York: St. Martin's Press, 1984), pp. 40–41.

16. Stephen T. Hosmer and Thomas W. Wolfe, *Soviet Policy and Practice Toward Third World Conflicts.* (Lexington: D. C. Heath and Company, 1983), p. 115.

17. Rubinstein, "Afghanistan," in Spiegel, p. 43.

18. Richard P. Cronin, *Afghanistan: Soviet Invasion and U.S. Response.* (Washington, D.C.: Congressional Research Service, 1982), p. 6.

19. John Kenneth Galbraith, "The Second Imperial Requiem," in Spiegel, *At Issue*, p. 20.

20. Shahram Chubin, "The Soviet Union and Iran," *Foreign Affairs*, Vol. 61, no. 4 (Spring 1983), p. 921.

21. Interview with Dr. Ronald Pope, Professor of Soviet Foreign Policy, Illinois State University, June 9, 1987.

22. Alfred L. Monks, *The Soviet Intervention in Afghanistan.* (Washington, D.C.: American Enterprise Institute for Public Policy Research, 1981), p. 8.

23. Alvin Z. Rubinstein, "Soviet Imperialism in Afghanistan," *Current History*, Vol. 79, no. 459 (October 1980), p. 81.

24. Arnold, *Afghanistan*, pp. 34, 38.

25. Keith A. Dunn, "Soviet Involvement in the Third World: Implications of U.S. Policy Assumptions," in Donaldson, *The Soviet Union and the Third World*, p. 415.

26. Statement by Roger E. Kanet in *The Soviet Role in Asia*, Hearings before the Subcommittees on Europe and the Middle East and on Asia and Pacific Affairs of the Committee on Foreign Relations, House of Representatives; 98th Congress, 1st Sess., July 19, 21, 26, 28; Aug. 2; Sept. 27; and Oct. 19, 1983 (Washington, D.C.: USGPO, 1983), p. 239.

27. John Tagliabue, "Soviet Defends Afghan Policy," *The New York Times*, April 24, 1983, p. 13.

28. Bradsher, *Afghanistan and the Soviet Union*, p. 241.

29. Norman Podheretz, "Appeasement by Any Other Name," *Commentary*, Vol. 76, no. 1 (July 1983), p. 29.

30. Arnold, *Afghanistan*, p. 39.

31. Rubinstein, in Spiegel, *At Issue*, p. 39.

32. Jagat S. Mehta, "Afghanistan: A Neutral Solution," *Foreign Policy*, No. 47 (Summer 1982), p. 147.

33. John C. Campbell, "The Gulf Region in the Global Setting," in *The Security of the Persian Gulf*, edited by Hossein Amirsadegh (New York: St. Martin's Press, 1981), p. 4.

34. Ibid.

35. Shahram Chubin, "The Soviet Union and the Persian Gulf," in *The Security of the Persian Gulf*, p. 50.

36. Ibid., p. 53.

37. Bradsher, *Afghanistan and the Soviet Union*, pp. 194–196; and Cronin, *Afghanistan: Soviet Invasion*, p. 15.

38. Barbara Crossette, "Pakistan Expects Rising Pressure," *The New York Times*, April 6, 1987, p. 13.

39. Bernard Gwertzman, "Soviet Discloses Decision to Trim its Armed Forces in Afghanistan," *The New York Times*, July 29, 1986, p. 1.

40. Nayan Chanda, "New Year Irresolution," *Far East Economic Review*, April 12, 1984, p. 24.

41. Alvin Rubinstein, *Soviet Policy Toward Turkey, Iran, and Afghanistan*. (New York: Praeger, 1982), p. 104.

42. Alvin Rubinstein, "The Soviet Union and Iran under Khomeini," *International Affairs*, (Autumn 1981), pp. 604–609.

43. Congressional Research Service, *NATO After Afghanistan*, Report prepared for the Subcommittee on Europe and the Middle East of the Committee of Foreign Affairs, U.S. House of Representatives Commission for a National Agenda for Eighties *The United States and the World Community in the Eighties*. (Englewood Cliffs: Prentice Hall Inc., 1980), p. 23.

44. John Stoessinger, *Why Nations Go to War*. (New York: St. Martin's Press, 1982), pp. 121–27.

45. Bradsher, *Afghanistan and the Soviet Union*, p. 95.

46. Selig S. Harrison, "Fanning the Flames in South Asia," *Foreign Policy*, No. 45, (Winter 1981–1982), p. 84.

47. Steven Weisman, "Hope Fading for Peace Accord in Afghan War," *The New York Times*, May 22, 1987, p. 1.

48. See Jagat S. Mehta, "Afghanistan: A Neutral Solution," *Foreign Policy*, No. 47 (Summer 1982), p. 148.

49. See Department of State, *Country Reports on Human Rights Practices*. (Washington, D.C.: USGPO 1981), pp. 1069–1077.

50. Stuart Schaar, "Our Blind Enthusiasm for Pakistan's Tyrant," *The New York Times*, June 14, 1984, p. 25.

51. Mustafar Khar, "Four Choices Facing Frontline Pakistan," *The Economist*, October 31, 1981, p. 25; and Khalid B. Sayeet, *Politics in Pakistan: The Nature and Directions of Change*. (New York: Praeger Publishers, 1980).

52. Harrison, "Fanning the Flames," p. 89.

53. Lawrence Ziring, Editor, *The Subcontinent in World Affairs*. (New York: Praeger Publishers, 1978), p. 103.

54. Amoury de Riencourt, "India and Pakistan in the Shadow of Afghanistan," *Foreign Affairs*, Vol. 61, no. 2 (Winter 1982–1983), p. 417.

55. Ibid., p. 418.

56. Author Stein, *India and the Soviet Union*. (Chicago: University of Chicago Press, 1969), p. 17.

57. Robert H. Donaldson, "The Soviet Union in India," in *The Pattern of Soviet Conduct in the Third World*, edited by Walter Laqueur, (New York: Praeger, 1983), p. 83.

58. Vyvyan Tenorio, "South Asian Nations Launch Bid for Greater Utility," *The Christian Science Monitor*, Dec. 6, 1985, p. 24.

59. Ibid., See Robert H. Donaldson, "Soviet Policy in South Asia," in *Soviet Policy in the Third World*, Edited by W. Raymond Duncan (New York: Pergamon Press, 1981), p. 212–213.

60. Robert C. Horn, *Soviet-Indian Relations: Issues and Influence.* (New York: Praeger, 1982), p. 1984.

61. Ibid.

62. Cronin, *Afghanistan: Soviet Invasion*, p. 14.

63. Horn, *Soviet-Indian Relations*, p. 184.

64. Francine Frankel, "Play the India Card," *Foreign Policy*, No. 62 (Spring 1986), p. 163.

65. Donald S. Zagoria, "The Moscow-Beijing Detente," *Foreign Affairs*, Vol. 61, no. 4 (Spring 1983), p. 861.

66., Yaacov Vertzberger, "China and Afghanistan," *Problems of Communism*, Vol 31, no. 3 (May–June, 1982), p. 12.

67. Edmund Lee, "Beijing Balancing Act," *Foreign Policy*, No. 51, (Summer 1983), p. 33.

68. See Ronald R. Pope, "Afghanistan and the Influence of Public Opinion on Soviet Foreign Policy," *Asian Affairs, An American Review*, July–August 1981, pp. 346–52; and Ronald R. Pope, "The Soviet Public and Moscow's Foreign Policy," *Asia Pacific Community*, Fall 1983, pp. 96–103; Anthony Arnold, "Afghanistan: Internal Incentives for Soviet Withdrawal," *The Christian Science Monitor*, September 10, 1985, p. 18. Also see Taras Kuzio, "Samizdat Against the Afghan War," *Soviet Analyst*, January 8, 1986, pp. 4–6; Dohdan Nahaylo, "Soviet Newspaper Reveals Antipathy Among Youth Towards War in Afghanistan," *Radio Liberty Research Bulletin*, January 14, 1987.

69. Ronald R. Pope, "Miscalculation in Soviet Foreign Policy," *Crossroads* (Winter-Spring 1982), pp. 107–123.

70. Selig S. Harrison, "A Breakthrough in Afghanistan?" *Foreign Policy*, no. 51 (Summer 1983), p. 11.

71. Ibid., p. 9; and Larry L. Fabian, "The Middle East: War Dangers and Receding Peace Prospects," *Foreign Affairs*, Vol. 62, no. 3 (Winter 1983), pp. 632–658.

72. Bradsher, *Afghanistan and the Soviet Union*, p. 252.

73. Drew Middleton, "Afghan Area Aiding Rebels," *The New York Times*, July 15, 1984, p. 9.

74. Peter Grier, "Afghan War Grinds to a Stalemate," *The Christian Science Monitor*, June 17, 1986, p. 3.

75. Jeri Laber, "The Overlooked War in Afghanistan," *The New York Times*, Oct. 17, 1986, p. 27.

76. Claude Malhuret, "Report from Afghanistan," *Foreign Affairs*, Vol. 62, no. 2, (Winter 1983–1984), p. 430; and William Borders, "For Afghan Rebels, a Holy War to the Last Man," *The New York Times*, Dec. 19, 1984, p. 6.

77. Ibid.

78. See Zalmay Khalilzad, "Moscow's Grip on Afghanistan," *The New York Times*, April 9, 1984, p., 19; and George Moffett, "Afghan Peace Outlook Seems Dim," *The Christian Science Monitor*, Feb. 26, 1986, p. 4.

79. Zalmay Khalilzad, "The War in Afghanistan," *International Journal*, Vol. 41, no. 2 (Spring 1986), p. 271.

80. Nancy P. Newell and Richard S. Newell, "The Struggle for Afghanistan," (Ithaca: Cornell University Press, 1981), p. 115.

81. Jeri Laber, "A Dilemma for Pakistan," *The New York Times*, Oct. 17, 1986, p. 27.

82. William Claiborne, "Tensions Erupt Between Afghan Refugees and Hosts in Pakistan," *The Washington Post*, Sept. 24, 1982, p. A12; and Barbara Crossette, "Pakistan Expects Rising Pressure as Fighting Grows," *The New York Times*, April 6, 1987, p. 13.

83. Selig Harrison, "Fanning the Flames in South Asia," p. 102.

84. *Pravda*, Feb. 26, 1986, p. 8; and Bernard Trainor, "War in Afghanistan," *The New York Times*, Feb. 18, 1987, p. 7; William G. Hyland, "Clash with the Soviet Union," *Foreign Policy*, No. 49 (Winter 1982–1983), p. 18. The Soviets are apparently willing to pay the price of controlling Afghanistan. See Richard Bernstein, "Remaking Afghanistan in the Soviet Image," *The New York Times Magazine*, March 24, 1985, p. 69; however, there are ambiguous signs that Moscow might be willing to accept a political solution. See Charlotte Saikowski, "Will the U.S.-Soviet Summit Dialogue Include Afghanistan," *The Christian Science Monitor*, Oct. 18, 1985, p. 1.

85. "Excerpts from Gorbachev's Speech," *The New York Times*, July 29, 1986, p. 4.

86. Barnett Rubin, "Helping the Soviet Union Quit Afghanistan," *The New York Times*, May 6, 1986, p. 27.

87. Bill Keller, "Gorbachev Indicates Afghan King Could Be Part of Future Coalition," *The New York Times*, May 21, 1987, p. 1.

88. Selig Harrison, "A Route Out of the Afghanistan Maze," *The New York Times*, May 20, 1987, p. 31.

89. John Kenneth Galbraith, "The Second Imperial Requiem," p. 20.

90. Harrison, "Fanning the Flames," p. 102.

91. Frankel, "Play the India Card," p. 166.

92. Shahram Chubin, "U.S. Security Interests in the Persian Gulf in the 1980s," *Daedalus: U.S. Defense Policy in the 1980s*, (Fall 1980), p. 33.

CHAPTER 4

1. Peter Smith, "The Origins of the Crisis," in *Confronting Revolution: Security through Diplomacy in Central America*, edited by Morris J. Blachman, William LeoGrande, and Kenneth Sharpe (New York: Pantheon Books, 1986), p. 4. Both Presidents Carter and Reagan shared a common perception of our role in Central America.

2. Robert A. Packenham, *Liberal America and the Third World*. (Princeton: Princeton University Press, 1973), pp. 132–133.

3. David D. Newsom, "U.S. Difficulty: Coping with Revolutions," *The Christian Science Monitor*, June 17, 1985, p. 18. Newsom points out that radical regimes that overthrow regimes friendly to the United States see America as their primary enemy, assume the U.S. will try to reverse the revolution, and are deeply suspicious of our moves and statements. However, this does not mean that being anti-American is necessarily pro-Soviet or communist.

4. James Chace, *Endless War*. (New York: Vintage Books, 1984), p. 5. The fear of revolution and the belief that other powers will try to infiltrate our hemisphere have allowed little if any room for the United States to consider the needs and desires of the Central American states themselves.

5. See Margaret Daly Hayes, *Latin America and the U.S. National Interest: A Basis for U.S. Foreign Policy*. (Boulder, Colorado: Westview Press, 1984), p. 221; and Wolf Grabendorff, "The U.S. and Western Europe: Competition or Cooperation in Latin America?" in *Latin America, Western Europe, and the United States*, edited by Wolf Grabendorff and Riordan Toett (New York: Praeger Publishers, 1985), pp. 259–260.

6. William A. Williams, *America Confronts a Revolutionary World*. (New York: William Morrow and Co., 1976, p. 18.

7. Hannah Arendt, *On Revolution*. (New York: The Viking Press, 1969), p. 91.

8. Robert Wesson, "Conclusion," in *U.S. Influence in Latin America in the 1980s*, edited by Robert Wesson. (New York: Praeger Publishers, 1982), p. 218.

9. Packenham, *Liberal America*, p. 133.

10. Robert E. White, "Central America: The Problem That Won't Go Away," *The New York Times Magazines*, July 18, 1982, p. 43.

11. Cole Blasier, *The Giant's Rival: The U.S.S.R. and Latin America*. (Pittsburgh: University of Pittsburgh, 1983), p. 43.

12. Arthur Schlesinger, Jr., "Foreign Policy and the American Character," *Foreign Affairs*, Vol. 62, no. 1 (Fall 1983), p. 5.

13. Smith, "Origins of the Crisis," p. 4.

14. Alan Riding, "The Central American Quagmire," *Foreign Affairs*, Vol. 61, no. 3 (1983), p. 641.

15. See Craig L. Dozier, *Nicaragua's Mosquito Shore: The Years of British and American Presence*. (Alabama: University of Alabama Press, 1985).

16. Samuel Flagg Bemis, *The Latin American Policy of the United States*. (New York: W.W. Norton and Co., 1967), p. 48.

17. Walter LaFeber, *Inevitable Revolutions: The United States in Central America*. (New York: W.W. Norton and Co., 1984), p. 28.

18. Ibid., p. 29.

19. Lars Schoultz, "Nicaragua: U.S. Confronts a Revolution," in *From Gunboats to Diplomacy*, edited by Richard Newfarmer, (Baltimore: Johns Hopkins University Press, 1984); and William O. Scroggs, *Filibusters, and Financiers: The Story of William Walker and His Associates*. (New York: Russell and Russell, 1969).

20. Piero Gleijeses, "Nicaragua: Resist Romanticism," *Foreign Policy*, No. 54 (Spring 1984), p. 125.

21. *The New York Herald Tribune*, Dec. 7, 1929, p. 11. Quoted in Piero, "Nicaragua: Resist Romanticism," p. 125.

22. See Richard Millett, *Guardians of the Dynasty*. (Maryknoll, New York: Orbis Books, 1977).

23. LaFeber, Inevitable Revolutions, p. 68.

24. Mark Falcoff, *Small Countries, Large Issues*. (Washington, D.C.: American Enterprise Institute for Public Policy Research, 1984), p. 63.

25. Ibid., p. 57.

26. Ibid.

27. Thomas W. Walker, *Nicaragua: The Land of Sandino*. (Boulder, Colorado: Westview Press, 1982), p. 155.

28. Dennis Gilbert, "Nicaragua," in *Confronting Revolutions*, p. 92.

29. Thomas P. Anderson, *Politics in Central America*. (New York: Praeger Publishers, 1982), p. 155.

30. Walker, *Nicaragua: The Land of Sandino*, p. 31.

31. William M. LeoGrande, "Cuba and Nicaragua," in *The New Cuban Presence in the Caribbean*, edited by Barry Levine, (Boulder, Colorado: Westview Press, 1983), p. 44.

32. Ibid.

33. Charles D. Ameringer, "Nicaragua: The Rock that Crumbled," in *U.S. Influence in Latin America*, p. 47.

34. Arturo J. Cruz, "Nicaragua's Imperiled Revolution," *Foreign Affairs*, Vol. 61, no. 5 (Summer 1983) p. 1033.

35. Anderson, *Politics in Central America*, (New York: Praeger Publishers, 1982), p. 158.

36. World Bank, *Nicaragua: The Challenge of Reconstruction*. (Washington, D.C.: October 9, 1981), p. 2.

37. Cruz, "Nicaragua's Imperiled Revolution," p. 1034; and Walker, *Nicaragua: The Land of Sandino*, p. 41.

38. See Joseph R. Thome and David Kaimowitz, "Agrarian Reform," in *Nicaragua: The First Five Years*, edited by Thomas W. Walker, (New York: Praeger, 1985), pp. 309–312.

39. Joseph Collins, *What Difference Could a Revolution Make*? (San Francisco: Institute for Food and Development Policy, 1985), p. 44.

40. Riding, "The Central America Quagmire," p. 651.

41. America Watch, *Miskitos in Nicaragua, 1981–1984*. (New York: Amnesty International, 1984).

42. George D. Moffett, "Exiled Nicaragua Editor Looks at Sandinistas' Failure," *Christian Science Monitor*, January 11, 1985, p. 3. According to this report, sometimes 70 percent of *La Prensa* was cut. On June 26, 1986, the Sandinista government closed down *La Prensa* indefinitely. See Violeta Barrios de Chamorro, "The Death of La Prensa," *Foreign Affairs*, Vol. 65, no. 2 (Winter 1986-87), p. 383; and Steven Kinzer, "In Nicaragua the Censors Stir Cynicism," *The New York Times*, April 20, 1987, p. 1.

43. Mario Vargas Llosa, "In Nicaragua," *The New York Times Magazine,* April 28, 1985, pp. 37–38.

44. Arturo Cruz Sequeira, "The Origins of Sandinista Foreign Policy," in *Central America: Anatomy of Conflict*, edited by Robert S. Leiken (New York: Pergamon Press, 1984), p. 98.

45. Ibid., p. 96.

46. Robert S. Leiken, *Soviet Strategy in Central America*. (New York: Praeger, 1982), p. 3; and Cole Blasier, *The Giant's Rival*, p. 19.

47. Cole Blasier, "Security: The Extracontinental Dimension," in *The United States and Latin America in the 1980s*, edited by Kevin Middlebrook and Carlos Rico (Pittsburgh : University of Pittsburgh Press, 1986), p. 530.

48. Ibid., p. 80.

49. W. Raymond Duncan, *The Soviet Union and Cuba: Interests and Influence*. New York: Praeger, 1985), p. 30.

50. See Michael S. Radu, "Soviet Proxy Assets in Central America and the Caribbean," in *The Red Orchestra*, edited by Dennis L. Bark (Stanford: Hoover Institution Press, 1986), pp. 84–107.

51. Duncan, *The Soviet Union and Cuba*, p. 157.

52. W. Raymond Duncan, "Castro and Gorbachev: Politics of Accommodation," *Problems of Communism*, March/April, 1986, p. 56.

53. Francis Fukuyama, "Gorbachev and the Third World," *Foreign Affairs*, Vol. 64, no. 4 (Spring 1986), p. 719.

54. Blasier, *The Giant's Rival*, p. 151.

55. W. Raymond Duncan, "Moscow and Latin America: Objectives, Constraints, and Implications," *Soviet Policy in the Third World*, edited by W. Raymond Duncan (New York: Pergamon Press, 1980), pp. 273–275.

56. Aldo Cesar Vacs, *Discreet Partners: Argentina and the U.S.S.R. Since 1917*. Translated by Michael Joyce, (Pittsburgh: University of Pittsburgh Press, 1984), p. 8.

57. LeoGrande, "Cuba and Nicaragua," in *The New Cuban Presence in the Caribbean*, edited by Levine, p. 44.

58. Ibid., p. 46.

59. Ibid., p. 49.

60. Alexander Haig, *Caveat*. (New York: Macmillan Publishing Co. 1984), p. 124.

61. Theodore Schwab and Harold Sims, "Relations with the Communist States," in *Nicaragua: The First Five Years*, pp. 45–55.

62. Morris Rothenberg, "The Soviet and Central America," in Leiken, *Central America*, p. 134.

63. Jiri Valenta and Virginia Valenta, "Soviet Strategy and Policies in the Caribbean Basin," in *Rift and Revolution*, edited by Howard J. Wiarda (Washington, D.C.: American Enterprise Institute for Public Policy Research, 1984), p. 217.

64. Department of State and Department of Defense, *The Sandinista Military Buildup*. (Washington, D.C.: USGPO, 1985), p. 3.

65. Department of State and Department of Defense, *The Soviet-Cuban Connection in Central America and the Caribbean*. (Washington, D.C., USGPO, 1985), p. 22.

66. Ibid., p. 26.

67. Miguel Acoca, "Why Fear Nicaragua?" *The New York Times*, March 26, 1985, p. 27.

68. Carl G. Jacobson, "Statement," *Soviet Posture in the Western Hemisphere*. Hearings before the Subcommittee on Western Hemisphere Affairs of the Committee on Foreign Affairs, House of Representatives, 99 Congress, 1st Session, Feb. 28, 1985 (Washington, D.C. USGPO, 1985), p. 49; See the Jacobson Report of June 1984 on *Soviet Attitudes Towards, Aid to, and Contacts With Central American Revolutionaries*. (Washington, D.C.: The State Department, 1984).

69. See Stephen Kinzer, "Nicaraguans elect President and Assembly Today," *The New York Times*, Nov. 4, 1984.

70. Howard Wiarda, "At the root of the problem," in Leiken, *Central America*, pp. 259–260.

71. Richard H. Ullman, "At War With Nicaragua," *Foreign Affairs*, Vol. 62, no. 1 (Fall 1983), p. 39.

72. Clifford Kraus, "Sniping among Contra leaders builds," *Wall Street Journal*, April 16, 1987, p. 23.

73. Christopher Dickey, "Central America: From Quagmire to Cauldron," *Foreign Affairs*, Vol. 62, no. 3 (1984), p. 662.

74. For an excellent summary of Carter's initial response to the Sandinistas see Charles Ameringer, "Nicaragua: The Rock that Crumbled," in *U.S. Influence in Latin America in the 1980s*, edited by Robert Wesson (New York: Praeger, 1982), p. 157.

75. Ameringer, "Nicaragua: The Rock that Crumbled," pp. 152–153.

76. Paul E. Sigmund, "U.S.-Latin American Relations from Carter to Reagan: Change or Continuity?" in *The Dynamics of Latin American Foreign Policies: Challenges for the 1980s*, edited by Jennie K. Lincoln and Elizabeth G. Ferris (Boulder, Colorado: Westview Press, 1984), p. 65.

77. Dickey, "Central America: From Quagmire to Cauldron," p. 659.

78. Haig, *Caveat*, p. 124.

79. Michael J. Kryzanek, *U.S.-Latin American Relations*. (New York: Praeger, 1985), p. 181.

80. Lt. Col. Edward L. King, U.S. Army (Retired), "Statement" in *Developments in El Salvador*. Hearings before the Subcommittee on Western Hemisphere Affairs of the Committee on Foreign Affairs, House of Representatives, 99 Congress, 1st Session, January 31, 1985 (Washington, D.C.: USGPO, 1985), p. 53.

81. "Transcript of Reagan Interview on a Range of Foreign Issues," *The New York Times*, Oct. 21, 1984, p. 6.

82. Philip Taubman, "U.S. is Reported to Oppose Electoral Challenge to Sandinistas," *The New York Times*, Oct. 21, 1984, p. 6.

83. "The C.I.A. and the Rebels: A Tangled History," *The New York Times*, March 18, 1985, p. 6.

84. Riding, "The Central American Quagmire," p. 652; and Dickey, "Central America: From Quagmire to Cauldron," p. 672.

85. "Excerpts from C.I.A. Primer Giving Pointers to the Nicaraguan Insurgents," *The New York Times*, Oct. 17, 1984, p. 6.

86. See "International Court of Justice: Case concerning Military and Paramilitary Activities in and against Nicaragua," in *International Legal Materials*, Vol. 25, no. 5 (Sept. 1986), pp. 1023–1293; and Keith Highet, "Evidence, the Court, and the Nicaraguan Case," *American Journal of International Law*, Vol. 81, no. 1 (January 1987), pp. 1–56.

87. Honduras wants Washington to resettle the Contras in the U.S. if their operations against the Sandinistas fail.

88. Stephen Kinzer, "Nicaraguan Rebels Step Up Raids in Coffee Areas," *The New York Times*, November 19, 1984, p. 1.

89. LaFeber, *Inevitable Revolutions*, p. 286.

90. "U.S. to Conduct Military Exercise in Central America," *Dallas Morning News*, March 22, 1987, p. 24A.

91. In late 1986 the United States had to ferry Honduran troops from the border with El Salvador to the Nicaraguan border.

92. Larry Rohter, "Nicaragua Offers Hope of Further Concessions," *The New York Times*, March 3, 1985, p. 8.

93. Susan Kaufman Purcell, "Mexico-U.S. Relations: Big Initiatives Can Cause Big Problems," *Foreign Affairs*, Vol. 60, no. 2 (Winter 1981–82), p. 388.

94. Ibid., p. 389; See Henry S. Gill, "Cuba and Mexico: A Special Relationship?" in Levine, pp. 75–76.

95. H. Michael Erisman, "Contemporary Challenge Confronting U.S. Caribbean Policy," in *The Caribbean Challenge: U.S. Policy in a Volatile Region*, edited by Erisman (Boulder, Colorado: Westview Press, 1984), p. 22.

96. Gill, "Cuba and Mexico," p. 79.

97. William M. LeoGrande, "Rollback or Containment? The U.S., Nicaragua, and the Search for Peace in Central America," *International Security*, Vol. 11, no. 2 (Fall 1986), p. 95.

98. Viron Vaky, "Reagan's Central American Policy: An Isthmus Restored," in Leiken, *Central America*, p. 243.

99. Tom J. Farer, "Contadora: The Hidden Agenda," *Foreign Policy*, no. 59 (Summer 1985), p. 59.

100. Philip Taubman, "Latin Peace Plan: Why the U.S. Balks," *The New York Times*, Oct. 2, 1984, p. 3; and Elaine Sciolino, *"U.S. is said to link Latin Aid to Support for Contras," The New York Times, May 18, 1987, p. 4.*

101. *"Contadora: A Text for Peace," International Policy Report*, (Washington, D.C.: Center for International Policy, November 1984).

102. Alan Riding, "U.S. Faulted at Talks on Latin Peace Treaty," *The New York Times*, Nov. 14, 1984, p. 7; Piero Gleijeses, "The Reagan Doctrine and Central America," *Current History*, (Dec. 1986), p. 403; and "The Procedure for the Establishment of a Strong and Lasting Peace in Central America," *The New York Times*, August 12, 1987, p. 6.

103. U.S. Department of State, *Misconceptions about U.S. Policy Toward Nicaragua*, (Washington, D.C.: USGPO, June, 1985), p. 2.

104. LeoGrande, "Rollback or Containment?" p. 89.

105. Morris J. Balckman, et al., "The Failure of the Hegemonic Strategic Vision," in *Confronting Revolutions*, p. 347.

106. See Frances Fitzgerald, "Reagan's Band of True Believers," *The New York Times Magazine*, May 10, 1987 p. 43.

107. Thomas Perry Thornton, *The Challenge to U.S. Policy in the Third World: Global Responsibilities and Regional Devolution*. (Boulder: Westview Press, 1986), p. 153.

108. Tom J. Farer, "Manage the Revolution?" *Foreign Policy*, No. 52, (Fall 1983), p. 116; and Cole Blasier, *The Hovering Giant: U.S. Responses to Revolutionary Change in Latin America*. (Pittsburgh: University of Pittsburgh Press, 1976), pp. 272–273.

109. Blasier, *The Hovering Giant*, p. 274.

110. "Summary of the Kissinger Communism Report," *The Congressional Quarterly*, Jan. 14, 1984, p. 64.

111. Government Accounting Office, *Foreign Aid: Questions on the Central American Regional Program Need to be Resolved*. (Washington, D.C.: USGPO, 1986), p. 20.

112. See William H. Bolin, "Central America: Economic Help is Workable Now," *Foreign Affairs*, Vol. 62, no. 5 (Summer 1984), pp. 1096–1106.

113. Alan Riding, "Revolution and the Intellectual in Central America," *The New York Times Magazine*, March 13, 1983, p. 37.

CHAPTER 5

1. Jeane Kirkpatrick, "United States Security and Latin America," *Commentary*, Vol. 71, no. 1 (January 1981), p. 29.

2. Abraham Lowenthal, "Troubles in the Caribbean," *The Wilson Quarterly*, Vol. 6, no. 2 (Spring 1982), p. 135.

3. Robert Leiken, "Eastern Winds in Latin America," *Foreign Policy*, No. 42, (Spring 1981), p. 95.

4. W. Raymond Duncan, "Soviet and Cuban Interest in the Caribbean," in *The Restless Caribbean: Changing Patterns of International Relations*, edited by Richard Millett and W. Marvin Will, (New York: Praeger Publishers, 1979), p. 138.

5. Robert S. Leiken, *Soviet Strategy in Latin America*. (New York: Praeger, 1982), p. 107.

6. Anthony Lake, "Defining the National Interest," in *The Power to Govern*, edited by Richard M. Pions. (New York: The Academy of Political Science, 1981), p. 210.

7. William M. LeoGrande, "Cuba Policy Recycled," *Foreign Policy*, No. 46, (Spring 1982), p. 105.

8. Wayne M. Smith, "Dateline Havana: Myopic Diplomacy," *Foreign Policy*, No. 48, (Fall 1982), p. 157.

9. Robert D. Crassweller, *The Caribbean Community: Changing Societies and U.S. Policy*. (New York: Praeger, 1972), p. 54.

10. See John B. Martin, *U.S. Policy in the Caribbean*. (Boulder, Colorado: Westview Press, 1978), p. 9.

11. Crassweller, *The Caribbean Community*, p. 55.

12. Ibid., p. 54.

13. W. Raymond Duncan, "Caribbean Leftism," *Problems of Communism*, May–June, 1978), p. 33.

14. J. Daniel O'Flaherty, "Finding Jamaica's Way," *Foreign Policy*, No. 31 (Summer 1978), p. 142.

15. President Reagan, "Self Determination, Economic Development, Collective Security," *The Washington Post*, February 25, 1982, P. A12.

16. Ransford Palmer, *Caribbean Dependence on the United States Economy*. (New York: Praeger, 1979), pp. 89–91.

17. "Economic Prospects Remain Dismal," *Latin America Regional Reports: Caribbean*, June 17, 1983, p. 8.

18. Ibid.

19. Lowenthal, "Troubles in the Caribbean," p. 120.

20. Daniel S. Rapp, *Soviet Perceptions of the Developing World in the 1980s*. (Lexington, Massachusetts: Lexington Books, 1985), p. 99.

21. W. Raymond Duncan, *The Soviet Union and Cuba: Interests and Influence*. (New York: Praeger, 1985), p. 158.

22. Ibid.

23. Rapp, *Soviet Perceptions*, p. 100.

24. Wendell Bell, "Independent Jamaica Enters World Politics: Foreign Policy in a New Stage," *Political Science Quarterly*, Vol. 92, no. 4 (Winter 1977–1978), p. 695.

25. Ibid.

26. Carla Anne Robins, *The Cuban Threat*. (New York: McGraw-Hill Book Company, 1983), p. 241.

27. "Cuba's Renewed Support for Violence in Latin America," *Department of State Bulletin*, February 1982, p. 5.

28. Ibid., p. 9.

29. Ibid.

30. Myles R. Frechette, "Cuban-Soviet Impact on the Western Hemisphere," *Department of State Bulletin*, July 1980, p. 78.

31. Anthony Payne, "Seaga's Jamaica After One Year," *The World Today*, Vol. 37, no. 11, (November 1981), p. 438.

32. Martin, *U.S. Policy in the Caribbean*, p. 136; and Ralph R. Premada, "Guyana: Socialist Reconstruction or Political Opportunism?" *Journal of Interamerican Studies and World Affairs*, Vol. 20, no. 2 (May 1978), p. 134.

33. Wendell Bell, "Independent Jamaica Enters World Politics: Foreign Policy in a New State", *Political Science Quarterly*, Vol. 92, no. 4 (Winter 1977–78), p. 700.

34. "Fund Assistance to Jamaica Has Sought to Check Decline and Restore Economic Growth," *IMF Survey*, Dec. 15, 1980, pp. 378–379.

35. Roger S. Leeds, "External Financing of Developing—Challenges and Concerns," *Journal of International Affairs*, Vol. 34, no. 1 (Spring/Summer, 1980), p. 3.

36. Bell, "Independent Jamaica," p. 703; and Martin, *U.S. Policy in the Caribbean*, pp. 130–132.

37. "Jamaica: Island in the Soup," *The Economist*, June 12, 1980, p. 52.

38. Winston Van Horne, "Jamaica: Why Manley Lost," *The World Today*, Vol. 37, no. 11 (November 1981), p. 430.

39. John Huey, "Jamaica's Cash Crunch Haunts Officials," *The Wall Street Journal*, Sept. 18, 1980, p. 35.

40. *Latin American Regional Reports: Caribbean*, January 16, 1981, p. 2.

41. See "Economic Prospects Remain Dismal, *Latin American Regional Report: Caribbean*, June 17, 1983, p. 8; and "Jamaica Private Sector at Odds with the Government," *Latin American Regional Reports: Caribbean*, July 16, 1982, p. 1.

42. *Latin American Regional Reports: Caribbean*, May 13, 1983, p. 1.

43. Ibid., p. 2.

44. Michael Manley, "Overcoming Insularity in Jamaica," *Foreign Affairs*, Vol. 49, no. 1 (October 1970), p. 100.

45. Ibid., p. 109.

46. Anthony Payne, Paul Sutton and Tony Thorndike, *Grenada: Revolution and Invasion*. (New York: St. Martin's Press, 1984), p. 16.

47. Ibid., p. 91.

48. Bruce Marcus and Michael Taber, Editors, *Maurice Bishop Speaks: The Granada Revolution 1979-1983*. (New York: The Pathfinder Press, 1983), p. 87.

49. A. Payne, *et al., Grenada*, p. 95.

50. Ibid., p. 82.

51. Deetrio Boersner, "Cuba and Venezuela," in *The New Cuban Presence in the Caribbean*, edited by Barry B. Levine (Boulder, Colorado: Westview Press, 1983), p. 97.

52. Nestor D. Sanchez, "What was Uncovered in Grenada," *Caribbean Review*, Vol. 12, no. 4 (Fall 1983), pp. 21-22.

53. "Progress Report of Commission #5: National Service and Labor Army," *The Grenada Papers*, edited by Paul Seabury and Walter A. McDougall (San Francisco: Institute for Contemporary Studies Press, 1984), pp. 117-118.

54. "Cuba's Renewed Support for Violence," *Department of State Bulletin*, p. 10; and Jiri Valenta, "The Soviet-Cuban Alliance in Africa and the Caribbean," *The World Today*, Vol. 37, no. 2 (February 1981), p. 50.

55. See *Latin American Report: Caribbean*, August 20, 1982, p. 3; July 16, 1982, p. 4; and December 4, 1981, p. 5.

56. "Grenada," *Latin American Report: Caribbean*, May 13, 1983, p. 3.

57. "Grenada's Relations with the U.S.S.R.," in *The Grenada Papers*, p. 207.

58. "Letter from Noel to Central Committee 10/17/83, in *The Grenada Papers*, p. 331.

59. Lowenthal, "Troubles in the Caribbean," op. cit., p. 137.

60. See William G. Bowdler, Assistant Secretary for Inter-American Affairs, "Foreign Assistance Proposals." Department of State, Bureau of Public Affairs, (April 15, 1980), p. 3. Juan de Onis, "Caribbean Leaders Appeal for More Economic Aid," *The New York Times*, February 3, 1980, p. 5.

61. Paul E. Sigmund, "Latin America: Change or Continuity," *Foreign Affairs: American and the World 1981*, Vol. 60, no. 3 (1982), pp. 643–644.

62. "U.S.-Jamaica Barter Agreement," *The Department of State Bulletin*, May 1982, p. 68.

63. "Grenada," *Latin America Regional Reports: Caribbean* March 31, 1983, p. 1; and "Setback for Washington as Caricom Votes for Tolerance," *Latin America Regional Reports: Caribbean*, December 10, 1982, p. 1.

64. Richard J. Payne, "The Lessons of Grenada," *Worldview*, Vol. 27, no. 2 (Feb. 1984), p. 13.

65. Errol Barrow, "The Danger of Rescue Operations," *Caribbean Review*, Vol. 12, no. 4 (Fall 1983), p. 3.

66. Charles Mohr, "Grenada Invasion: Roots of Purported Shortcomings Traced," *The New York Times*, Oct. 26, 1984, p. 4.

67. Bill Keller, "Reports Cite Poor Planning for Grenada Invasion," *The New York Times*, Dec. 4, 1984, p. 4.

68. Dennis Volman, "Grenadians are Uneasy as Last U.S. Troops Leave Islands," *The Christian Science Monitor*, Jun 12, 1985, p. 9.

69. Payne, *et al, Grenada*, p. 25.

70. President Reagan, "Self-determination," p. A12.

71. Ibid.

72. See William Chapman, "Reagan Rebuffed on Caribbean Basic Plan," *The Washington Post*, May 12, 1982, p. A24; and John M. Goshko, "President, Warnings of Latin Unrest, Sends Caribbean Plan to Hill, *The Washington Post*, March 18, 1982, p. A20.

73. Lou Cannon, "Reagan Opens Five-Day Visit to the Caribbean," *The Washington Post*, April 8, 1982, p. A6.

74. Abraham F. Lowenthal, "Caribbean Basin Initiative: Misplaced Emphasis," *Foreign Policy*, No. 47 (Summer 1982), pp. 115–117; and Robert Pastor, "Sinking in the Caribbean Basin," *Foreign Affairs*, Vol. 60 (Summer 1982), p. 1047.

75. Pastor, "Sinking," p. 1046; Jane Seabury, "Caribbean Policy Hit at Hearings," *The Washington Post*, March 24, 1982, p. D9; and Jean Seabury, "Sugar Draws Caribbean Plan Critics," *The Washington Post*, February 25, 1982, p. D9.

76. Raphael Hernandez-Colon, "CBI: Puerto Rico, Partner or Victim?" *Foreign Policy*, No. 47, (Summer 1982), p. 123.

77. Ibid., p. 125.

78. State Department and Department of Defense, *The Soviet-Cuban Connection in Central America and the Caribbean* (Washington, D.C., March 1985), p. 1.

79. Carl Stone, *Class, State and Democracy in Jamaica.* (New York: Praeger, 1986), pp. 181–182.

80. George Moffett, "Despite Reagan's Initiative, Caribbean Basin Trade Woes Worsen," *The Christian Science Monitor*, March 19, 1987, p. 5.

81. GAO, *Caribbean Basin Initiative*, (Washington, D.C.: USGPO, December 1986), p. 5.

82. Clyde Farnsworth, "The 'Good Neighbor' Offers Little Aid and Less Trade," *The New York Times*, Feb. 1, 1987, p. 6.

CHAPTER 6

1. Hedley Bull, "The West and South Africa," *Daedalus: Journal of the American Academy of Arts and Sciences*, Vol. III no. 2 (Spring 1982), p. 266.

2. John Lenczowski, *Soviet Perceptions of U.S. Foreign Policy.* (Ithaca: Cornell University Press, 1982), p. 212.

3. Colin Legum, "Africa Outlooks toward the U.S.S.R.," in *Communism in Africa*, edited by David E. Albright (Bloomington: Indiana University Press, 1980), p. 24.

4. Seth Singleton, "The Natural Ally: Soviet Policy in Southern Africa," in *Changing Realities in Southern Africa: Implications for American Policy*, edited by Michael Clough (Berkeley: Institute of International Studies, 1982), p. 192.

5. See L. H. Gann and Peter Duigan, *Why South Africa Will Survive.* (New York: St. Martin's Press, 1981), p. 286; and The Study Commission on U.S. Policy toward Southern Africa, *South Africa: Time Running Out.* (Berkeley: University of California Press, 1981), p. 325. Another stated Soviet objective is to establish military bases in the region and to control the sea lanes through which Westen oil passes.

6. "An Appeal for Thought: An Interview with George F. Kennan," *The New York Times Magazine*, May 7, 1978 p. 126.

7. Kenneth Adelman, "The Black Man's Burden," *Foreign Policy*, No. 28 (Fall, 1977), p. 94. See also Elliot J. Berg, "The Economic Basis of Political Choice in French West Africa," *American Political Science Review*, Vol. 54 (1960), pp. 398–9.

8. Maurice Halperin, "The Cuban Role in Southern Africa," in *Southern Africa Since the Portuguese Coup*, edited by John Seiler, (Boulder, Colorado: Westview Press, 1980), pp. 26-27.

9. Ibid., p. 28.

10. William M. LeoGrande, *Cuba's Policy in Africa, 1959-1980* (Berkeley: Institute of International Studies, 1980), p. 10.

11. Halperin, "The Cuban Role," pp. 29-30.

12. LeoGrande, *Cuban Policy in Africa*, p. 29-30.

13. Ibid., p. 12.

14. Senator Dick Clark, "American Policy Toward Southern Africa," *Issue*, Vol. 7 no. 1 (Spring 1977), p. 2. See John Marcum, "Lessons From Angola," *Foreign Affairs*, Vol. 54 (April 1976), p. 408; President Richard Nixon, *U.S. Foreign Policy for the 1970s: A New Strategy for Peace*. (Feb. 18, 1970), pp. 83-89; and Mohamad A. El-Khawas and Barry Cohen, ed., *The Kissinger Study of Southern Africa*. (Westport, Conn.: Lawrence Hill, 1976), pp. 105-106.

15. Arthur Jay Klinghoffer, *The Angolan War: A Study in Soviet Policy in the Third World*. (Boulder, Colorado: Westview Press, 1980), p. 98.

16. Gerald J. Bender, "Angola: Left, Right, and Wrong," *Foreign Policy*, No. 43, (Summer 1981), p. 56.

17. LeoGrande, *Cuba in Africa*, p. 16; and Alexander George, "Missed Opportunities for Crisis Prevention: The War of Attrition and Angola," in *Managing U.S.-Soviet Rivalry: Problems of Crisis Prevention*, edited by Alexander George. (Boulder, Colorado: Westview Press, 1983), p. 201.

18. Klinghoffer, *The Angolan War*, p. 70.

19. Bender, "Angola: Left, Right and Wrong," p. 57.

20. Klinghoffer, *The Angolan War*, p. 95.

21. Gerald Bender, "American Policy Toward Angola: A History of Linkage," in *African Crisis Areas and U.S. Foreign Policy*, edited by Gerald Bender, James Coleman, and Richard Sklar (Berkeley: University of California Press, 1985), p. 113.

22. John Stockwell, *In Search of Enemies: A CIA Story*. (New York: W.W. Norton, 1978), p. 68. Stockwell was the chief of the CIA Angolan Task Force in 1975-76.

23. Raymond L. Garthoff, *Detente and Confrontation: America-Soviet Relations from Nixon to Reagan*. (Washington, D.C.: The Brookings Institution, 1985), p. 513; Abraham F. Lowenthal, "Cuba's African Adventure," *International Security*, Vol. 2 (Summer 1977), pp. 3-10; and Jorge I. Dominguez, "Cuban Foreign Policy," *Foreign Affairs*, Vol. 57 (Fall 1978), pp. 96-98.

24. Garthoff, *Detente and Confrontation*, p. 508.

25. Ibid., p. 512.

26. William J. Durch, "The Cuban Military in Africa and the Middle East," *Studies in Comparative Communism*, Vol. II (Spring–Summer 1978) p. 68.

27. See Chester A. Crocker, "The African Dimension of Indian Ocean Policy," *Orbis: A Journal of World Affairs*, Vol. 20 (Fall, 1976), p. 663. "Soviet Union and Angola," *African Affairs* Vol. 75 (April, 1976), pp. 1147-51.

28. Garthoff, *Detente and Confrontation*, p. 535.

29. John Marcum, "Lessons from Angola," p. 422; and Wayne Smith, "A Trap in Angola," *Foreign Policy* No. 62 (Spring 1986), p. 61-74.

30. See David Ottaway, "Failure in Angola: How the Side Backed by U.S. Crumbled," *The Washington Post*, Feb. 19, 1976, p. A1; Christopher S. Wren, "Africa: An Inviting Arena for Moscow," *The New York Times*, Dec. 28, 1975, Sec. 4, p. 1; Statement by Senator Dick Clark, *United States Policy Toward Africa*. Hearings before the Subcommittee on Foreign Relations of the U.S. Senate, 94th Congress, 2nd Sess. March 5, 1976, p. 1; and Statement by Hon. Henry A. Kissinger, Secretary of State, *U.S.-Involvement in Angola*. Hearings before the Subcommittee on African Affairs of the Committee on Foreign Relations of the U.S. Senate, 94th Congress, 2nd Sess. January 29, 1976, p. 7.

31. Alexander George, "Detente," in *Managing U.S.-Soviet Rivalry*, edited by Alexander George (Colorado: Westview Press, 1983), p. 201.

32. Robert I. Rotberg, *Suffer the Future: Policy Choices in Southern Africa.* (Cambridge: Harvard University Press, 1980), p. 4.

33. Leonard Thompson and Andrew Prior, *South African Politics.* (New Haven: Yale University Press, 1982), p. 35.

34. Rotberg, *Suffer the Future*, p. 35.

35. See Elizabeth S. Landis and Michael I. Davis, "Namibia," in *Southern Africa: The Continuing Crisis*, edited by Gwendolen M. Carter and Patrick O'Meara, (Bloomington: Indiana University Press, 1982), p. 144; and John Dugard, *The South West Africa/Namibia Dispute.* (Berkeley: University of California Press, 1973).

36. Hidipo L. Hamutenya and Gottfried H. Geingob, "African Nationalism in Namibia," in *Southern Africa in Perspective*, edited by Christian P. Potholm and Richard Dale, (New York: The Free Press, 1972), pp. 88-91.

37. *South Africa: Time Running Out*, p. 328.

38. Thomas M. Callaghy, "Apartheid and Socialism: South Africa's Relations with Angola and Mozambique," in *South Africa in Southern Africa*, edited by Callaghy, (New York: Praeger, 1983), p. 273.

39. Leonard M. Thompson, *The Republic of South Africa.* (Boston: Little, Brown and Co., 1966), p. 168.

40. Thomas Karis, "Revolution in the Making: Black Politics in South Africa," *Foreign Affairs*, Vol. 62, no. 2 (Winter, 1983-84), p. 382.

41. Ibid., pp. 398. Moscow's influence on the ANC is significant but not pervasive. This influence stems from the ANC's dependence on Soviet weapons. See Gary Thatcher, "Soviets Found to Influence ANC but not Control it," *The Christian Science Monitor*, Aug. 8, 1986, p. 1.

42. Paul Van Slambrouck, "South African Blacks Regroup as Friends Make Pacts with Pretoria," *Christian Science Monitor*, May 15, 1984, p. 11; and Rotberg, "Suffer the Future," p. 71.

43. "State of Emergency Imposed Throughout South Africa," *The New York Times*, June 13, 1986, p. 1. Under the state of emergency security forces may arrest anyone who is considered a threat to public order, and detain them as long as the state of emergency continues.

44. "As Expected, Black Curbs Extended in South Africa," *The Christian Science Monitor*, June 11, 1987, p. 2.

45. Gwendolen Carter, "South Africa: Growing Black-White Confrontation," in *Southern Africa*, Carter, p. 125. A "Super Federation of Black Labor Unions," formed in 1982, is a potentially powerful political organization.

46. John de St. Jorre, "South Africa: Is Change Coming?" *Foreign Affairs*, Vol. 60, no. 1 (Fall, 1981), p. 110; and see "South Africa: A Desperate Drive to Import Skilled Labor," *Business Week*, Nov. 30, 1981, pp. 64-65; and Joseph Lelyveld, "South Africa Growth Lets a Few Blacks Aim Higher," *The New York Times*, Dec. 27, 1981, p. 1.

47. Gavin Relly, "The Costs of Disinvestment," *Foreign Policy*, No. 63 (Summer 1986), p. 132; and "The Rand: A Fraction of its Former Self" The Christian Science Monitor, Sept. 6, 1985, p. 13.

48. "Comprehensive Anti-Apartheid Act of 1986," *International Legal Materials*, Vol. 26, no. 1 (January 1987), pp. 77-136.

49. Joseph Lelyveld, "A Ruling on Residency Agitates South Africa," *The New York Times*, June 19, 1983, p. E3. In 1985 the South African government decided that blacks now living in urban areas would be allowed to remain. Even advocates of the Homelands policy had realized that it was unworkable.

50. Joseph Lelyveld, "Church in South Africa calls Apartheid Heresy," *The New York Times*, Oct. 10, 1982, p. 10.

51. John D. Battersby, "South Africa Seiges 120 at Campus Rally," *The New York Times*, May 5, 1987, p. 3.

52. Allister Sparks, "South Africa Planning 'Confederal' Role for Blacks," *The Washington Post*, August 12, 1982, p. A24.

53. Gary Thatcher, "Prospects bleak for Ciskei After Independence," *The Christian Science Monitor*, April 8, 1981, p. 5.

54. Rotberg, "Suffer the Future," p. 7.

55. Patrick Laurence, "South African Reforms Wilt Under Scrutiny," *The Christian Science Monitor*, July 29, 1986, p. 1.

56. Alan Cowell, "South African Whites Approve Chapter for Limited Power Sharing," *The New York Times*, November 4, 1983, p. 2. The obvious attempt to continue excluding blacks from the political life of South Africa helped to fuel the violence which began in 1984.

57. Ibid., By 1985 Coloureds and Indians had moved further away from white minority governments, and were moving closer to the black majority.

58. Joseph Lelyveld, "The Afrikaners Are Torn Over Botha's Constitution," *The New York Times*, October 9, 1983, p. 1.

59. John D. Battersby, "Botha Outlines Terms for Any Changes," *The New York Times*, May 20, 1987, p. 3.

60. Alan Cowell, "South Africa: 'Yes' to Botha," *The New York Times*, November 5, 1983, p. 3. Elections in 1985 showed greater polarization between Afrikaners.

61. Christopher R. Hill, "Regional Cooperation in Southern Africa," *African Affairs*, Vol. 82, no. 327 (April, 1983), pp. 222-223; and Callaghy, "Apartheid and Socialism," p. 305. South Africa attempted to influence Western opinion against the imposition of sanctions by threatening to send foreign workers back to neighboring states.

62. Pamela S. Falk, "Cuba in Africa," *Foreign Affairs*, Vol. 65, no. 5 (Summer 1987), p. 1086.

63. I. William Zartman, "Issues of African Diplomacy in the 1980s," *Orbis*, Vol. 25, no. 4 (Winter 1982), p. 1035.

64. Neil A. Lewis, "Angolan Rebels to Get New Aid, Reagan Decides," *The New York Times*, June 11, 1987, p. 1. Formal congressional approval is not required to send $15 million to Savimbi. The money comes out of the CIA's budget.

65. Callaghy, "Apartheid and Socialism," p. 286.

66. James Brooks, "Angolans Flee Both Sides in Civil War," *The New York Times*, Feb. 10, 1987, p. 7.

67. Ibid., p. 287.

68. "South Africa Says 1,000 Namib Rebels are Poised to Cross Border from Angola," *The New York Times*, Dec. 27, 1983, p. 8. Cuban troops increased from 20,000 in 1984 to 30,000 in 1985, and the number of Soviet advisors doubled during the same period.

69. Ibid.

70. "Soviet Announces an Accord to Bolster Angolan Defense," *The New York Times*, January 12, 1984, p. 1.

71. Falk, "Cuba in Africa," p. 1086.

72. Robert M. Press, "Soviets Lead Angola Buildup," *The Christian Science Monitor*, April 7, 1987, p. 1.

73. Jill Jolliff, "Rising Tension in Angola Heightens Nation's Reliance on the Soviets," *The Christian Science Monitor*, May 4, 1987, p. 18.

74. John F. Burns, "Call to Arms: Africa Hears Different Drummers," *The New York Times*, June 4, 1978, Sec. 4, p. 1.

75. Bull, "The West and South Africa," p. 260.

76. J. E. Spence, "South Africa: Reform versus Reaction," *The World Today*, Vol. 37, no. 12 (December, 1981), p. 464.

77. W. Scott Thompson, "U.S. Policy Toward Africa: At America's Service?" *Orbis*, Vol. 25, no. 4 (Winter 1982), p. 1021. For the policy of constructive engagement see Chester A. Crocker, "South Africa: Strategy for Change," *Foreign Affairs*, Vol. 59 (Winter 1980/81), p. 324–350; Chester Crocker, "An Update of Constructive Engagement in South Africa," *Department of State Bulletin*, (January 1985), pp. 5–6; Kenneth W. Dam, "South Africa: The Case Against Sanctions," *Department of State Bulletin* (June 1985), p. 37; and "Test of President Reagan's Remarks on South Africa," *Department of State Bulletin* (October 1985), p. 1.

78. Clyde Ferguson and William R. Cotter, "South Africa — What is to be Done?" *Foreign Affairs*, Vol. 56, (January 1978), p. 267. Faced with overwhelming support in the Senate for sanctions against South Africa, Reagan imposed relatively minor sanctions against the white minority government.

79. "Excerpts from Crocker's Speech on Washington's Policy in Southern Africa," *The New York Times*, August 30, 1981, p. 10.

80. William Chapman and John M. Goshko, "U.S. Lifts Curbs On Certain Sales to South Africa," *The Washington Post*, Feb. 27, 1982, p. 1.

81. "Excerpts from Eagleburger's Address on Africa," *The New York Times*, June 24, 1983, p. 6.

82. Sanford Ungar and Peter Vale, "Why Constructive Engagement Failed," *Foreign Affairs*, Vol. 64, no. 2 (Winter 1985/86) pp. 234–258.

83. John De St. Jorre, "Africa: Crisis of Confidence," *Foreign Affairs*, Vol. 61, no. 3 (1983), p. 686.

84. Bull, "The West and South Africa," p. 264.

85. Jennifer Seymour Whitaker, *Conflict in Southern Africa*. (New York: Foreign Policy Association, 1978), p. 80.

86. Joanne Gowa and Nils H. Wessell, *Ground rules: Soviet and American Involvement in Regional Conflicts.* (Philadelphia: Foreign Policy Research Institute, 1982), p. 69.

87. Anthony Lake, "Africa: Do the Doable," *Foreign Policy*, No. 54, (Spring 1984), p. 109.

88. Commission on U.S. Policy toward Southern Africa, *South Africa: Time Running Out*, p. 412; for black protest see Tom Lodge, *Black Politics in South Africa Since 1945.* (New York: Longman, 1983). Chapter one discusses early protest movements.

89. Lake, "Africa: Do the Doable," pp. 108–109. The U.S. was Angola's largest customer in 1985, taking 38 percent of its exports (mainly oil) and providing 10 percent of its imports.

90. Karis, "Revolution in the Making," p. 400. Due to South African raids into Angola, growing acts of sabotage by UNITA, and efforts by the Reagan administration to fund UNITA, the number of Cuban troops actually increased from 20,000 in 1984 to 35,000 in 1987. Schultz and Tambo met in Washington. See Ned Temko, "United States' South Africa Policy: Signs of a Shift," *The Christian Science Monitor*, Dec. 22, 1986, p. 7.

91. Xan Smiley, "Inside Angola," *The New York Review of Books*, Feb. 17, 1983, p. 42; and Bender, "Angola: Left, Right, and Wrong," p. 66. Washington (in 1987) pledged $93 million in new aid to SADCC to reduce its dependence on South Africa. See Serge Schmemann, "U.S. Pledges Aid to South Africa's Neighbors," *The New York Times*, Feb. 6, 1987, p. 7.

92. Helen Kitchen, *U.S. Interests in Africa.* (New York: Praeger, 1983), p. 21. In 1985 Gavin Kelly, the new chairman of the Anglo American Corporation of South Africa, met with ANC leaders in Zambia to discuss the future of South Africa. Business is aware that only fundamental change in South Africa will provide the kind of stability they desire.

93. Elizabeth Valkenier, "Moscow is not Winning in Africa," *The Christian Science Monitor*, May 20, 1981, p. 22.

94. "Sullivan: All U.S. Firms out of South Africa in 9 Months," *The Christian Science Monitor*, June 4, 1987, p. 2.

95. Bernard Simon, "At a Crossroad in South Africa," *The New York Times*, Nov. 6, 1983, p. F9; and Tamar Lewin, "Rev. Sullivan Steps up his Anti-Apartheid Fight," *The New York Times*, Nov. 6, 1983, p. F13.

CHAPTER 7

1. Roger Fisher and William Ury, *Getting To Yes.* (New York: Penguin, 1984), p. 53.

2. Seyom Brown, "Power and Prudence in Dealing with the U.S.S.R.," in *Neither Cold War nor Detente*, edited by Richard Melanson (Charlottesville: University of Virginia Press, 1982), p. 233.

3. Thompson R. Buchanan, "The Real Russia," *Foreign Policy*, No. 47 (Summer 1982), p. 45.

4. Fisher and Ury, *Getting To Yes*, p. 53.

5. Buchanan, "The Real Russia," p. 43.

6. Walter C. Clemens, Jr., *National Security and U.S.-Soviet Relations.* (Muscatine, Iowa: The Stanley Foundation, 1981), p. 25.

7. Richard Nixon, *Memoirs.* (London: Sidgwick and Jackson, 1978), p. 884.

8. Ibid.

Bibliography

Adelman, Kenneth. "The Black Man's Burden." *Foreign Policy* 28 (1977), pp. 391–405.

Adelman, Kenneth L. *African Realities*. New York: Crane, Russak, and Co., 1980.

Africa South of the Sahara 1984–1985. London: Europa Publications, Ltd., 1984.

Albright, David E. *The U.S.S.R and Sub-Saharan Africa in the 1980s*. New York: Praeger, 1983.

Albright, David E. "The U.S.S.R. and Africa in 1982: Quest for Global Power Status." in *Africa Contemportary Record, 1982–1983*, edited by Colin Legum. New York: Africana Publishing Company, 1984.

Almond, Gabriel. *The American People and Foreign Policy*. New York: Frederick A. Praeger Publishers, 1960.

Americas Watch, *Miskitos in Nicaragua, 1981–1984*. New York: Amnesty International, 1984.

"An Appeal for Thought: An Interview with George F. Kennan." *New York Times Magazine*, May 7, 1978.

Anderson, Thomas P. *Politics in Central America*. New York: Praeger, 1982.

Arendt, Hannah. *In Revolution*. New York: The Viking Press, 1969.

Arnold, Anthony. *Afghanistan: The Soviet Invasion in Perspective*. Stanford: Hoover Institution Press, 1981.

Ball, George. *Diplomacy for a Crowded World: An American Foreign Policy*. Boston: Little, Brown and Co., 1976.

Barios de Chamorro, Violeta. "The Death of LaPrensa." *Foreign Affairs 65 (Winter 1986–87)*.

Barrow, Errol. "The Danger of Rescue Operations." *Caribbean Review* 12 (1983), pp. 3–4.

Bemis, Samuel Flagg. *The Latin American Policy of the United States*. New York: W.W. Norton and Co., 1967.

Bender, Gerald J. "Angola: Left, Right, and Wrong." *Foreign Policy* 43 (1981), pp. 53–69.

Bernstein, Richard. "Remaking Afghanistan in the Soviet Image." *The New York Times Magazine* March 24, 1987, p. 69.

Bhargave, G. S. *South Asia Security After Afghanistan*. Lexington: D.C. Heath and Co., 1983

Bialer, Seweryn and Joan Afferica. "Reagan and Russia." *Foreign Affairs* 61 (1982–83), pp. 249–271.

Blasier, Cole. *The Giant's Rival: The U.S.S.R. and Latin America*. Pittsburgh: University of Pittsburgh Press, 1983.

Boersner, Deetrio. "Cuba and Venezuela." in *The New Cuban Presence in the Caribbean*, edited by Barry B. Levine. Colorado: Westview Press, 1983, pp. 89–97.

Bolin, William H. "Central America: Economic Help is Workable Now." *Foreign Affairs* 62 (1984), pp. 1096–1106.

Bradsher, Henry S. *Afghanistan and the Soviet Union*. Durham, North Carolina: Duke University Press, 1983.

Brind, Harry. "Soviet Policy in the Horn of Africa." *International Affairs* 60 (1983–84).

Brown, Ed. "The U.S. and Africa in 1983." in *Africa Contemporary Record 1983–1984*, edited by Colin Legum. New York: Africana Publishing Company. 1985.

Brown, Seyom. *On the Front Burner: Issues in U.S. Foreign Policy*. Boston: Little, Brown and Co., 1983.

Buchanan, Thompson. "The Real Russia." *Foreign Policy* 47 (1982), pp. 26–45.

Bull, Hedley. "The West and South Africa." *Daedalus: Journal of the American Academy of Arts and Sciences* 3 (1982), pp. 255–270.

Callaghy, Thomas M. "Apartheid and Socialism: South Africa's Relations with Angola and Mozambique." in *South Africa in Southern Africa*, edited by Thomas Callaghy. New York: Praeger, 1983.

Campbell, John C. "The Gulf Region in the Global Setting." in *The Security of the Persian Gulf*, edited by Hossein Amirsadegh. New York: St. Martin's Press, 1981.

Chace, James. *Endless War*. New York: Vintage Books, 1984.

Chanda, Nayan. "New Year's Irresolution." *Far East Economic Review* April 12, 1984, pp. 24–26.

Chavarria, Ricardo E. "The Nicaragua Revolution." in *Revolutions: Theoretical, Comparative, and Historical Studies*, edited by Jack Goldstone. San Diego: Harcourt Brace, Javanovich, 1986.

Chubin, Shahram. "The Soviet Union and Iran." *Foreign Affairs* 61 (1983), pp. 921–949.

Chubin, Shahram. "U.S. Security Interests in the Persian Gulf in the 1980s." *Daedalus: U.S. Defense Policy in the 1980s* (Fall 1980) pp. 33–50.

Clark, Dick. "American Policy Toward Southern Africa." *Issue* 7 (1977), pp. 1–4.

Clemens, Walter C. "National Security and U.S.-Soviet Relations." in *Toward Nuclear Disarmament and Global Security*, edited by Burns H. Weston. Colorado: Westview Press. 1984.

Clemens, Walter C. Jr. *National Security and U.S.-Soviet Relations*. Iowa: The Stanley Foundation, 1981.

Collins, Joseph. *What Difference Could a Revolution Make*. San Francisco: Institute for Food and Development Policy, 1985.

"Contadora: A Text for Peace." *International Policy Report*. Washington, D.C.: Center for International Policy, November 1984.

Cottam, Richard. *Foreign Policy Motivations*. Pittsburgh: University of Pittsburgh Press, 1977.

Crocker, Chester A. "The African Dimension of Indian Ocean Policy." *Orbis: A Journal of World Affairs* 30 (1976), pp. 663–670.

Cronin, Richard P. *Afghanistan: Soviet Invasion and U.S. Response*. Washington, D.C.: Congressional Research Service, 1982.

Cruz, Arturo J. "Nicaragua's Imperiled Revolution." *Foreign Affairs* 61 (1983), pp. 1031–1047.

De St. Jorre, John. "Africa: Crisis of Confidence." *Foreign Affairs* 61 (1983), pp. 675–691.

Department of Defense. *Soviet Military Power*. Washington, D.C., USGPO, 1985.

Department of State and Department of Defense. *The Sandinista Military Buildup*. Washington, D.C.: USGPO, 1985.

Department of State and Department of Defense. *The Soviet-Cuban Connection in Central America and the Caribbean*. Washington, D.C.: USGPO, 1985.

Dickey, Christopher. "Central America: From Quagmire to Cauldron." *Foreign Affairs* 62 (1984), pp. 658–662.

Dil, Shaheen F. "The Cabal in Kabul: Great Power Interaction in Afghanistan." *American Political Science Review* 71 (1977), pp. 468–478.

Dominguez, Jorge, I. "The United States and its Regional Security Interests: The Caribbean, Central America, and South America." *Daedalus* 109 (1980), pp. 42–56.

Dominguez, Jorge I. "Cuban Foreign Policy." *Foreign Affairs* 57 (1978), pp. 83–108.

Donaldson, Robert H. "Soviet Policy in South Asia." in *Soviet Policy in the Third World*, edited by W. Raymond Duncan. New York: Pergamon Press, 1981.

Donaldson, Robert H. "The Soviet Union in India." in *The Pattern of Soviet Conduct in the Third World*, edited by Walter Laqueur. New York: Praeger, 1983.

Dougherty, James E. *The Horn of Africa: A Map of Political-Strategic Analysis*. Cambridge, Massachusetts: Institute for Foreign Policy Analysis, 1982.

Dozier, Craig L. *Nicaragua's Mosquito Shore: The Years of British and American Presence*. Alabama: University of Alabama Press, 1985.

Dugard, John. *The South West Africa/Namibia Dispute*. Berkeley: University of California Press, 1973.

Duncan, Raymond W. *The Soviet Union and Cuba: Interests and Influence*. New York: Praeger, 1985.

Duncan, Raymond W. "Soviet and Cuban Interest in the Caribbean." in *The Restless Caribbean: Changing Patterns of International Relations*, edited by Richard Millet and W. Marvin Will. New York: Praeger, 1979.

Duncan, W. Raymond. "Moscow and Latin America: Objectives, Constraints, and Implications." in *Soviet Policy in the Third World*, edited by W. Raymond Duncan. New York: Pergamon Press, 1980.

El-Khawas, Mohamad A. and Barry Cohen, eds. *The Kissinger Study of Southern Africa*. Westport, Connecticut: Lawrence Hill, 1976.

Erisman, H. Michael. "Contemporary Challenge Confronting U.S. Caribbean Policy." in *The Caribbean Challenge: U.S. Policy in a Volatile Region*, edited by H. Michael Erisman. Colorado: Westview Press, 1984.

Falcoff, Mark. *Small Countries, Large Issues*. Washington, D.C.: American Enterprise Institute for Public Policy Research, 1984.

Farer, Tom J. "Manage the Revolution?" *Foreign Policy* 52 (1983), pp. 96–117.

Farer, Tom. *War Clouds on the Horn of Africa*. New York: Carnegie Endowment of International Peace, 1976.

Farer, Tom J. "Contadora: The Hidden Agenda." *Foreign Policy* 59 (1985), pp. 59–72.

Ferguson, Clyde and William R. Cotter. "South Africa—What is to be Done?" *Foreign Affairs* 56 (1978), pp. 253–274.

Fisher, Roger. *Dear Israelis, Dear Arabs: A Working Approach To Peace*. New York: Harper and Row, 1972.

Fisher, Roger. *Points of Choice*. New York: Oxford University Press, 1978.

Fisher, Roger and William Ury. *Getting to Yes: Negotiating Agreement Without Giving In*. New York: Penguin Books, 1983.

Fitzgerald, Frances. "Reagan's Band of True Believers." *The New York Times Magazine* May 10, 1987, pp. 43–45.

Fukuyama, Francis. "Gorbachev and the Third World." *Foreign Affairs* 64 (Spring 1986), pp. 715–731.

Gabriel, Marcella and Daniel S. Papp. "The Soviet-Cuban Relationship." in *The Soviet Union and the Third World: Successes and Failures*, edited by Robert H. Donaldson. Colorado: Westview Press, 1981.

Gaddis, John Lewis. "Containment: Its Past and Future." in *Neither Cold War Nor Detente? Soviet-American Relations in the 1980s*, edited by Richard A. Melanson. Charlottesville: University Press of Virginia, 1982.

Gann, L. H. and Peter Duignan. *Why South Africa Will Survive*. New York: St. Martin's Press, 1981.

Garrett, Stephen A. "Illusion and Reality in Soviet-American Relations." *International Journal on World Peace* 3 (April/June, 1986), pp. 19–30.

Gegum, Colin. "Africa Outlooks toward the U.S.S.R." in *Communism in Africa*, edited by David E. Albright. Bloomington: Indiana University Press, 1980.

George, Alexander. "Detente: The Search for a Constructive Relationship." in *Managing U.S.-Soviet Rivalry: Problems in Crisis Prevention*, edited by Alexander George. Colorado: Westview Press, 1983.

George, Alexander. "Missed Opportunities for Crisis Prevention: The War of Attrition and Angola." in *Managing U.S.-Soviet Rivalry: Problems of Crisis Prevention*, edited by Alexander George. Colorado: Westview Press, 1983.

Gleijeses, Piero. "Nicaragua: Resist Romanticism." *Foreign Policy* 54 (1984).

Gleijeses, Piero. "The Reagan Doctrine and Central America." *Current History* December 1986, pp. 403–408.

Gorman, Robert F. *Political Conflict on the Horn of Africa*. New York: Praeger, 1981.

Government Accounting Office. *Foreign Aid: Questions on the Central American Regional Program Need to be Resolved*. Washington, D.C.: USGPO, 1986.

Gowa, Joanne and Nils H. Wessell. *Ground Rules: Soviet and American Involvement Regional Conflicts*. Philadelphia: Foreign Policy Research Institute, 1982.

Grabendorff, Wolf. "The U.S. and Western Europe: Competition or Cooperation in Latin America?" in *Latin America, Western Europe, and the United States*, edited by Wolf Grabendorff and Riordan Toett. New York: Praeger, 1985.

Grande, William Leo. "Cuba and Nicaragua: From the Somozas to the Sandinistas." in *The New Cuban Presence in the Caribbean*, edited by Barry B. Levine. Colorado: Westview Press, 1983.

Griffiths, John C. *Afghanistan: Key to a Continent*. Colorado: Westview Press, 1981.

Halliday, Fred and Maxine Molyneux. *The Ethiopian Revolution*. London: N. B., 1981.

Halperin, Maurice. "The Cuban Role in Southern Africa." in *Southern Africa Since the Portuguese Coup*, edited by John Seiler. Colorado: Westview Press, 1980.

Hamutenya, Hidipo L. and Gottfried H. Geingob. "African Nationalism in Namibia." in *Southern Africa in Perspective*, edited by Christian P. Pothlom and Richard Dale. New York: The Free Press, 1972.

Harrison, Michael. "Reagan's World." *Foreign Policy* 43 (1981), pp. 3–16.

Harrison, Selig S. "Fanning Flames in South Asia." *Foreign Policy* 45 (1981–82), pp. 84–102.

Harrison, Selig S. "A Breakthrough in Afghanistan?" *Foreign Policy* 51 (1983), pp. 3–26.

Hartman, Frederick H. *The New Age of American Foreign Policy*. New York: The Macmillan Co., 1970.

Hayes, Margaret Daly. *Latin American and the U.S. National Interest: A Basis for U.S. Foreign Policy*. Colorado: Westview Press, 1984.

Henze, Paul B. "Ethiopia." *The Wilson Quarterly* 8 (1984).

Hernandez-Colon, Raphael. "CBI: Puerto Rico, Partner or Victim?" *Foreign Policy* 47 (1982), pp. 12–127.

Hill, Christopher R. "Regional Cooperation in Southern Africa." *African Affairs* 82 (1983), pp. 222–239.

Horn, Robert C. *Soviet-Indian Relations: Issues and Influence*. New York: Praeger, 1982.

Hosmer, Stephen T. and Thomas W. Wolfe. *Soviet Policy and Practice Toward Third World Conflicts*, Lexington: D.C. Heath and Co., 1983.

Hough, Jerry F. *The Struggle for the Third World*. Washington, D.C.: The Brookings Institution, 1986.

Hyland, William G. "Clash with the Soviet Union." *Foreign Policy* 49 (1982–83), pp. 3–19.

"International Court of Justice: Case Concerning Military and Paramilitary Activities in and against Nicaragua." In *International Legal Materials* 25 (September 1986), pp. 1023–1295.

"Jamaica: Island in the Soup." *The Economist* June 1980, pp. 51–54.

Joyce, John M. "The Old Russian Legacy." *Foreign Policy* 55 (1984), pp. 137–153.

Kanet, Roger. *Soviet Foreign Policy in the 1980s.* New York: Praeger, 1982.

Karis, Thomas. "Revolution in the Making: Black Politics in South Africa. *Foreign Affairs* 62 (1983-84), pp. 378-406.

Kennan, George. *The Cloud of Danger: Current Realities of American Foreign Policy.* Boston: Little, Brown and Co., 1977.

Khar, Mustafar. "Four Choices Facing Frontline Pakistan." *The Economist* October 31, 1981, p. 25.

Kheli, Shirin Tahir. "The Soviet Union in Afghanistan: Benefits and Costs." In *The Soviet Union and the Third World: Successes and Failures*, edited by Robert H. Donaldson. Colorado: Westview Press, 1981.

Kissinger, Henry A. *American Foreign Policy.* 3rd ed. New York: W.W. Norton and Co., 1977.

Kitchen, Helen. *U.S. Interests in Africa.* New York: Praeger, 1983.

Klinghoffer, Arthur Jay. *The Angolan War: A Study in Soviet Policy in the Third World.* Colorado: Westview Press, 1980.

LaFeber, Walter. *Inevitable Revolutions: The United States in Central America.* New York: W.W. Norton and Co., 1984.

Lake, Anthony. *Third World Radical Regimes: U.S. Policy Under Carter and Reagan.* New York: Foreign Policy Association, 1985.

Lake, Anthony. "Africa: Do the Doable." *Foreign Policy* 54 (1984), pp. 102-121.

Landis, Elizabeth S. and Michael I. Davis. "Namibia." in *Southern Africa: The Continuing Crisis*, edited by Gwendolen M. Carter and Patrick O'Meara. Bloomington: Indiana University Press, 1982.

Lauren, Paul G. "Theories of Crisis Decision Making." in *Diplomacy*, edited by Paul Lauren. New York: Free Press, 1979, pp. 105-115.

Lee, Edmund. "Beijing Balancing Act," *Foreign Policy* 51 (1983), pp. 27-46.

Leiken, Robert S. *Soviet Strategy in Central America.* New York: Praeger, 1982.

Leiken, Robert S. *Soviet Strategy in Latin America.* New York: Praeger, 1982.

Lenczowski, John. *Soviet Perceptions of U.S. Foreign Policy.* Ithaca: Cornell University Press, 1982.

LeoGrande, William. "Rollback or Containment? The U.S., Nicaragua, and the Search for Peace in Central America." *International Security* 11 (Fall, 1986).

LeoGrande, William. "Cuba and Nicaragua." in *The New Cuban Presence in the Caribbean*, edited by Barry Levine. Colorado: Westview Press, 1983.

LeoGrande, William M. *Cuba's Policy in Africa, 1959-1980.* Berkeley: Institute of International Studies, 1980.

LeoGrande, William M. "Cuban-Soviet Relations and Cuban Policy in Africa." in *Cuba in Africa*, edited by Carmelo Mesa-Lago and June S. Belkin. Pittsburgh: University of Pittsburgh Press, 1982.

LeoGrande, William M. "Cuba Policy Recycled." *Foreign Policy* 46 (1982), pp. 104-119.

Lowenthal, Abraham F. "Caribbean Basin Initiative: Misplaced Emphasis." *Foreign Policy* 47 (1982), pp. 113-131.

Malhuret, Claude. "Report from Afghanistan." *Foreign Affairs* 62 (1983-84), pp. 426-435.

Mandelbaum, Michael and Strobe Talbott. "Reykjavik and Beyond." *Foreign Affairs* 65 (Winter 1986–87), pp. 212–220.

Manley, Michael. "Overcoming Insularity in Jamaica." *Foreign Affairs* (1970), pp. 100–110.

Marcum, John. "Lessons From Angola." *Foreign Affairs* 54 (1976), pp. 407–425.

Marcus, Bruce and Michael Taber, eds. *Maurice Bishop Speaks: the Grenada Revolution 1979–1983*. New York: The Pathfinder Press, 1983.

Martin, John B. *U.S. Policy in the Caribbean*. Colorado: Westview Press, 1978.

McColm, Bruce R. "Castro's Ambitions Amid New Winds from Moscow." *Strategic Review* 14 (Summer 1986), pp. 47–59.

Medvedev, Zhores A. *Gorbachev*. New York: W.W. Norton, 1986.

Mehta, Jagat S. "Afghanistan: A Neutral Solution." *Foreign Policy* 47 (1982), pp. 143–151.

Millett, Richard. *Guardians of the Dynasty*. New York: Orbis Books, 1977.

Monks, Alfred L. *The Soviet Intervention in Afghanistan*. Washington D. C.: American Enterprise Institute for Public Policy Research, 1981.

Nuechterlein, Donald E. *America Overcommitted: U.S. National Interests in the 1980s*. Lexington: University of Kentucky Press, 1985.

Newell, Nancy P. and Richard S. Newell. *The Struggle for Afghanistan*. Ithaca: Cornell University Press, 1981.

Nixon, Richard. *Memoirs*. London: Sidgwick and Jackson, 1978.

Nye, Joseph. "Can America Manage Its Soviet Policy?" *Foreign Affairs* 62 (1984), pp. 857–878.

Ottaway, Mariana. "Superpower Competition and Regional Conflicts in the Horn of Africa." in *The Soviet Impact in Africa*, edited by R. Craig Nation and Mark V. Kauppi, Lexington, Massachusetts: Lexington Books, 1984.

Ottaway, Mariana and David. *Ethiopia: Empire in Revolution*, New York: Africana Publishing Company, 1978.

Packenham, Robert A. *Liberal America and the Third World*. Princeton: Princeton University Press, 1973.

Parenti, Michael. *The Anti-Communist Impulse*. New York: Random House, 1969.

Pastor, Robert. "Sinking in the Caribbean Basin." *Foreign Affairs* 60 (1982), pp. 1038–1058.

Payne, Richard J., "The Lessons of Grenada." *Worldview* 27 (1984), pp. 13–17.

Payne, Anthony, Paul Sutton and Tony Thorndike. *Grenada: Revolution and Invasion*. New York: St. Martin's Press, 1984.

Payne, James L. "Foreign Policy for an Impulsive People." in *Beyond Containment: Alternative American Policies Toward the Soviet Union*, edited by Aaron Wildavsky. San Francisco: Institute for Contemporary Studies Press, 1983.

Pipes, Richard. "Soviet Global Strategy." *Commentary* 76 (1983), pp. 31–39.

Podheretz, Norman. "Appeasement by Any Other Name." *Commentary* 76 (1983), pp. 25–38.

Purcell, Susan Kaufman. "Mexico-U.S. Relations: Big Initiatives Can Cause Big Problems." *Foreign Affairs* 60 (1981–82), pp. 379–392.

Remmek, Richard B. "Soviet Policy in the Horn of Africa: The Decision to Invervene." in *The Soviet Union and the Third World: Successes and Failures*, edited by Robert H. Donaldson. Colorado: Westview Press, 1982.

Riding, Alan. "Revolution and the Intellectual in Central America." *The New Times Magazine* March 13, 1983.

Riding, Alan. "The Central American Quagmire." *Foreign Affairs* 61 (1983).

Riencourt, Amoury de. "India and Pakistan in the Shadow of Afghanistan." *Foreign Affairs* 61 (1982–83), pp. 416–437.

Rivera, Joseph de. *The Psychological Dimension of Foreign Policy*. Ohio: Charles E. Merrill, 1968.

Robins, Carla Anne. *The Cuban Threat*. New York: McGraw-Hill Book Co., 1983.

Rotberg, Robert I. *Suffer the Future: Policy Choices in Southern Africa*. Cambridge: Harvard University Press, 1980.

Rothenberg, Morris. *The U.S.S.R. and Africa: New Dimensions of Soviet Global Power*. Miami: Advanced International Studies Institute, 1980.

Rubinstein, Alvin Z. *Soviet Policy Toward Turkey, Iran, and Afghanistan*. New York: Praeger, 1982.

Rubinstein, Alvin Z. "Afghanistan: Embraced by the Bear." in *At Issue: Politics in the World Arena*, edited by Stephen L. Speigel. New York: St. Martin's Press, 1984.

Rubinstein, Alvin Z. "Soviet Imperialism in Afghanistan." *Current History* 79 (1980), pp. 80–83.

Rubinstein, Alvin Z. "The Soviet Union and Iran under Khomeini." *International Affairs* (Autumn 1981), pp. 599–617.

Saivetz, Carol R. and Sylvia Woodby. *Soviet-Third World Relations*. (Colorado: Westview Press, 1985.

Sanchez, Nestor D.. "What Was Uncovered in Grenada." *Caribbean Review* 12 (1983), pp. 21–23.

Sayeet, Khalid B. *Politics in Pakistan: The Nature and Direction of Change*. New York: Praeger, 1980.

Schlesinger, Arthur Jr. "Foreign Policy and the American Character." *Foreign Affairs* 62 (1983), pp. 1–16.

Schoultz, Lars. "Nicaragua: U.S. Confronts a Revolution." in *From Gunboats to Diplomacy*, edited by Richard Newfarmer. Baltimore: Johns Hopkins University Press, 1984.

Scroggs, William O. *Filibusters and Financiers: The Story of William Walker and His Associates*. New York: Russell and Russell, 1969.

Sequeira, Arturo Cruz. "The Origins of Sandinista Foreign Policy." in *Central America: Anatomy of Conflict*, edited by Robert S. Leiken. New York: Pergamon Press, 1984.

Shipler, David K. "Russia: A People Without Heroes." *The New York Times Magazine* October 1983, p. 94.

Sigmund, Paul E. "Latin America: Change or Continuity." *Foreign Affairs: America and the World 1981* 60 (1982), pp. 629–657.

Sigmund, Paul E. "U.S.-Latin American Relations from Carter to Reagan: Change or Continuity?" in *The Dynamics of Latin American Foreign*

Policies: Challenges for the 1980s, edited by Jennie K. Lincoln and Elizabeth G. Ferris. Colorado: Westview Press, 1984.

Simes, Dimitri. "The New Soviet Challenge." *Foreign Policy* 55 (1984), pp. 113–131.

Singleton, Seth. "The Natural Ally: Soviet Policy in Southern Africa." in *Changing Realities in Southern Africa: Implications for American Policy*, edited by Michael Clough, Berkeley: Institute of International Studies, 1982.

Smith, Peter. "The Origins of the Crisis." in *Confronting Revolution: Security Through Diplomacy in Central America*, edited by Morris J. Blachman, William LeoGrande, and Kenneth Sharpe. New York: Pantheon Books, 1986.

Spence, J. E. "South Africa: Reform Versus Reaction." *The World Today* 37 (1981).

St. Jorre, John de. "South Africa: Is Change Coming?" *Foreign Affairs* 69 (1981), pp. 106–122.

Steele, Jonathan. *Soviet Power: The Kremlin's Foreign Policy*. New York: Simon and Schuster, 1983.

Stein, Author. *India and the Soviet Union*. Chicago: University of Chicago Press, 1969.

Stevens, Christopher. "Soviet Union and Angola." *African Affairs* 75 (1976), pp. 137–151.

Stoessinger, John. *Why Nations Go to War*. New York: St. Martin's Pres, 1982.

Stroder, Rebecca V. and Colin S. Grey. "Empire and Soviet Power." *Problems of Communism* 30 (1981), pp. 1–32.

The Study Commission on U.S. Policy Toward Southern Africa. *South Africa: Time Running Out*. Berkeley: University of California Press, 1981.

"Summary of the Kissinger Communism Report." *The Congressional Quarterly*, January 14, 1984.

Taylor, Maxwell D. "The Reality of the Soviet Threat." in *the Soviet Threat: Myths and Realities*, edited by Grayson Kirk and Nils H. Wessell. New York: The Academy of Political Science, 1978.

Theberge, James D. "Soviet Policy in the Caribbean." in *Soviet Seapower in the Caribbean: Political and Strategic Implications*, edited by James D. Thebrege. New York: Praeger, 1972.

Thome, Joseph R. and David Kaimowitz. "Agrarian Reform." in *Nicaragua: The First Five Years*, edited by Thomas W. Walker. New York: Praeger, 1985, pp. 309–312.

Thompson, Leonard and Andrew Prior. *South African Politics*. New Haven: Yeal University Press, 1982.

Thompson, W. Scott. "U.S. Policy Toward Africa: At America's Service?" *Orbis* 25 (1982), pp. 1011–1024.

Thornton, Thomas Perry. *The Challenge to U.S. Policy in the Third World: Global Responsibilities and Regional Devolution*. Colorado: Westview Press, 1986.

Tocqueville, Alexis De. *Democracy in America*, edited by J.P. Mayer. New York: Doubleday and Co., 1969.

Tonelson, Alan. "The Real National Interest." *Foreign Policy* 61 (Winter) 1985–86), pp. 49–72.

U.S. Department of State. *Misconceptions about U.S. Policy Toward Nicaragua*, Washington, D.C.: USGPO, June 1985.

Ullman, Richard H. "At War With Nicaragua." *Foreign Affairs* 62 (1983).

Valenta, Jiri. "The Soviet-Cuban Alliance in Africa and the Caribbean." *The World Today* 37 (1981), p. 50.

Valenta, Jiri and Virginia Valenta. "Soviet Strategy and Policies in the Caribbean Basin." in *Rift and Revolution*, edited by Howard J. Wiarda. Washington, D.C.: American Enterprise Institute for Public Policy Research, 1984, pp. 215–221.

Vertzberger, Yaacov. "China and Afghanistan." *Problems of Communism* 31 (1982), pp. 1–23.

Volsky, George. "The Soviet-Cuban Connection." *Current History* 80 (1981), pp. 325–328, 335–346.

Walker, Thomas W. *Nicaragua: The Land of Sandino*. Colorado: Westview Press, 1981.

Wesson, Robert. "Conclusions." in *U.S. Influence in Latin America in the 1980s*, edited by Robert Wesson. New York: Praeger, 1982.

Whitaker, Jennifer Seymour. *Conflict in Southern Africa*. New York: Foreign Policy Association, 1978.

White, Robert E. "Central America: The Problem That Won't Go Away." *The New York Times Magazine* July 18, 1982, pp. 21–28.

Williams, William A. *America Confronts a Revolutionary World*. New York: William Morrow and Co., 1976.

Zagoria, Donald S. "The Moscow-Beijing Detente." *Foreign Affairs* 61 (1983), pp. 853–873.

Zartman, William. "Issues of African Diplomacy in the 1980s." *Orbis* 25 (1982), pp. 1025–1043.

Ziring, Lawrence, ed. *The Subcontinent in World Affairs*. New York: Praeger, 1978.

Index